Exploring the Moral Heart of Teaching

D1113965

Exploring the Moral Heart of Teaching

TOWARD A TEACHER'S CREED

David T. Hansen

Teachers College, Columbia University
New York and London

Published by Teachers College Press, 1234 Amsterdam Avenue, New York, NY 10027

Cover art, *Eratosthenes Teaching in Alexandria* by Bernardo Strozzi, c. 1635. Courtesy the Montreal Museum of Fine Arts, Horsley and Annie Townsend Bequest. Photo, the Montreal Museum of Fine Arts, Christine Guest.

Excerpt from Rilke's *Duino Elegies* from *Selected Poetry of Rainer Maria Rilke*, by Rainer Maria Rilke, copyright © 1982 by Stephen Mitchell. Reprinted by permission of Random House, Inc.

Excerpt from Rilke's *Book of Hours* from *Rilke's Book of Hours: Love Poems to God* by Rainer Maria Rilke, translated by Anita Barrows and Joanna Macy, copyright © 1996 by Anita Barrows and Joanna Macy. Used by permission of Riverhead Books, a division of Penguin Putnam, Inc.

Chapter 1 is adapted in part from *Teaching and Teacher Education, 14*, David T. Hansen, "The Moral Is in the Practice," pp. 643–655, copyright © 1998, with permission from Elsevier Science.

Chapter 1 is adapted in part from "Conceptions of Teaching and Their Consequences," by David T. Hansen, in *Changing Schools/Changing Practices*, edited by M. Lang, J. Olson, H. Hansen, and W. Buender, 1999, Louvain, Belgium: Garant Publishers. Copyright © 1999 by Garant Publishers Ltd. Adapted with permission.

Library of Congress Cataloging-in-Publication Data

Hansen, David T., 1952–
    Exploring the moral heart of teaching : toward a teacher's creed / David T. Hansen.
      p. cm.
    Includes bibliographical references and index.
    ISBN 0-8077-4093-4 (pbk. : alk. paper)—ISBN 0-8077-4094-2 (cloth: alk. paper)
    1. Teaching—Moral and ethical aspects. 2. Teachers. 3. Teachers—Professional ethics. I. Title.

LB1775 .H282 2001
371.102—dc21   00-066996

ISBN 0-8077-4093-4 (paper)
ISBN 0-8077-4094-2 (cloth)

Printed on acid-free paper
Manufactured in the United States of America

08 07 06 05 04 03 02 01   8 7 6 5 4 3 2 1

To Alix, Nora, Alana, Chryste, Kelly,
Ariana, Andrew, Jeremy, Matthew, and Amanda—
may your teachers always remember

Contents

Preface

MY POINT OF DEPARTURE in this book is the premise that good teaching centers around a set of time-honored, dynamic terms. Good teaching involves enriching, not impoverishing, students' understandings of self, others, and the world. It means expanding, not contracting, students' knowledge, insight, and interests. It means deepening, not rendering more shallow, students' ways of thinking and feeling. And it entails paying intellectual and moral attention as a teacher. Good teaching does not imply moral and intellectual apathy, indifference, or inattentiveness to students and the curriculum.

In an earlier work, *The Call to Teach*, I sought to shed light on these terms by conceiving teaching as a vocation or calling. I still believe, more so than ever, that the idea of a calling holds considerable promise for teachers and for the practice of teaching wherever it takes place. To perceive the work in these terms, rather than as merely a job or occupation, brings teachers closer to the significance and the rewards of teaching as a human endeavor.

However, in framing this idea I also stated—and I still believe this, too—that it would be a mistake to try to convert the sense of vocation into an obligation. Teachers cannot be made to see their work as a calling, anymore than a person can wake up in the morning and decide to have a calling. Countless men and women do enter teaching with a strong desire to work with children, youth, or adults. But for many teachers, what seems to happen is that becoming involved in the enterprise generates an enduring spirit of service. They take on the call to teach, rather than beginning their careers with their minds made up about it. For these and other reasons, I wrote in that earlier book about the value for teachers of acting "as if" they had a calling. Such a posture can propel them to become that much more engaged, from the very start, with the intellectual and moral terms of teaching that I touched on above. To treat teaching as a calling can help teachers hold true to these core aspects of the work and to resist forces that bear down on them to lower their expectations, to cut corners in the name of expediency, or, in the worst cases, to lose heart.

The studies presented here extend and deepen this way of thinking about teaching and teachers. I examine why teaching constitutes a moral and intellectual practice with a rich tradition. I show how this conception spotlights the outlook, the conduct, and the sensibility of the person in the role of teacher. The person in the role is decisive, because teaching necessitates paying persistent attention to the (usually) younger human beings who are in the role of student. I develop an image of a growing, educated person that can help guide a teacher in paying attention. I examine how this image coheres with cultivating a classroom environment that can support teaching and learning. I illustrate the process by taking an extended look at a course I have taught for a number of years in a teacher education program. I embed this analysis in a study of teaching and the sense of tradition. My premise here is that teaching is a long-standing human endeavor that has a distinctive identity and a distinctive contribution to make to overall human flourishing. Finally, I link the discussion to ideals in teaching. I examine the place of ideals in the work by identifying their dangers and limitations, but also by highlighting their moral vitality.

I intend the subtitle of this book, TOWARD A TEACHER'S CREED, to be evocative rather than descriptive. As I understand it, a creed describes a set of beliefs, convictions, and commitments that serve as a guide through life or through one of life's endeavors. A creed is like a compass. It provides direction, pointing the way toward some courses of action and away from others. A creed can shore up a person's sense of purpose, especially in times of doubt and confusion when the very idea of having a purpose—for example, to make a difference in human affairs—can seem foolish and unrealistic. To articulate a creed can become a clarifying act, helping to dispel mist and fog surrounding self-understanding and providing a view of where one stands in the world.

A creed can denote a code of conduct or a system of principles. People speak of subscribing to a creed and of joining a community or order that adheres to such a creed. One of the most famous tracts in the history of educational writing employs the term: John Dewey's "My Pedagogic Creed," published in 1897. It contains, in germ, ideas Dewey would analyze in great detail in subsequent years. Dewey rendered his text into a kind of educational constitution. It contains five "articles" in which he states what he believes about education, schools, subject matter and method, and social progress. Dewey's writing is powerful, still timely, and often moving. In his hands, a teacher's creed becomes a banner to be unfurled in the face of an uncertain but promising world.

I esteem the idea of a teacher's creed, which is one reason why it appears in the book's subtitle. But I do not know what it is like to arrive at a final creed or testament of belief. Posed differently, the idea of attaining a last word about teaching seems to contradict the dynamics of the practice. Dewey, incidentally, did not believe he was providing the last word, nor did he wish to. After all, he entitled his text "My Pedagogic Creed," rather than speaking on behalf of other educators. The point is that educational inquiry and practice often seem to share the fate of philosophy. They keep returning to the same kinds of questions and concerns, even if cloaked in different guises and idioms. To those who dream of a last word or of final insight into such questions, this state of affairs can feel frustrating, even maddening. But that response seems to mean that the rediscovery of a forgotten or overlooked question constitutes a reason to shake one's head, rather than a reason for joy and hope. From the latter perspective, the human propensity to return to questions of meaning and purpose borders on the marvelous. It is remarkable enough, as many have said, that people exist in the first place. Why should there be a human world at all? But the human capacity to question, again and again, values, actions, knowledge, beliefs, and hopes astonishes and amazes. Because that capacity is not always realized, and because persons so often need others to help them substantiate it, teachers will always have a reason for being.

The present book is less a personal testament of pedagogical convictions, à la Dewey, than a study of what might contribute to the making of a teacher's sense of purpose. I hope the notion of *exploring* in the book's title, as well as the subtitle TOWARD A TEACHER'S CREED, suggest an image of movement rather than one of final rest. The words evoke the familiar idea of a journey or a quest. That idea is useful for understanding what it means to be a teacher. A teacher's creed stands for an ideal endpoint, a place where everything she or he might conclude about teaching comes together. As an ideal, that place can never be reached, a fact I examine in Chapter 8. Serious-minded teachers know there is always more to learn about how to perform the work well. They know there is always room for growth, and they know that being a good teacher means keeping space open in their minds and hearts for that growth. This process implies that their beliefs and convictions also evolve, even if subtly and slowly. The image of arriving at a creed helps guide the journey or quest to become the teacher one most aspires to be. Like final wisdom, a final creed in teaching may not be attainable. But like trying to become wise, it is worth pursuing in order to keep oneself going in the right direction.

The chapters ahead seek to shed light on what it means to strive toward a teacher's creed.

A NUMBER OF colleagues in universities and schools have helped me think more clearly about what I am trying to say. Several anonymous reviewers for Teachers College Press provided comprehensive and useful criticism. Whipp Johnson read an entire draft of the manuscript and raised many telling and beautiful questions. Deborah Kerdeman read a draft of Chapters 1 and 8, and offered generous, wide-ranging, and helpful insights. Catharine Bell provided timely and thoughtful perspective on the discussion in Chapters 3, 4, and, especially, 5. Caroline Heller and her students shared lively and useful comments on a shorter version of Chapter 5. Rene Arcilla raised provocative and inspiring questions about the arguments as originally crafted in Chapters 6 through 8. Joe Becker did the same with respect to a shorter version of Chapters 6 and 7. Rebecca Bushnell's response to what is now Chapter 7 was heartening and gracious. Susan McDonough, Janice Ozga, and Michelle Piercyznski-Ward offered provocative comments on an earlier version of Chapter 8. None of these persons, to be sure, is committed to agreeing with what I say.

I presented a preliminary version of Chapter 5 (on "indirect" teaching) at the Midwest Faculty Seminar, University of Chicago, in February 1998. I want to record my thanks to Elizabeth Chandler, the seminar organizer, and to the participating college faculty for their generative comments and questions. I presented earlier versions of Chapters 6 and 8 at successive meetings of the Philosophy of Education Society, in April 1999 (New Orleans) and March 2000 (Toronto). I much appreciate the audience's response at both sessions, and I am particularly grateful to the sessions' discussants, Paul Farber and Emily Robertson, for their criticism. I also presented preliminary versions of several chapters at successive meetings of the American Educational Research Association, in April 1999 (Montreal) and April 2000 (New Orleans). My deep thanks to colleagues at those occasions for their reactions and comments.

Brian Ellerbeck at Teachers College Press has provided steady and sure assistance throughout. My wife, Elaine, has heard me talk endlessly about the ideas in this book, and, through her listening, she has helped me give them form.

Finally, my mother, Anne, helped as always through her sheer presence. She passed away as this book went to the publisher. Hers was a wondrous life, rich in countless ways. I will miss our talk of words, ideas, books, and all the things that matter.

Exploring the Moral Heart of Teaching

❧ 1 ❧

Overview: Teaching as a Moral and Intellectual Practice

CONCEPTIONS OF TEACHING have consequences. They influence how teachers think about and conduct their work. They shape what researchers investigate. They guide how teacher educators prepare new candidates. They play a role in what students come to expect from their teachers. And they underlie how administrators, policy makers, politicians, businesspersons, and parents perceive and judge teachers. In short, conceptions of what teaching is, and of what it is for, make a difference in educational thought and practice.

My aim in this book is to contribute to a conception of teaching that does justice to its time-honored importance in human life. I investigate why teaching is a moral and intellectual practice with a rich tradition. Those terms help capture why teaching has been such a long-standing, priceless human activity. I mean "priceless" in the sense of having no substitute. No other practice, be it medicine, parenting, law, or social work, accomplishes what teaching does, even though there may be occasional overlap between them. This viewpoint turns attention to the importance of the person—the distinctive, irreproducible human being—who inhabits the role of teacher. It spotlights, in turn, why teaching entails paying attention to the persons who fill the role of student. These persons, whether they be children or adults, are themselves unique and noninterchangeable. They need teachers, at timely moments, to help them fulfill their promise.

In this introductory chapter, I outline this perspective on the practice by, first, examining current conceptions of teaching. I raise questions about them that center on the issue of whether teaching is an "empty cell" whose terms and meaning derive from outside the practice, in various

1

political, economic, social, or other interests. I argue that teaching is an enduring practice whose moral and intellectual terms can be derived, to a vital degree, from *within*. Teaching has its own integrity, just as do the individual men and women who occupy the role in a serious-minded, thoughtful way. I discuss why the integrity of both the practice of teaching and of individual teachers threatens to fall out of sight whenever people cast teaching as merely a means to an end, with that end shaped from outside the practice. Public concerns and interests do merit a permanent place in talk about teaching. But such talk should be balanced by a grasp of why teaching is a moral and intellectual endeavor.

To support these claims, I sketch a conception of teaching that pivots around the ideas of *practice* and *tradition*. This sketch provides a background for why I focus, throughout the book, on the question of what it means to be a person in the role of teacher. The remarkable ways in which individual teachers, over the generations, have responded to that question help account for why the practice remains vibrant and why it continues to support the human prospect. I conclude with an overview of subsequent chapters in the book.

CONCEPTIONS OF TEACHING MATTER

Public talk about education today features a range of conceptions of what teaching is or should be. For purposes of exposition, I divide current conceptions into two groups: those that focus on the kind of activity teaching is presumed to be and those that emphasize outcomes that teachers should presumably promote. The first group tends to highlight instructional *means*; the second group, instructional *ends*.

A Focus on Means

There exist numerous activity-based conceptions of teaching that underlie contemporary talk about teaching, captured in such words as *job, occupation*, and *profession*. According to one viewpoint, teaching is a job whose tasks are clear-cut and obvious. Teachers must transmit knowledge and skills to the young. This perspective also assumes that both the knowledge and the skills, as well as the methods of transmitting them, are determined not primarily by teachers but by others in the educational system who are seen as holding the major reins of responsibility. The root meaning of the word *job* is "lump," or object or product. That meaning leaves out of the equation the human being who performs the work, raising the idea that persons who do the work are interchangeable—or intersubstitutable, as Bernard Williams (1981, p. 15) puts it—and can be replaced without affecting the nature of the task.

Another conception current today treats teaching as an occupation. Teaching is seen as one occupation among several that are housed within schools, which, in turn, constitute one structural level of the educational system. The idea of an occupation bestows more dignity and status on teaching than does the notion that it is a job pure and simple. The idea connotes an established and valued set of activities carried out by a group of people trained and perhaps licensed to perform it, such that they are not as replaceable or interchangeable as may be assumed in the case of jobs. However, as with jobs, the terms of the occupation tend to be set by those who stand outside it, meaning that occupants remain dependent on others to define the activities that constitute the endeavor.

A third and final activity-based conception of teaching I address is the notion that it is a profession. Professionals perform a range of specialized activities based on preparation that is (typically) accredited, systematic, and continuing. It is also preparation over which professionals themselves tend to have considerable control, unlike the case with many jobs and occupations. In general, professionals differ from persons in jobs or occupations because they have greater autonomy and voice in setting the terms of the work. They influence the range and the content of the activities in which they engage (Langford, 1978; Sockett, 1993). However, in actual practice the idea of a profession can be more outward- than inward-looking. That is, it can lead members of a profession, ironically perhaps, to focus less on the moral and intellectual dimensions of their daily work and more on conserving autonomy and securing political, social, and economic resources (Abbott, 1988; Friedson, 1994). As recent debates in education, in nursing, and elsewhere have suggested, the push for professional status and prerogatives can sometimes override a spirit of service that, in theory, goes hand-in-hand with many forms of professional activity (Benner, 1994; Benner & Wrubel, 1989; Burbules & Densmore, 1991; Downie & Telfer, 1980; Gotz, 1988; Labaree, 1992). I will return in a moment to these and other problems with activity-centered conceptions of teaching.

A Focus on Ends

A second set of contemporary conceptions of teaching emphasizes not what kind of activity teaching supposedly is—job, occupation, profession—but what the activity should produce. From one point of view, teaching means promoting academic learning. Many persons presume that this outcome should be the main concern of teachers. They argue that teachers' methods and activities take their meaning from the extent to which they serve this result. Other conceptions underscore the importance of socializing or acculturating the young into the larger society. Teachers should help produce graduates who know how to participate in the social world and who can slowly assume responsibility for sustaining that world as their elders retire to the sidelines. Still other conceptions highlight the need to prepare the young to be productive members of the economic system. Teachers must help students develop sound skills, good work habits, and cooperative and flexible attitudes that will render them effective and successful workers in whatever economic domain they enter.

Outcome-centered conceptions of teaching do not stop with these familiar notions of academic, social, and economic preparedness. For some educators and members of the public, teaching should foster political attitudes in students, such as a democratic orientation. According to this viewpoint, teachers should encourage students to develop qualities of citizenship and personal political agency. Practitioners should continue to teach subject matter, but they should do so in the spirit of serving political capability. Other conceptions of teaching underscore the aim of promoting cultural understanding, awareness, and respect. According to this standpoint, teachers should be culturally focused and responsive, regardless of whether they work in schools that implement forms of multiculturalism, in schools that advance the identity of a particular group, or in public schools generally. Still other conceptions of teaching treat the work as a vehicle for promoting religious values and beliefs. Accordingly, teachers should conduct themselves in the service of these values and beliefs in both their curriculum and in their instruction.

Academic learning, socialization and acculturation, readiness for work, political agency and understanding, cultural identity and awareness, religious faith and practice: Here are just a few of the outcomes advocated today that exist alongside conceptions of teaching conceived primarily in terms of job, occupation, or profession. In everyday talk about the work, the conceptions overlap. I have divided them into two groups, one focusing on what the activity is, the other on what it should produce, for expositional purposes. The overview seems to suggest that in the public realm there are as many conceptions of teaching as there are conceptions of what is important in life. It also seems to imply that from the point of view of both logic and values, people should first determine what they care about, and then craft a conception of teaching that coheres with that determination.

I will comment in subsequent chapters on the character of some of these perspectives. Here, I want to question the proposition that teaching should be conceived primarily in terms of activity *or* outcome. Conceptions of teaching that unduly privilege desirable outcomes can take the focus away from the actual world of teaching and learning in classrooms. Such conceptions may shine too strong a light on predetermined results and treat them as "finalities to which everything must be bent and sacrificed" (Dewey, 1916/1997, p. 175). This outlook renders teaching into an instrumental activity, into a means to an end defined apart from the means. In my view, accenting any particular outcome in this manner narrows the vision of what teaching encompasses and, paradoxically, can undercut the potential of teaching to lead to such outcomes in the first place. These conceptions too easily gloss over what might be called the present educational moment, the moment when teacher and student are together in the often uncertain and unpredictable terrain of teaching and learning. However, that is the only moment, as numerous educators have reminded us, in which teaching and learning can occur. Harold Loukes (1976) writes that "there can be no teaching without seriousness: without a drawing of the teacher's will and purpose in face of a challenge, and a drawing of the pupil's will and purpose in face of a challenge—both of them concentrating on teaching-and-learning, the whole personal force now, just-this-minute, engaged to the exclusion of all else" (p. 144).

The consequence of focusing unduly either on outcomes or on the kind of activity teaching supposedly comprises is a blurring of the relation between means and ends in the work. Activity-based conceptions can presume too rigid a view of the nature of teaching and, as a result, can reduce the practice to a set of procedures. The procedures take on a life of their own. Technique and method drive the work, divorced from a conception of worthwhile ends or purposes. According to David Carr (1999), however, teaching is a moral endeavor that should be undertaken with skill. It does not comprise a set of value-neutral, discrete skills that should be carried out morally. Posed differently, as I argue below, teaching is a practice that generates the need for particular skills and methods. It is not a set of occupational skills pieced together to fulfill a social function defined apart from those skills. The purposes of teaching both inform and come alive in method and technique.

Outcome-based views, on the other hand, can focus so heavily on results or ends that the means of their realization are treated in an instrumental manner. But that means that *teachers* are regarded instrumentally, as merely a means to an end, just as they are according to activity-based conceptions that picture the work as merely a job or occupation. The poet Octavio Paz warns that any enterprise that converts persons into a means to some future end, however laudable or desirable that end may sound, implies "preparing a prison for the present" (quoted in Brann, 1999, p.

152). Paz's stark terms underscore the possible consequences of overlooking the individual persons who occupy the roles of teacher and student.

Critics might remark that this attenuated overview of current conceptions of teaching reflects the worries of academics more than it does those of schoolteachers. The latter fret much more about how to work well with children, how to fashion successful lesson plans, how to evaluate reams of homework and tests, and more. Their focus is wise. When in the midst of teaching and working with students, teachers want to be on the ground rather than moving into abstract reflection about what they are doing. My argument is that one of the conditions that drives teachers to abstraction—and, perhaps, to distraction, too—is the contested and often ambiguous nature of the work they do. Teachers at all levels of the system work in an ethos characterized by assumptions, claims, and policies that reflect the activity- and outcome-based conceptions of teaching outlined above. Although teachers might not use the language I have employed here, they would be the first to appreciate the often conflicting public expectations that characterize their surroundings. They understand what it is like to be treated by the system as hired hands, while also being expected to educate well each and every student. They feel the weight of trying to promote various desired outcomes—academic, social, political, economic— while also having to fashion successful ways of working with the young in the immediate moment. Sometimes, it seems clear, the politically relevant trumps the pedagogically relevant in the shaping of curricular and school policies.[1] Such circumstances generate tension, frustration, and anxiety, the sources of which teachers, from preschool through higher education, may not know how to identify even if they feel their impact (cf. Burbules & Hansen, 1997).

I hope the studies presented here will help provide teachers, teacher educators, researchers, and others interested in the practice with a standpoint that can assist them in appreciating the nature and significance of teaching. This outlook can help teachers confront the tensions and frustrations that accompany their work more efficaciously. Teachers are members of a practice with a long history. Across the generations, their predecessors have had to deal with multiple and sometimes conflicting demands. The argument in this book will not yield, in itself, strategies for resolving current problems. Moreover, to picture oneself as part of a tradition—that is, as a participant in a practice with a long history—will not dissolve the tensions, ambiguities, and predicaments that accompany the work. But such a standpoint gives one grounds for responding to these conditions, rather than merely reacting to them. A response is more than a reaction. It implies an ability to think matters through, to attain a broadened perspective, to be patient rather than impulsive in how one joins issue with the challenges of the day. A response implies a capacity to take ownership of one's work, rather than to conceive oneself as merely carrying out the dictates of others. Those dictates are often so varied and riddled with clashing expectations that it is small wonder they can drive teachers inward and lead them to accept a narrow, routinized, or idiosyncratic approach to their work. But that is a defensive, reactive posture, and it does not have to be the only recourse. A central claim I make is that cultivating a sense of tradition about the values in teaching points the way to a richer perspective. It does so in at least two ways. A sense of tradition generates for the teacher a critical distance from contemporary conceptions of what teaching is supposedly about. At the same time, it spurs the teacher to engage in self-scrutiny and to keep in view the question of what it means to be a teacher in the first place.

DERIVING THE TERMS OF TEACHING FROM THE PRACTICE

The idea of critical distance discloses an underlying premise of this book. When the question arises regarding what kind of activity teaching is or what its outcomes or purposes are—in other words, when the question of the relation between means and ends in the work that I touched on earlier is raised—educators can turn to the practice of teaching itself for insight. I will have much to say about the concept "practice" below and in subsequent chapters, especially about how it both presumes and promotes the importance of the individual human being in the role of teacher. My point here is that educators do not have to turn first to formal theories of education and society, nor do they have to turn first to the wishes of a particular community, in order to make sense of teaching. I say "first" because, to be sure, at various points educators can profitably consider formal theoretical perspectives and at other points must, from a moral and political point of view, seriously respond to the aspirations of various communities. Such a response is indispensable if only because most teachers work in public institutions financed by the public, whose children those teachers are in a strong position to influence.[2]

However, I believe that turning first to teaching itself can shed critical light on the strengths and the limitations in the activity- and outcome-based conceptions I outlined above. Such a turn recalls the fact that many such conceptions come and go. That is, conceptions of teaching informed by concerns, interests, and reform efforts that originate from *outside* the practice tend to be as numerous, and to have the same life span, as those concerns, interests, and reform projects. However warranted they may be, none of them supersede what resides at the heart of the practice. None of them provide an adequate source for characterizing the terms and the significance of teaching. In my view, one cannot search for meaning outside the practice (or wholly so, at any rate) if the aim is to account for what is embedded *within* it. Nor can any external set of concerns and interests ensure that the practice will survive to serve humanity's best possibilities. History shows that practices have blossomed and then withered. A given practice cannot always contain an emerging set of internal or external aims and pressures, and it is either sundered, folded into some other endeavor, or transformed into a new (and not necessarily better) way of living. But teaching has endured for an extraordinarily long time. That is one reason why it is worthwhile to turn first to teaching in order to understand its terms and to identify resources to sustain its integrity.

The Vitality of Tradition

Teaching as a human practice is not an empty cell that awaits filling from some purely external source of meaning. This fact does not imply that people can, or should, approach teaching without a conceptual outlook. All persons perceive and act in the world through a prism of evolving viewpoints. But teaching comprises something other than merely a contingent "social construction." That term describes a widely held presumption about the work (not to mention about other human practices). In crude terms, the idea of social construction presumes that, over time, human beings conceive aims, interests, and hopes, and then construct social arrangements to enable them to realize those aims, interests, and hopes. The process is not always as intentional, articulate, or orderly as this statement suggests. It is rarely so, according to some perspectives. Anthropologists and sociologists alike have contended that people are often unaware of the intricate processes in what is called social construction. They may come to regard so-called social constructions—ways of teaching, of organizing family life, of practicing medicine, and so forth—as natural or God-given. They may view challenges to them as strange, frightening, and ideologically or politically driven. They may regard such challenges as the only actual social constructions.

In a literal sense, the theory of social construction seems true to the mark. Unless one is, say, a strict biological or religious determinist, one has to grant that human beings are responsible for their ways of living. Human beings fashion ways of rearing and educating the young, of caring for (or ignoring) the elderly, of managing economic affairs, and so forth. From a critical point of view, the theory of social construction spotlights political, cultural, economic, and other factors at play in any society in which teaching occurs. The perspective it provides can help educators avoid a thoughtless embrace of past or current educational methods and goals.

However, the theory cannot capture or account for the moral tradition that has animated teaching since the practice first arose through the agency of figures such as Socrates, Confucius, and many, many others. In Chapters 6 and 7, I examine the idea of tradition in teaching. I contrast it with traditionalism, a standpoint characterized by a dogmatic, often reactionary, espousal of previous forms of life. I emphasize the distinction because a number of right-wing movements in recent years have sought to co-opt the terms *moral* and *tradition* (e.g., the so-called Moral Majority in the United States). As I understand the terms, tradition in teaching symbolizes a dialogue across human generations. In that dialogue, the encounter with the past questions and curbs "presentist" impulses, among them the tendency to regard the fashionable views of today as infallibly wiser and more urgent than any alternatives that might come to mind (if they come to mind at all). The alternatives I have in view are not ideologies or educational formulae from days of yore. I will argue throughout the book that the practice of teaching, as it has come down to us through time and human effort, does not constitute a hardened, unchangeable endeavor to which teachers must bend themselves unquestionly. Rather, it is a living practice. It evolves as a result of the initiative and imagination of teachers, part of whose task is to respond (but not to "react") to external pressures and social demands.

According to Jaroslav Pelikan (1984), a living practice nurtured by tradition has the "capacity to develop while still maintaining its identity and continuity" (p. 58). In my view, there exists a certain continuity in the practice of teaching over human time. I do not mean that all teachers participate in the practice, nor that every individual teacher always conducts him- or herself as a "practitioner" or feels him- or herself to be such. Many serious-minded teachers sometimes doubt themselves and their ability to teach, even after many years of service, and perhaps even after a whole lifetime spent in teaching. In addition, the actual conduct of much teaching in the United States and elsewhere has been more in keeping with the idea of a job or occupation, in which external actors determine what teachers do and many teachers more or less simply follow their lead. Moreover, there have always been teachers who perform poorly and in whose hands the practice suffers—meaning, in starker terms, that students suffer. But it is equally clear that there have always been sizable numbers of teachers who genuinely assist students in realizing their powers and potential. I base that claim on educational research and on other sources that I draw upon throughout the book. Such teachers shape the role. They give it distinctive intellectual and moral substance. And yet that substance comprises recognizable components that have arisen in the practice over a long period of time. Those components include helping students learn to think in broader rather than in narrower terms. They include fueling rather than draining students' sense of agency and confidence, strengthening rather than weakening students' skills in reading, writing, numerating, and more, and deepening rather than rendering more shallow students' engagement with the larger world they inhabit.

These components, or terms of the practice, suggest that teaching obliges teachers to give sustained intellectual and moral attention to students, regardless of the subject at hand or the grade or age level. This attentiveness implies that teachers of auto mechanics, literature, art, chemistry, and meditation share extensive common ground. To be sure, there are countless factors that differentiate them. But while intellectual and moral attentiveness can take many forms, although not just any form, the prospect of not attending at all to students' learning and growth is not an option for those who genuinely participate in the practice. I have argued elsewhere (Hansen, 1999) that intellectual attentiveness involves focusing on what students know, feel, and think about the subject matter at hand, with an eye toward their building both knowledge of the world and a sense for how to continue learning about the world. Moral attentiveness means being alert to students' responses to opportunities to grow as persons—for example, to become more rather than less thoughtful about ideas and more rather than less sensitive to others' views and concerns. Moral attentiveness issues, in part, from being mindful that each student is a unique, irreproducible human being who embodies a distinctive, evolving set of dispositions, capacities, understandings, and outlooks. From this perspective, the central bonds between teacher and student are not ideological (cf. Wilson, 1998, p. 151). Rather, the bonds between them are intellectual and moral, pertaining to their emerging knowledge, understanding, and growth as persons. In Chapters 2 and 3, I examine the all-too-familiar concept "person" and try to show how central it is in the practice of teaching.

In recent years researchers have illuminated the moral dimensions of teaching.[3] One lesson I draw from this body of work is that a teacher's moral and intellectual attentiveness to students is not a means to an end. That is, teachers do not attend to students in order to promote learning. They attend because that is what it means to be a teacher. Posed differently, teaching entails a moral, not just academic, relation between teacher and student. That relation surfaces in how teachers treat both subject matter and students. The teacher's curricular choices presume a value or normative judgment—"This is worth studying, that is not (at least not now)" (cf. Tom, 1984, p. 78). Any mode of addressing or working with students reveals moral perception and judgment. A teacher might ask him- or herself, "Why is this student not grasping the issue?" and take action—or the teacher might not care enough to ask the question, which is itself a moral posture (and an inadequate one, an observer might argue). Recent research underscores why the moral relation between teacher and student cannot be argued away if we are to hold onto the idea of *teaching*, rather than replacing it with images of, say, anonymous supplier on one side of the transom passing information over to anonymous customer on the other side. The practice of teaching, as contrasted with merely supplying information to others, obliges its practitioners to cultivate their capacity to attend intellectually and morally to students.

A second lesson I draw from research on the moral aspects of teaching is that the idea of an intellectual and moral relation between teacher and student makes possible what is often called the social construction of meaning. Posed differently, the relation generates the opportunity to "construct" meaningful experiences of teaching and learning in the first place. The relation suggests that teaching, as a distinctive human endeavor, is not an empty cell that awaits filling from a purely external source. Teaching is not a societal epiphenomenon (cf. McCarty, 1997, p. 392). The moral and intellectual relation embedded in the work cannot be "constructed" away if teaching is the object of discussion.[4]

This relation is not constructed into being either, as if it were a matter of choosing or deciding what teaching shall mean. Teachers do not have to decide what the practice means. Instead, they take on its terms and, through time and effort, they mold, shape, criticize, and influence them depending upon local circumstances and needs. In this process, to be sure, teachers do make many decisions, and they do have to choose among multiple options—to perform this experiment rather than another in class, to call on this student now rather than another, to use this rubric for grading rather than another, and so forth. But these choices and decisions do not occur in a temporal or purposive vacuum. They derive their significance and their necessity from the terms of the practice. The many questions that any teacher faces about what to do get their answers not in isolation from the practice but by discovering *who* one is in relation to the practice (cf. Horton & Mendus, 1994, p. 9). That unpredictable, ongoing experience includes pondering who one is in relation to students. Once again, the importance of the person in the role of teacher—a central theme of this book—comes to the fore.

Teachers can and do innovate. I would hope teachers do so all the time, every year, with every group of students, if only because no student is identical with another and thus cannot be treated in an identical way. However, the point is that this very quality of imaginative responsiveness on the part of the teacher is a moral and intellectual dimension of the work. It is one of the terms of the practice of teaching that has emerged out of its tradition. Perhaps no teacher anywhere has ever fully succeeded in recognizing all students' distinctiveness and in supporting all students' intellectual and moral flourishing. Like people in other practices, such as nursing and law, teachers are not miracle workers. But the terms of teaching serve them as a source of guidance, direction, and inspiration.

My argument does not imply that good teaching in classrooms today is good because it mimics the past. Quite on the contrary. My claim is that we can no more derive an adequate sense of what constitutes good teaching from an external principle than we could determine, for example, what constitutes good painting today by ignoring all past painting, and all past reflection on painting, and turning to, say, a political, economic, or hedonistic principle. To do so would mean dissolving painting as a distinctive endeavor and imperialistically absorbing it into some external principle that is now supposed to become the guide for what painters do and for how to interpret their work. The analysis of different conceptions of teaching with which I began suggests that this kind of pressure on teaching has been real. Both activity- and outcome-based views of teaching can ignore, or even dismiss, the dynamic human element at the heart of teaching and learning.

Moreover, any turn to an external principle for guidance must confront the fact that any and all such principles, assuming they are nonarbitrary, themselves derive from some tradition of thought and action—or else they could not even be grasped as principles. Karl Popper (1963) cautions against presuming that persons can fashion a meaningful principle, theory, or plan of action that is entirely divorced from tradition. He regards "rationalist" critiques of tradition as untenable because they presume people can wipe the slate clean, so to speak, and act independently from any and all traditions. Popper argues that

> the idea of canvas-cleaning . . . is impossible, because if the rationalist cleans the social canvas and wipes out the tradition he necessarily sweeps away with it himself and all his ideals and all his blue-prints of the future. The blue-prints have no meaning in an empty social world, in a social vacuum. They have no meaning except in a setting of traditions and institutions—such as myths, poetry, and values—which all emerge from the social world in which we live. Outside it they have no meaning at all. Therefore the very incentive and the very desire to build a new world must disappear once we have destroyed the traditions of the old world. (pp. 131–132)[5]

Popper's remarks highlight the standpoint that resides at the opposite extreme from strong versions of the theory of social construction.[6] That standpoint is rationalism, understood (in crude terms) as the claim that human reason can operate apart from, and unaffected by, all social circumstance, context, or aspiration. Popper and other critics (e.g., Langford, 1985; Taylor, 1989) would point out that the very notion that reason can function in this way reflects traditions of thought and outlook, even if the connections between them may be opaque. The critics' perspective does not imply that human beings inhabit a forest, much less a prison, of traditions from which there is no escape, although some observers of the human condition may feel that way, at least at times.[7] On the contrary, I will try to show how the sense of tradition in teaching generates a basis for a rich, critical view of practice, but one always anchored in human time and continuity. I elucidate these claims more fully in Chapters 6 and 7 as well as elsewhere in the book.

The ideas of practice and tradition make it possible to reach beyond differences between concepts such as "natural" and "discovery," on the one side, and "construction," on the other. The idea of the natural suggests that the entrant to the practice of teaching *discovers* its moral and intellectual terms, not alone but through engagement with students, with colleagues, and with others. In contrast, the idea of construction implies that the entrant *creates*, or constructs, its moral and intellectual terms, not alone but through working with students and many others. Discovery implies continuity with humanity's past. The notion of construction suggests a more tenuous, and perhaps even dispensable, connection. However, here is the premise I will work through in the pages to come: A serious-minded teacher responds imaginatively to the moral and intellectual terms she or he discovers are inherent in the practice of teaching.

As mentioned previously, those terms center around notions of broadening, deepening, and enriching students' understandings, knowledge, and outlooks, rather than rendering them more narrow, shallow, or impoverished. They have to do with helping students to learn rather to become more ignorant and assisting them to think rather than hamstringing their minds. They include spending time with students rather than ignoring them, raising questions with them rather than dampening their curiosity, immersing them and oneself in subject matter, acting in patient if determined ways throughout, and more. The fact that some teachers, or even all teachers from time to time, have failed to realize these terms does not call into question the integrity and meaning of the practice. Those failures attest more to the genuine challenges in teaching well.

Teaching and Its Qualifiers

Another way to characterize the view of teaching that orients this book is to call attention to the widespread use of qualifiers in today's discussions of teaching. Consider, for example, terms such as *"constructivist* teaching," *"culturally responsive* teaching," *"democratic* teaching," *"emancipatory* teaching," *"indirect* teaching," *"multicultural* teaching," *"progressive* teaching," *"reflective* teaching," *"reform-minded* teaching," and *"student-centered* teaching." In all such pairings, the qualifier appears to take precedence, both philosophically and practically. The qualifier highlights particular ends and/or means that proponents suggest give teaching its identity, direction, and warrant. Some proponents treat teaching as an empty category that takes its entire meaning and social relevance from the featured qualifier. That outlook mirrors arguments about teaching that start with desired outcomes and then treat those outcomes as the source of teaching's identity and purpose. Both tendencies, it seems to me, reflect the socially and politically charged nature of public education.

Each of the qualifiers could be said to underscore a particular aspect of teaching, regardless of the age level or subject under consideration. For example, constructivist teaching urges us, at least in some of its forms, to remember the learner's agency and capacity for autonomous growth. Culturally responsive teaching, in some of its versions, highlights ways in which teachers can draw on students' cultural values and customs to spur genuine learning. Democratic teaching, according to some accounts, shines a light on how classroom practices can promote civic dispositions and a sense of public responsibility. And the list goes on. One could argue that these and other qualifiers emphasize phases in the ongoing, complicated process of teaching and learning. At one moment, for instance, teachers might em*phasize* themes in the reading at hand, at others their em*phasis* will be on students' background experience, at still others the *phase* they and their students enter is one where mindfulness of moral qualities becomes paramount (e.g., "Please give her the respect you would want when you speak up in class"). In Chapters 3 through 5, I provisionally employ a qualifier myself, in speaking about "indirect" teaching. Among other things, I suggest that the qualifier represents the value to teachers of attending to the environment in which they and their students work together.

But that qualifier does not supplant the meanings embedded in the practice of teaching. It helps clarify them, or at least it is intended to do so. If the qualifier "indirect" were eliminated, along with all the others mentioned above, teaching would not reduce to an empty category. Its history and tradition attest to the contrary, for the practice constitutes more than the sum of its parts. I believe that something vital is lost, or becomes confused, whenever particular outcomes or qualifiers are given the first and last word about teaching. My claim is not that these conceptions are themselves inherently faulty. My concern is with the way in which educators craft such conceptions of teaching in the first place. Something important is placed in the shadows, and may be forgotten, whenever educators concerned about teaching operate solely from a standpoint outside the practice. The same holds true whenever educators unhesitantly adopt the theory of social construction (or any formal theory of social life, one might add). If the theory is taken to suggest that human beings, rather than, say, occult forces, shape ways of teaching, well and good. However, if it is then assumed to imply that the meanings and terms embedded in the practice of teaching derive entirely from external interests or forces—in other words, if it regards teaching as merely a means to some end conceived apart from the work—it becomes problematic. In this book, I want to approach teaching from a different origin. In metaphorical terms, I want to discern whether it is possible to catch hold of a tune that has been playing, often in the background, for a very long time.

A critic might wonder whether this talk about activity- and outcome-centered views of teaching, of social construction, and of the use of qualifiers implies the view that because teaching seems to be a singular concept, it therefore must have a singular meaning. The critic might ask if this book represents a search for the one best definition of teaching that could bring all debate to a close, calm the waters, and allow teachers to go about their work peaceably. I would entertain any idea or project that might help teachers do their work well, at any level of the system. But I do not seek a final definition of teaching. Rather, I hope to characterize enduring aspects of the work in as rich a fashion as possible. In order to do so, I draw on ideas and experiences from a wide variety of writers, including John Dewey, Dorothy Emmet, Etty Hillesum, Immanuel Kant, and Michael Oakeshott, whose views on many substantive matters differ (I do not share their outlooks *in toto* either).

The practice of teaching embodies continuity, not to be confused with mimicry or sameness, in thought and action. This understanding of the work presumes the value of dialogue about its terms. I believe the image of a unity in teaching opens the door to an inquiry into what serious-minded teachers everywhere might have to say to one another about how to articulate and to realize in action the enduring terms of the practice. Such an inquiry can generate productive ways of talking critically together across differences, whether these pertain to institutional or grade or disciplinary contexts, to political or religious or national creeds, to racial, ethnic, gender, or class identities, and so forth. That conversation, in turn, can continually revitalize the practice of teaching and keep it attuned to humanity's most compelling notions of what it means to lead a flourishing life. I will write of teaching without any a priori qualifiers and without focusing either on means or ends alone, because my interest is in pondering aspects of the terrain all teachers share or might come to share. I do not presume to know how large or small, how firm or unstable, that terrain might turn out to be. But I believe it exists—and has for some time. It may be ground that teachers and those who care about teaching have to keep clearing away and tending. To support that endeavor, I try in this book to clarify some long-standing features of the practice, as well as to suggest ways of vindicating them.

This approach incorporates what Anthony Cua (1998) describes as an "ideal of coherence." According to Cua, an ideal of coherence "provides a unity or unifying perspective for viewing the diversity of interpretations as interpretations of the same tradition" (p. 244). Teachers have, for generations, pondered and debated the terms of their work. Scholars have done the same. They have advanced a variety of theories about the nature and purposes of teaching. However, to borrow from Pelikan (1984), these changes in theory and outlook can be understood as "attempts to make sense of a continuing practice and, even in purely historical terms (whatever that may mean), do not themselves make sense apart from that continuing practice" (p. 49). Like all ideals, an ideal of coherence does not directly map concrete realities. Rather, it points to possibilities for communication, to broad connections, to productive directions for thought and action. Tradition in teaching constitutes a coherent entity, in at least two senses of the term. First, it describes something that co-heres, or holds together, across time and vicissitude, even (or especially) through moments of intense self-questioning and change. Second, tradition can be identified and understood. Teachers can take hold of tradition, rather than merely being held by it, through teaching, through study, and through conversation with peers. Such is the orientation toward teaching, sketched in the widest possible terms, that animates the studies I undertake in the pages to come.

ORGANIZATION OF THE BOOK

In Chapter 2, I discuss how a teacher or teacher candidate might respond to the hypothetical question, Why should *you* be allowed to teach children, adolescents, or adults? The response I commend involves thinking about three closely related terms: *person, conduct,* and *sensibility.* I discuss what a person is, a subject that people normally take for granted but that has an enormous bearing on how a teacher might interact with students. Then, I show how conduct differs from behavior. The idea of conduct helps capture the intellectual and moral presence a teacher develops as he or she works with students. I suggest that students may learn as much from a teacher's conduct as from the subject matter he or she teaches. Finally, the notion of a sensibility, or *moral sensibility*, becomes helpful in picturing the overall attitude a teacher brings to bear in the classroom. I draw on the concepts developed in this chapter throughout the remainder of the book.

Chapters 3 and 4 take up the related question of what image of a growing, educated person might guide a teacher's work with students. The analysis presumes that teachers do not educate students directly, as if they could reach inside students' hearts and minds. Rather, they teach indirectly, or so I suggest, through the medium or intermediary of the environment. Consequently, teachers need to think long and hard about just what kind of environment they want to bring into being in the classroom. Part of that process involves considering what it means to be a growing, educated person and what kinds of activities can promote such growth. I make extensive use of pioneering ideas from Jean-Jacques Rousseau and John Dewey both to discuss the idea of teaching indirectly and to craft an image of a learner. Ultimately, the conception of a growing person I depict merges with a more fundamental image of a *living* person—an odd way to speak, perhaps, until one ponders how much human time feels uneventful, forgettable, even meaningless.

Chapter 5 makes direct use of the analysis undertaken in Chapters 3 and 4. I examine in detail a course I teach every year to teacher candidates preparing to work in middle and high schools. In this discussion-based course, I seek to act on the principle that teachers cannot directly educate other human beings. Teachers are not magicians or wizards; they cannot enter unmediatedly into another person's mind or spirit. Posed differently, the immediate aim for teachers is not student learning, strange as this may sound at first hearing. Rather, a teacher's concrete aim is to engage students in meaningful classroom activities—discussing, experimenting, listening to a good lecture, completing a project—on the principle that such engagement can foster learning. The teacher makes use of the environment and actively strives to cultivate a particular kind of environment. I argue that who the teacher is as a person, as well as who the students are, figures centrally into the making of a classroom environment. The teacher's image of a growing, living person plays its dynamic part as well. Although focused on my own course, I undertake this analysis in a way that I hope addresses teachers at *any* level of the system, from preschool through graduate education.

In Chapters 6 and 7, I step back from the classroom scene, metaphorically speaking, and consider how developing a sense of tradition can assist teachers in attaining critical distance from everyday cares and concerns. A sense of tradition helps teachers keep hold of the larger purposes of their work. It helps them gain perspective on contemporary debates about what teaching is, debates that swirl through state, university, and school district offices and whose outcomes often find their way into local educational policies, much to teachers' surprise, shock, disappointment, or delight. A sense of tradition overcomes the ahistorical ethos surrounding so much talk about teaching. It helps teachers, and those in a position to support them, to perceive the limitations as well as the strengths in present policies and educational expectations. A sense of tradition enriches the meaning and value of being a teacher, in part by enabling teachers to see themselves as members of a practice that has a very long history. Teachers help connect the human past and future through their critical efforts in the present moment.

Finally, in Chapter 8, I examine the place of ideals in teaching. I discuss the fears and concerns various critics have expressed about the role of ideals and idealism in human affairs. Critics have argued that ideals can sometimes lead people to ignore the reality of other persons, with their distinctive viewpoints and hopes. I respond to these legitimate worries by suggesting that "big" ideals, such as social justice and developing caring citizens, can have ambiguous consequences in education. They can serve teachers as sources of motivation and inspiration, but they can also work against genuine teaching and learning. I argue that such ideals do not override the terms and obligations in the practice. In other words, no ideal conceived *apart* from teaching trumps the values built into the very endeavor itself. I have touched on some of those values, terms, and obligations in this chapter, and I will continue to elucidate them throughout the book. My argument in Chapter 8 is that in order to fulfill the responsibilities of teaching, and to amend and vitalize them (since they are not static), teachers might pursue an ideal of personhood. They might ponder what it means to be a certain kind of person—for example, a person who can be a force for good in the first place. The name I give to this ideal of personhood in teaching is *tenacious humility*. Like all ideals, what it means to be tenaciously humble in one's work is difficult to pin down and to define in precise terms. I return the discussion full circle to the analysis in earlier chapters by showing how this ideal of personhood can serve as a source of good teaching.

In summary, the themes I examine in the chapters ahead include person, conduct, and sensibility in teaching, an image of a growing person that can guide teachers' work, what it means to craft an environment that cultivates such growth, teaching and the sense of tradition, and the place of ideals in teaching. These themes spring from the idea that teaching is a moral and intellectual practice with a rich tradition. To my knowledge, the themes have not been examined in the systematic, integrated fashion I undertake here. The themes point to ways in which educators can fuse what are often treated separately in both the scholarly literature and in the classroom: theory and practice, philosophy and action, ideas and conduct.

The themes also pivot around the question I raised at the start of the chapter: what it means to be a person in the role of teacher. Much of my focus in the book will be on the individual who occupies the role. That emphasis should not be taken to discount the very real values to teachers of collaboration, of collegiality, of keeping productive company with parents, social workers, and others involved in the education of children and youth. Many recent studies rightfully underscore these and related considerations. Such studies also highlight broad issues of school reform and the reform of teacher education, which are hot topics in the United States and elsewhere. Still, "broader" does not mean "more important" when it comes to teaching. As argued previously, we can turn to teaching first, and last, in order to grasp its terms and its significance. The question of what it means to be a person in the role of teacher is best answered not from an occupational context but from a context of tradition and practice. Teaching has been and will remain, above all, the work of individual persons communicating with usually younger human beings and participating with them in educational endeavors. In writing this book, I have sought to tether myself to that fundamental fact.

≈ 2 ≈

Person, Conduct, and Moral Sensibility in Teaching

TO JUDGE FROM its long tradition, the most important factor in the practice of teaching is the person who occupies the role of teacher. No other factor has greater weight in influencing the intellectual and the moral quality of the instruction children, youth, and adults receive during their years of classroom experience. Curricular materials, technology, and support from other professionals are all significant. But their impact in the classroom is dependent on the teacher's understanding, knowledge, initiative, and receptivity.

These premises underlie a family of questions that societies and cultures have had to address ever since teaching first emerged as a practice. Who should fill the role of teacher? What kind of persons should they be? What should they do in the classroom? What should they know? How much autonomy, or freedom of action, should they be granted? Who should prepare them for their work, and how? Who should evaluate them, and how? Democratic societies have found these questions particularly vexing. By their very nature, such societies tend to embody different and even contrasting views of the purpose of education. Some persons regard education as preparation for work, others as a way to develop qualities of citizenship, still others as a means of fostering a whole or well-rounded person—and the list goes on.

The questions about who should teach, and how they should teach, attest to the public interests and hopes that swirl around a society's corps of teachers. To the individual teacher, or person considering becoming a teacher, the questions—if faced squarely and honestly—may seem overwhelming, if not intimidating. Think of the young high school teacher nervously checking and rechecking materials in the rapidly waning minutes before his first class, or of the new assistant professor swallowing every time she checks the clock as it ticks down to her first course meeting. At such moments, the questions about who should teach may seem to boom down like echoes from an Olympian mountaintop, transfixing the mortals below and making their knees knock. And, in a genuine sense, they should. Such questions should stop any thoughtful person short, given how crucial formal education can be to the welfare of individuals and societies.

However, like an artist who reacts to the question "What is art?" by painting, composing, or performing well, a teacher can respond to the question "Who should teach?" by teaching well. Posed differently, a teacher can answer society's unspoken but ever-present question "Why should we let *you* be a teacher of our young?" by saying, in effect: Let me show you why. A good showing entails being mindful of the person one is and of the conduct one enacts when in the presence of students. Such mindfulness goes hand-in-hand with developing a moral sensibility, by which I mean a disposition of mind and feeling centered around attentiveness to students and their learning. In this chapter, I examine each of the core terms *person, conduct*, and *moral sensibility*. I suggest that the invitation to become a certain kind of person, as teacher, presents an opportunity rather than a forbidding burden. In making this case, I hope to demonstrate the value of dwelling on what may seem, at first glance, to be obvious features of teaching, but that turn out to be more complicated, and more significant, the longer one ponders them. Such features sometimes fall into the shadows, or are elbowed aside, in the often impersonal, bureaucratic, and hectic world of educational systems.

THE PERSON IN THE ROLE OF TEACHER

Who, or, better perhaps, what is a person? On first hearing, this question may appear strange. A sympathetic reader might respond: "What kind of a question is that? 'Who or what is a person?' You can ask what is a *good* person, a *bad* person, a *thoughtful* person, a *caring* person. We can develop answers to those questions. But what can it mean to ask about a 'person'?" The reader's commonsensical response is on the mark. As a Shakespearean character might put it, there is madness in asking about certain things. Life would come to a standstill, and would be ridiculous, if everyone suddenly stopped and asked their friends, family, and colleagues, "Who or what are you?" However, while it may be odd or even mad in some way, anthropologists, philosophers, and psychologists, not to mention painters, poets, and novelists, have frequently explored what it means to be a person. They have thought it worthwhile to investigate what goes into making us the persons we are. They have found that, unexpectedly perhaps, the concept of a person is "imprecise, delicate, and fragile" (Mauss, 1985, p. 1).

In taking for granted the notion of a person, as we typically do, we take for granted human qualities that would strike us as wondrous if they were not so commonplace. For example, when we encounter one another in offices, homes, restaurants, schools, and on the street, we treat each other as having agency. That is, we presume that we have both the capacity and the disposition to engage in certain actions—as simple as avoiding barging into one another and as complex as initiating a conversation. In assuming that other people can act as agents rather than as robots, we also regard them as having the related qualities of intentionality and will. We presume that others have intentions, in the everyday sense of that word, just as we ourselves do: to read a book, go to the store, have coffee with a friend, take a nap, and so forth. We take for granted that others have a will. They not only form intentions, but they realize them in action. They can and will read the book, go to the store, and show up for the rendezvous.

We also assume that a person—whether a neighbor, friend, colleague, or stranger—is a being who thinks and feels, who has a sense of imagination, a memory, and a diverse if not incalculable array of human contacts. We treat others not as having empty heads but as being able to think. We talk to them as if they were thinking beings, and we take for granted that they regard us in a similar way (at least most of the time). We presume that persons feel things. We try to avoid saying or doing things that hurt them. Even cruel people often take it as given that others feel things. We also assume that people imagine possibilities in their lives. They have dreams, hopes, and aspirations, however muted these may be, just as we ourselves do. We presuppose that persons have memories and can retain knowledge, thereby freeing us from a nightmare world in which we would have to explain everything to everyone every time we saw them. Finally, we regard a person as a social being, as having grown up, like ourselves, in a social world in which we take on language, customs, beliefs, and more. We take for granted the fact that persons live in a world populated with other persons.

If this bare-bones picture of who or what a person is makes sense, it provides a start to answering the question "Who do we believe should be allowed to teach?" In a nutshell, we would like the teacher to be a person.

At this juncture, our sympathetic reader might feel compelled to interject: "I have to say that this conclusion is less than profound. We want a teacher to be a person, you say. Three cheers! In technical terms, all you have done is kept us within the confines of a sentence. That is, in the sentence 'The teacher is or should be a person,' the predicate you employ, *person*, is *contained* in the subject, *teacher*. There is no such thing as a teacher, at any rate a human one, who is not a person. To understand teaching, we need propositions in which the predicate is not contained in the subject. A good example would be: The teacher is a person *who knows subject matter well and can teach it effectively to students*. Here, the long predicate is not contained in the idea of a person. After all, we do not expect all persons, such as taxi drivers, florists, and sports stars, to 'know subject matter well and [be able] to teach it effectively to students.' We do expect teachers to have that capacity. So all your talk thus far about a person falls well short of the mark."

Once again, one hears the echoes of common sense. Teachers should understand what they are teaching, and they should be skillful in their classroom instruction. I will address these and other qualities of a teacher as I proceed. However, as many educational commentators have cautioned (e.g., Buchmann & Floden, 1993; Jackson, 1986), there are dangers in relying solely on common sense when it comes to comprehending teaching. Teaching involves a host of uncommon actions. For example, in everyday life we often tell people things we know or would like them to do. Many teachers steer clear of such talk or at least are deliberate about when to employ it. They often ask students to figure matters out for themselves, guiding them along the way with questions and possibilities but not directly telling them what to do or what to think. To take another example, in everyday life people evaluate and judge each other's ideas and actions all the time. Most of this commentary is casual, spur of the moment, simply a part of daily interaction. However, teachers must develop *formal* methods of judging other people's ideas and actions. As public servants, they cannot be arbitrary in so doing. They cannot, for example, give a high mark to a student on a math test simply because they like the student's taste in ice cream. They have to work with warranted criteria of what it means to learn and to articulate or to demonstrate one's learning. In order to fulfill their mandate responsibly, teachers cannot operate in a casual, ad hoc manner. Moreover, even the most successful teachers sometimes find it very difficult to understand students and to evaluate their work. Prior experience and knowledge do not guarantee that such teachers will have smooth sailing in each and every class, with each and every student. In short, teachers cannot rely on common sense alone. That is why it is worthwhile to dwell, in a perhaps uncommon way, on terms such as "person," "conduct," and "sensibility."

Consider once more the assumptions that comprise the apparently simplistic claim that the teacher must be a person. In accepting that proposition, we are saying that the teacher has a sense of agency, can fashion intentions, can act on them, can think about what he or she does, can feel things (for example, caring and positive regard for students), can use imagination, and can remember things pertinent to the work. We also presume that the teacher, as a person, is a social being, a being who recognizes and can partake in the sorts of everyday interactions between people that occur in schools and classrooms. We take for granted *all* of these qualities just by presuming that the teacher should be a person. Posed differently, we act as if there is no need to discuss such qualities at all.

But what a list! Would everyone say that every teacher they have ever had embodied them all or embodied them to similar degrees? The answer is no. This fact does not imply the drastic conclusion that weaker, less effective, and less memorable teachers are not persons. Rather, it may suggest that such teachers have not occupied the role as fully as others whom we regard as more successful. It may mean that such teachers are not yet the persons they are capable of becoming, at least within the terms of the role. They are not, say, as broad-minded, knowledgeable, curious, enthusiastic, or patient with students as they might be. Perhaps they remain on a more comfortable plane, or they may still be finding their way. It would be a mistake to assume that acting patiently with students, for instance, is natural and simple, even if some teachers make it look that way. Patience seems so essential to teaching and learning that a teacher who lacks this quality, or at least the willingness to develop it, is bound to have difficulties, even if he or she possesses all the knowledge in the world.

There are at least two alternatives to the idea that teachers should be persons: (1) that they be replaced by machines or (2) that they become functionaries mechanically carrying out the dictates of others. I will not make a case for either alternative, even for heuristic purposes, because I cannot imagine defending them. Who could ever program a machine to perform the nuanced, sensitive interpretations teachers must constantly make of students' ideas, explanations, concerns, capabilities, questions, interests, doubts, and hopes? Would not the ability and knowledge to program a machine in such a way mean that the programmers were themselves masters of those gifts? What group of programmers possess that qualification? What group of persons have ever had such Olympian understanding of human development?

Machines and technology have been and doubtless will remain useful resources for teachers. But nothing nonhuman will ever be able to do what teachers-as-persons do, namely, recognize and cultivate the emergence of personhood in the young. Moreover, the basic claim that a teacher must be a person becomes even richer when we recall that to intend, to will, or to think are not states of being in and of themselves. In other words, we always intend, will, or think *something*. Nor do we feel, imagine, or remember in a vacuum. We always feel, imagine, or remember *something*. Dewey (1916/1997) helps keep these fundamental facts before our eyes. Dewey describes as "mythological" the idea that persons have faculties, such as perceiving and listening, that must be "fed" by external stimuli. "There are no such ready-made powers," he argues, "waiting to be exercised and thereby trained" (p. 62). Perception is nonexistent without a percept. Listening is nonexistent without something to listen to. Perception is more than the functioning of the eye, just as listening constitutes more than the functioning of the ear. The biological conditions that make perceiving and listening possible are not the same as the power to observe or the ability to listen (for thoughtful discussion of this point, see Elkins, 1996, and Wolfe, 1993). The latter have to be built up through life experience, including education, and they can be developed in better and worse ways. We all know perceptive people who can see into human affairs, just as we know people who seem blind to the very world in front of them.

Here the sympathetic reader's request for further insight can be met. What does a teacher intend, will, or think? Nothing random, to say the least. As a teacher, the person intends to promote student learning. That intention materializes in the will to act: to craft a good curriculum, to conceive and enact sound lesson plans, to pay attention to students individually, and so forth. The person thinks regularly and persistently about such matters. We might say that such thoughts occupy his or her mind. They do not do so at every waking moment. The person will be many other things, too: parent, spouse, friend, weekend golfer, filmgoer, walker of the dog, and much more. In those roles other thoughts are paramount, although some of them can and often do cross over into the province of teaching. However, as a *teacher*, thoughts of students, curriculum, lessons, the whole classroom and school world are never absent from the person's mind. Posed differently, such thoughts and their associated actions *are* the mind of the teacher. This statement is worth elucidating, since common sense often presumes that the mind is strictly mental and removed from the world of objects and things.

"Too frequently mind is set over the world of things and facts to be known," Dewey (1916/1997) writes; "it is regarded as something existing in isolation, with mental states and operations that exist independently" (p. 130; see also Oakeshott, 1991, pp. 109–110). But that conception is "mythical," Dewey argues. Mind does not exist apart from human aspirations, actions, perceptions, and anticipations. Mind "appears in experience"—it literally comes into being—as the "ability" to respond to situations in light of purposes, hopes, and possible consequences (p. 130). Mind "is not a name for something complete by itself; it is a name for a course of action in so far as that is intelligently directed; in so far, that is to say, as aims, ends, enter into it, with selection of means to further the attainment of aims" (p. 132). Boisvert (1998) writes that mind "should be treated more as a verb than as a substantive. . . . Children are told to 'mind' their parents. An individual has a 'mind' to engage in some project. We are re-'minded' of past events. A father 'minds' his children, and a tourist in Britain must 'mind' low archways" (pp. 99–100). We are mindful of others' concerns and questions, or we are unmindful of them. In short, mind describes not a self-contained receptacle in the head but a human enactment. Serious-minded teachers literally "mind" what they do in the school and classroom.

What does a teacher feel? A great many things, with a range as wide as thought itself. However, as with thought, a teacher's feelings exist neither in a vacuum nor in the privacy of some black box in the head or red box in the chest. They center around the terms of teaching. For example, the teacher feels joy in helping students learn, anguish over a student who rejects his or her efforts, delight in a student composition or drawing, despair over a student who keeps failing, frustration at being subject to so many bureaucratic imperatives, hope in being able to accomplish things despite such institutional pressures, and lassitude during the doldrums that set in from time to time during the schoolyear when it seems next to impossible to energize oneself for the work ahead. The list goes on, stretching as far as the boundaries of pedagogical work.

The person in the role of teacher imagines how tomorrow's activities will play out and how students might respond to them. The person imagines where she would like the class to be 3 months hence and plans accordingly. The person imagines how a particular student might react to a particular project or academic suggestion. She may imagine the contours of her own life a year from now, or 5 years from now, and ask herself what kind of person and teacher she hopes to be. The imaginative gaze turns to the past, too, and profitably so. The person in the role of teacher reimagines last year's classes and realizes in a whole new way what she learned from the experience. She reimagines what drew her into teaching in the first place and suddenly perceives how she has grown as well as how she has developed some bad habits that need changing.

Memory figures into intentions, will, thought, feeling, and imagination. In fact, all of these aspects of the person in the role of teacher overlap and come to life together. They can be distinguished only for purposes of exposition. The teacher remembers his original curricular plans when revising them. He strengthens his will by recalling how things went awry last week or by recalling how well the lesson went in the earlier period that day. He fuels his thoughts about students with memories of what they have said and done so that he can connect with them better in the future. He recollects what he felt at the previous faculty meeting so that he can conduct himself at the forthcoming one more prudently. And he remembers his hopes for his classes when the schoolyear began, how he imagined things would turn out, and thereby restarts himself as he enters a new semester.

The qualities of a person outlined here not only overlap and merge, they also have a social dimension. As suggested previously, a person is a social being raised in a social world characterized by language, custom, belief, and much more. Thus the teacher is also a social being. But this is so not just because the teacher may speak the local language, believe the local beliefs, and observe the local customs. It is so because every feature of teaching touched upon thus far has social aspects. In saying that the teacher thinks or feels *something*, rather than doing so in a vacuum, I am suggesting that the teacher thinks and feels within a social medium. To think about a lesson plan intended to promote student learning is to engage in an endeavor with social overtones, even if the thinking takes place in the privacy of one's office or home. This is because one is thinking about matters with social import and is thinking with concepts and terms with a social origin. And to feel delight or despair in the role of teacher also has a social aspect, since the delight or the despair originate, at least in part, in the social context of educational practice.

This perspective does not dissolve the person in the role of teacher into a purely social entity. It does not mean the teacher's thoughts and emotions can be causally traced to social circumstances and forces, as if the latter have an independent agency of their own. That belief would be the mirror image of the view that mind and emotion exist quite independently of the world and have their own quite independent laws and operations. To be sure, a person's thoughts, perceptions, feelings, hopes, fears, loves, and more depend on social, not to mention biological, conditions. But it would be rash to assume that they are caused by those conditions, as contrasted, say, with suggesting they are made possible by them. Michel Serres contends that "you can always proceed from the product to its conditions, but never from the conditions to the product" (quoted in Donoghue, 1998, p. 73). Human beings have an unfathomable capacity to cultivate their intellectual and moral sensibilities and conduct (see below). The concepts with which they think, and the feelings they hold, may originate in the social or public world. But the significance and the meaning of those concepts and feelings do not end there.

Persons can color the concepts they use in distinctive ways. Their feelings, as they fuse with or uncouple from various thoughts, can take unique trajectories. As Iris Murdoch (1970) shows, a 20-year-old may have a different understanding of and feeling for courage than a 60-year-old. Moreover, the same human being will often find his or her understanding of a concept changing over time. A person may comprehend a concept, such as learning, in ways that evolve, to the extent that the person may come to see his or her earlier understanding as shortsighted. In addition, the person's new outlook may differ from that of others. Consider also a person who becomes absorbed in a new endeavor, such as poetry or basketball. To the would-be poet, familiar words may take on entirely new meanings, and they may generate new emotions, too—perhaps, as Dewey says about the plenitude of virtues (1916/1997, p. 357), emotions for which we do not have names. The poet may one day show others how to understand more richly particular concepts and feelings. A person new to the basketball court will likely discover new meanings and feelings in notions of teamwork, movement, rhythm, coordination. That person, too, might take what she or he learns and infuse it into other walks of life, perhaps to the surprise and benefit of others. I will illustrate this point further as I proceed.

Nonetheless, what bears underscoring at this juncture is that teaching, like being a person, has social dimensions. This conclusion implies that a misanthrope—that is, someone who has contempt for people—should be discouraged (to put it mildly) from entering the ranks of teaching. The same can be said for a misologist—that is, an individual who rejects or hates thought and inquiry. Misanthropy and misology are recipes for an oppressive, unhappy classroom.

So much for a brief outline of the person in the role of teacher. How might this person conduct him- or herself in the classroom and school? That question has been partially answered, but the next section provides a fuller response.

CONDUCT IN TEACHING

Statements such as "She behaved well today in the assembly" and "He is very respectful" are familiar and straightforward in meaning. They bring to mind terms such as "decorum," "manners," and "etiquette." Those words have to do with a person's public behavior and how others perceive and judge it.

However, *conduct* means something other than whether children sit quietly in their seats or whether fancy-dressed people at a ball bow appropriately to one another. Conduct differs from merely sanctioned or expected behavior. It derives its meaning from more than social convention or from how others tend to perceive what an individual does. This is not to say that conduct necessarily clashes with socially approved or expected behavior. However, like the idea of a person, conduct is more complicated than first meets the eye.[1]

Conduct comprises the characteristic doings of a person. In other words, it reveals and expresses his or her character. Character has to do with how the person regards and treats others. It embodies what makes the person irreproducible or noninterchangeable with others; no two persons have the same character. In this light, person and conduct are inseparable. In an almost literal sense, a person materializes in his or her conduct. And conduct becomes empty formality, or even something biologically determined, in the absence of a person with qualities such as intentionality, will, and imagination, as discussed in the previous section. We speak of a butterfly's behavior but not of its conduct, and we do not ascribe conduct to stones, stars, or the rain. We associate it with persons.

While the idea of a person helps us understand human agency—that is, the potential and the ability to act—the idea of conduct highlights patterns of action. Conduct describes the continuity, or unity, in what a person does. "Where there is conduct," Dewey argues, "there is not simply a succession of disconnected acts but each thing done carries forward an underlying tendency and intent, *conducting*, leading up, to further acts and to a final fulfillment and consummation" (1932/1989, p. 168). Dewey implies that human beings are not always engaged in conduct. "Where there is conduct," as he puts it, there is a person with intentions and aims, such that each thing she undertakes "carries" an aim forward. In turn, that aim invests her subsequent acts with meaning. Her actions become more than a "succession of disconnected" doings, as if someone or something else were in control. Rather, her acts merge and propel her forward, toward fulfilling or consummating the aim, as Dewey puts it. Where there is no conduct, there is potential disconnection. Acts may be undertaken in a haphazard, perhaps thoughtless way. Instead of conduct, we get mere behavior, a jumping around from one thing to another in reaction to external stimuli. We can see looming on the horizon the idea that a teacher should aspire to engage in conduct rather than in mere behavior and should endeavor to help students appreciate the difference between them.

Where there is no conduct, there is no person, or so it seems. In the absence of conduct, one may expend energy here, there, and everywhere. The person may become dispersed, dislocated, disoriented. Consider the lampooned image of a television couch potato, mindlessly channel surfing hour after hour. No sense of personhood can grow under these conditions. The development of the person is on hold, as it were. Worse, the longer one remains aimless, the more likely it becomes that what has been gained in terms of personhood may begin to dissolve. Personhood has to be cultivated throughout the course of a life, and education can be conceived as the ongoing process of fueling personhood.[2]

An individual who connects acts creates the possibility of fulfilling aims and thus travels the road of a person. Acts begin to lead up to subsequent acts, thereby sustaining and developing human purposes and interests. I do not mean just any acts. A teacher who bullies children, which most educators would regard as an indefensible act, hardens him- or herself into a bullying kind of individual. Nor is there anything grandiose intended in this language. It pertains as much to the child at play—play surely involves connecting one act with another—as it does to the physicist at work on an experiment, for work entails connecting one's acts, too. Dewey (1916/1997), Hans-Georg Gadamer (1960/1996), and Johan Huizinga (1955), among others, object to the ways in which contemporary thinking and institutional life often divorce play and work. They argue that play and work do not describe necessarily unrelated activities but rather can denote phases or aspects of a person's engagement in a single undertaking (see also Dewey, 1934/1980, pp. 278–279).

The fact that every act can lead to further acts strengthens what Dewey calls our "permanent tendencies to act" (1932/1989, p. 170). Another term for "permanent tendencies" is disposition. That concept describes the mainspring for how a person undertakes tasks—for example, mindfully and diligently—and how he or she relates with other people—for example, patiently and attentively. In this light, person, conduct, and character become complementary terms. Dewey claims that conduct is "strictly correlative" with character, for "*potentially* conduct is one hundred percent of our conscious life. For all acts are so tied together that any one of them may have to be judged as an expression of character" (1932/1989, p. 170). In arguing that conduct is "potentially" the entirety of our conscious life, Dewey conjures an ideal of wholeness, or of continuity, in the self. The ideal state, it seems, is like that of an electric current in which there are no breaks. It is like the playing of a symphony, in which conductor and orchestra attend to each movement and note, rather than skipping some or jumping randomly from one to the other. Like all ideals (see Chapter 8), Dewey's image serves as a source of inspiration or guidance rather than as something truly attainable. The multiple facets and obligations of social life, and the psychological twists and turns to which most of us are subject, make it virtually impossible to sustain complete continuity. But Dewey highlights the powers and the potential an individual embodies to harmonize person and conduct and thus to bring his or her life into greater rather than lesser continuity.

The concept of narrative supports the value of thinking about continuity in one's actions. Alasdair MacIntyre (1984) makes powerful use of the concept in his influential study of the moral dimensions of human life. MacIntyre suggests that an individual becomes a person through knitting his or her acts together over time and across particular social environments. Those acts come to constitute, metaphorically speaking, the story of the individual's life, or what MacIntyre (p. 218) calls the narrative unity that helps substantiate the person's identity. The idea of such a unity seems to be built into the idea of continuity. If we wish to understand a person's acts—or, as MacIntyre (pp. 206–210, 214) puts it, if those acts are to be "intelligible"—we have to consider their larger life context or setting, much as we interpret a character's actions in a story by drawing on the background and events the author has provided. However, in actual lives the author of the story is the individual him- or herself. That fact implies that we must consider the person's acts in light of his or her history of conduct.

MacIntyre emphasizes the social dimension of such authorship. At the end of the day, he argues, we are but the "co-authors" of our lives (p. 213). As Stephen Preskill (1998) puts it, "The work of making the self is the labor of a lifetime occurring in concert with others, not in isolation from them" (p. 344). An individual becomes a person, in part, through participating in social life with all of its many influences, possibilities, and constraints. An individual person becomes a teacher through embracing the responsibilities of the work and through engaging in the social world of the school and classroom. If this argument is acceptable, the concepts of continuity and narrative describe something other than what psychologists call the maintenance of the self. Rather, the concepts highlight how a person *emerges*, or comes into being, through time, striving, and interacting with others.[3]

In summary, while the concept of a person highlights a human being's agency, that of conduct describes the pattern a person's acts can take. Conduct differs from mere behavior, which can be thoughtless and mechanistic. Conduct instantiates the person's intentions, will, thought, feeling, and hope. It helps us appreciate what Kant (1785/1990) describes as the "dignity" of individual human beings: their distinctiveness, their irreproducibility. Conduct is also a medium through which people influence each other and who they are becoming as persons. Moreover, persons can improve or enrich their conduct throughout a lifetime, and persons can influence one another throughout their lifetimes.

What does this account of conduct imply for a teacher? What does it mean to think about one's actions as a teacher in this spirit? To respond more fully to these questions, I turn now to the third term I introduced at the start of the chapter, *moral sensibility.*

MORAL SENSIBILITY AND TEACHING

The idea of a person's "sensibility" calls to mind words such as *thoughtful, reflective,* and *unhasty.* In this light, a sensibility contrasts with "feeling" or "emotion"—with matters of the heart, the spirit, the passions. However, human flourishing requires both thought and emotion, both mind and heart. Part of the project of becoming a person is learning to harmonize them in conduct.

One way to bring the terms together is to qualify them. For example, we could speak of sympathetic sensibility, meaning a quality of reasoning and foresight in which the welfare of other people, not just of oneself, is front and center. Or we could talk about thoughtful emotion, meaning a form of emotion or feeling guided, or educated, by thought itself. This might mean, for example, that in the face of human loss and distress a person feels others' pain but, at the same time, considers what can be done to alleviate the pain and perhaps also what can be done to work on the conditions that have caused it. Nancy Sherman (1997), among other recent writers, argues that neither reason nor emotion alone can reliably guide people through difficult moral predicaments. She suggests that moral conduct depends on the person having cultivated both human capacities. The person must learn to let reason and emotion mutually inform each other. Moreover, Sherman argues, that process pivots around the individual's agency. It cannot be forced or ordered by others. A school or school district cannot *make* a teacher be patient and attentive with students. Institutions have no jurisdiction over these aspects of a teacher's person and conduct. They hinge on the teacher's willingness to foster such qualities in him- or herself.

In light of the discussion of person and conduct in the previous two sections, I propose employing the term *moral sensibility* to bring reason and emotion together. The qualifier *moral* adds something both to feeling and to sensibility. Posed differently, it merges what I have said about sympathetic sensibility and thoughtful emotion. A moral sensibility embodies a person's disposition toward life and the people and events he or she encounters. It describes how a person fuses humaneness and thought in the way he or she regards and treats others. A moral sensibility features a critical orientation. It is neither blind nor sentimental. It includes a reflective capacity: the ability to stand back from the scene at certain moments in order to discern the issues at stake, to appreciate differences in point of view that may be involved, and more.[4] Such moments occur time and again in teaching. However, a moral sensibility does not trigger aloofness. To stand back from a classroom situation is not to stand apart from it. A moral sensibility presupposes a quality of engagement. It implies involvement in the outcome of the issue or problem. It embraces the premise that how one approaches a situation influences not only students but also the person and teacher one is becoming.

The idea of a moral sensibility underlines the importance of the *way* in which a teacher thinks and acts, rather than solely what he or she says or does. For example, two teachers might provide the same instructions for a small-group activity or identical explanations of a method for interpreting poetry. However, one teacher might be brusque and impatient, conveying the message that he does not trust or like his students. Or he might perform in a blasé or casual manner, signaling that he does not care about the outcome of the activity. Another teacher, offering the same remarks, might do so in an enthusiastic and supportive spirit, thereby expressing her involvement in teaching and her confidence in her students' power to learn. It is not hard to imagine which classroom students might prefer. Their choice would reflect the fact that the teachers differ not so much in their technical knowledge or expertise as in their moral sensibility. The terms that help capture the difference between them— *trust, care, support, involvement*—are saturated with moral meaning. They illustrate why we can speak of a teacher's moral presence in the lives of students, even if the teacher never thinks in those terms or employs the word "moral."

Some examples of a teacher's influence can clarify and dramatize the meaning of a moral sensibility.

Moral Being

The philosopher Michael Oakeshott (1989) describes how some of his teachers helped form his character as a person. He emphasizes that they did so indirectly, rather than through precept or admonition. For example, he writes that

> if you were to ask me the circumstances in which patience, accuracy, economy, elegance and style first dawned upon me, I would have to say that I did not come to recognize them in literature, in argument or in geometrical proof until I had first recognized them elsewhere; and that I owed this recognition to a Sergeant gymnastics instructor who lived long before the

days of "physical education" and for whom gymnastics was an intellectual art—and I owed it to him, not on account of anything he ever said, but because he was a man of patience, accuracy, economy, elegance and style. (p. 62)

As a result of being with such teachers, Oakeshott began to realize that "there was something else in learning than the acquisition of information" (p. 62). He began to discern the sensibility of the individual in the role of teacher, just as he perceived that academic subject matter itself revealed human sensibilities. He learned these things not because they were a topic of instruction but rather in "concrete situations," such as when historical facts were "suspended in an historian's argument" or when, while reading a passage of literature, he recognized "the reflection of a mind at work in a language" (p. 62). Oakeshott discovered that "how" a person is, in the world, can carry as much weight as "what" a person is. Those terms are another way of speaking of conduct and person. They point to why a moral sensibility can help to unify the two in ways that support, rather than undermine, human flourishing.

Moral Grace

The musician and scholar Suzanne Hoover offers comparable testimony about her music teacher, Nadia Boulanger. In Hoover's experience, Boulanger was much given to direct pedagogy and moral exhortation. "[G]enius without character is nothing," Boulanger would say, while "character without genius is nearly everything. Untiringly, day after day, she preaches discipline and devotion" (quoted in Epstein, 1981, p. 99). However, what emerges from Hoover's account is the power of Boulanger's sensibility. Her every word and gesture seem to express how to love music, how to devote oneself to its study, and how to reveal its wonders to other people. Boulanger showed Hoover the meaning of concentration, hard work, patience, deliberation, and the joy that can come from such commitment. Slowly but surely, Hoover deepened these qualities in herself, to the point of anticipating her teacher's expectations even while exceeding her own. "As usual," she writes at one point,

> nothing specific had been assigned [by Boulanger]—it was all up to me, and I knew what had to be done . . . I had decided that I would like to conduct the whole [concerto] from beginning to end; we had never considered more than one movement at a time. I worked, therefore, on the continuity. When I arrived at the lesson, N. B. asked simply, "What are you going to do?" I said I would like to play and beat the whole concerto from memory, at the piano. That was, of course, what she had hoped I would do. So away I

went—no pauses, no interruptions, and a minimum of stumbling. . . . When I had come to the end . . . she said, "Well, and tell me—don't you feel good?" (quoted in Epstein, 1981, p. 100)

Hoover grew not only in her musical knowledge and prowess. She grasped the enduring moral impact her serious-minded teacher had on her. She concludes her reminiscence by describing a concert Boulanger conducted in a centuries-old chapel:

The musical climax of the service was the *Salve Regina* of Fauré, . . . a quietly ravishing piece for soprano solo and instruments. N. B. was conducting it minimally . . . left hand resting elegantly on her hip, right hand making small arabesques in three-quarter time, when suddenly the soprano lost her place. An expression of despair spread over the singer's face. One understood instantly its cause: the sensation of having let N. B. down.

Still beating, N. B. took a step to the right, toward the girl. Then, smiling serenely, she took up the beat with her left hand as she laid her right hand gently on the soprano's shoulder and sang the music softly to her as it went along. The girl looked into N. B.'s eyes, smiled back, and in a moment or two resumed singing and continued without the score to the end. . . . [I]t is the memory of her in the chapel, conducting—so totally given to the music and the moment, and at the same time so close to her students—that will remain with me longest. (quoted in Epstein, pp. 101–102)

Like Oakeshott, Hoover came to understand something about the workings of a teacher's moral sensibility. She saw how her teacher embodied the very qualities that she now gazes upon with insight and gratitude.

Moral Presence

Children and adolescents can be equally responsive to a teacher's moral sensibility. I will illustrate this claim with several vignettes drawn from an extended classroom-based research project. That project centered around an inquiry into the moral life of schools (Jackson, Boostrom, & Hansen, 1993) and also became the occasion for a study of teachers' reasons for teaching in the first place (Hansen, 1995). I have commented on the vignettes before, but not in the way I shall undertake here.

The episodes feature three teachers. Ms. Smith was teaching sixth-grade social studies in an independent middle school when my research began. Prior to joining its faculty 4 years previously, she had taught for 10 years in public schools. Mr. Peters was teaching religious studies in a Catholic high school for boys. He had been in the classroom for 2 years. The third teacher, Ms. Walsh, had been teaching English for 25 years in public high schools when my inquiry started. The teachers' urban schools and communities differ from one another in noteworthy ways. However, I want to touch briefly on aspects of who they are as persons, aspects that cut across differences in setting and that shed further light on the significance of a moral sensibility.

In the middle of one of the 3 years I spent observing their practice, a sixth-grade student in Ms. Smith's school attempted suicide. This action threw the entire school off its stride. Many of the child's peers were deeply troubled, and some began to share their concerns directly with Ms. Smith. To help them regain their composure and confidence, Ms. Smith began to invite individual students to sit with her during her otherwise free lunch period. In a matter of days, the lunch group mushroomed to some 25 students. It began to take on the feel of a formal gathering. In due time, students' anxieties about their now fully recovered peer eased. However, the lunch group continued for a few days more as students took advantage of the opportunity to share other troubles and worries with Ms. Smith. These included concerns about the climate of the school and about how other adults were treating them.

One morning in April of that same year, Mr. Peters's Catholic school (located about a mile and a half away from Ms. Smith's school) was preparing for a memorial service for a student named Robert Williams who had been shot and killed several days before in a public park. During the homeroom period just before the service, in one of Mr. Peters's colleague's classes, the teacher quietly asked her students if they wanted to talk about their feelings. After a moment of silence, a boy raised his hand. "In my journal here," offered the boy, holding up his writing notebook that is a required part of Mr. Peters's religion class, "I wrote about how depressed I was to hear of Robert's being murdered. I was afraid. So I just stayed inside, I didn't want to go out, I was afraid what happened to him would happen to me. But then Mr. Peters, he said once that 'Goodness rules the world.' I asked him if he still believed that now and he says he still sees Good overall, and I feel I have to come outside, I want to see that Goodness, because there must *be* something Good if Mr. Peters sees it and believes it." The teacher acknowledged the boy's words in a manner that signaled her esteem for how Mr. Peters works with students. I heard other comments from students about Mr. Peters and his influence on them during my 3 years as an observer in the school.

During fourth period one morning in March of that year, Ms. Walsh and her Public Speaking class were listening to a student give a speech up at the podium (their large public high school is about a mile away from the other two schools mentioned previously). In his presentation, the student was recounting problems in the city's crowded prison system. The boy described how one inmate who was prematurely released promptly robbed a woman on the street, at the same time breaking her nose with a blow from a bottle. Ms. Walsh's students are neither unaware of nor always immune to the violence in the world. However, on hearing this report from their classmate, many students gasped spontaneously. Several girls turned and glanced at Ms. Walsh, who had stationed herself in a back corner of the classroom. Ms. Walsh's face registered both shock and anger in response to the incident reported by the student. The girls turned back to the front, still with disquieted faces as they shifted in their seats, a few audibly letting out a breath. They picked up the speaker's thread again. In the ensuing discussion, Ms. Walsh asked students to comment not just on the quality and structure of their peer's speech—learning to evaluate each other's presentations is a central part of their work in the course—but also to share any concerns it generated. Among other topics, the class discussed the issue of violence against women, children, and the poor, and what society should do about it.

These episodes attest to the kind of relationship with students that Ms. Smith, Mr. Peters, and Ms. Walsh have fashioned in their respective schools and classrooms. The moral dimensions of that relationship come to light in the students' words and actions, not to mention in the specific human issues they confront. Those dimensions speak volumes about the teachers' moral sensibilities. Ms. Smith's students took up the offer to visit with her during her lunch period not because they regarded her as a trained suicide counselor with expertise to share. Mr. Peters's student took seriously his teacher's words about goodness in the world not because he regarded Mr. Peters as an expert in theology or cosmology. And Ms. Walsh's students sought her reaction to an incident of violence against a woman in poverty not because they perceived her as a violence counselor or spokesperson for women and the poor. What these students signaled is that they are morally receptive to Ms. Smith, Mr. Peters, and Ms. Walsh. They put faith in the teachers' judgment and example. Unhesitantly, they turn to them in moments of doubt and concern (and of joy—on many occasions I witnessed students happily describing their successes to the teachers). They want to know these teachers' views, attitudes, and outlooks. Moreover, their moral receptivity issues from more than the fact that the three are teachers per se. There are other teachers whom these same students do not approach when they are troubled and who, to judge from their extensive informal testimony, do not embody qualities that draw students to heed them. The students' actions reveal the moral sensibility that Ms. Smith, Mr. Peters, and Ms. Walsh enact in their everyday practice. Their sensibilities infuse their work with an ethos of involvement to which their students respond, just as Oakeshott and Hoover responded to some of their teachers.

Dynamics of a Moral Sensibility

The teachers' influence in the incidents described here is unrehearsed and unpremeditated. In other words, the teachers do not undertake their everyday efforts in order to have students come see them during lunch, as did Ms. Smith's students, or to mention them favorably in other contexts, as did one of Mr. Peters's students. I make this perhaps obvious point to stress that the teachers do not treat their conduct as a means to an end (more on this in a moment). Ms. Smith created a classroom environment, through her day-by-day attentiveness and hard work, that positioned students to discern that she was a person to trust. Mr. Peters's student wrote about him because he had been affected by his teacher's steady, serious-minded efforts. Ms. Walsh's students turned to her when unnerved because she had showed them time and again, through her everyday conduct, that she believed in her obligations as a teacher. In later chapters, I discuss in greater detail what it means to say that teachers often influence their students indirectly. The point here is that a teacher's moral sensibility can figure prominently in whatever impact he or she might have in the classroom.

As I have suggested, the three teachers' actions, as a means, embody ends, which are to fuel students' intellectual and moral growth. That fact gives rise to the idea that a teacher's moral sensibility should be understood as an achievement in its own right. Its worth and meaning do not hinge solely on what kind of consequences it produces. A moral sensibility is not like a tool that a teacher pulls out of a box and then replaces once she or he has done the sensible and sensitive thing. However substantial or narrow it may be, a moral sensibility accompanies the teacher's conduct. In short, the value of a moral sensibility results from its being not a tool for success, but a mark of a meaningful life. Oakeshott's and Hoover's testimony, and the actions of the three teachers' students, reveal what students can learn from a teacher engaged in crafting a meaningful life, even if the teacher may not employ such a self-description.

A person's moral sensibility plays an indirect role, although no less powerful for that fact, in whatever influence he or she might have on others. At the same time, like the quality of personhood itself, an individual has to develop a moral sensibility. It does not come prepackaged at birth. It is best understood, as Oakeshott (1993, p. 35) argues, as an achievement. A person cultivates, deepens, and refines it over the course of a lifetime. However, just as an individual's sensibility tends to have an indirect impact on others, so a person shapes his or her sensibility indirectly. It is not like a muscle that can be built up steadily and predictably through weight training, or a skill that can be picked up through repetition. A moral sensibility takes form slowly and unpredictably. Most of the time, it is not a direct object of the person's attention or perception. Rather, it is funded, indirectly, by attending to people and to the situations in which they dwell. The individual's intentions, thoughts, feelings, and actions all figure into the equation. Each leaves a trace, however minute, on the individual's sensibility. Consequently, rather than focusing directly on one's evolving moral sensibility, a process that might lead to self-absorption rather than to self-development, the wiser course seems to be to try to conduct oneself well, both in one's dealings with others and with oneself. To strive and to act in this spirit can influence, however indirectly, the growth of one's moral sensibility. It can also enable a person to help others do the same.

CONCLUSION: ENTERING A WORLD OF MEANINGFUL ACTIVITY

Person, conduct, and *moral sensibility* are terms that highlight the dispositions, the knowledge, and the practical wisdom that an individual brings to life in the role of teacher. The terms substantiate the claim with which this chapter began, that the individual in the role of teacher is a more decisive factor in the quality of classroom instruction than are curricula, methods, and technology taken by themselves. As we have seen, conduct contrasts with mere behavior and with unconnected actions. Conduct in teaching constitutes a pattern of action that supports meaningful teaching and learning. That pattern reflects, or emerges from, the teacher's agency, intentions, will, thought, feeling, imagination, and memory—all those facets of who and what a person is discussed previously. Person and conduct come to light in complementary fashion.

An evolving moral sensibility helps to fuse and to harmonize them. A moral sensibility brings person and conduct together under a unifying outlook or orientation. The teacher's acts begin to carry significance. They *mean* something positive, which would not necessarily be the case if the acts were undertaken casually and thoughtlessly, uninformed by a sense of purpose and value. Through time and experience, teachers can learn to build connections between what they say and do, such that focusing on any single act they undertake can shed light on the persons they are and on the student learning and growth they promote. Just as a painter's choice of color, line, and texture can illuminate his entire philosophy of art—if he paints in such a way that the parts comprise a whole, or a pattern—so any single act by a teacher can reveal his philosophy of education.

I suggested at the start of the chapter that the task of becoming a person, as teacher, constitutes an opportunity rather than an intimidating burden. To be sure, with that opportunity comes a host of demanding responsibilities, some of which I have touched on here, others which I will clarify in the chapters to come. Teaching is not easy, and it is not for everyone. However, it remains equally true that accepting the responsibilities that accompany the role opens the door to what might be called a new world. I mean this in several senses. First, teaching ushers a person into the world of one of humanity's oldest and most vital practices. In some respects this is an astounding opportunity, at least if we stop to think about where we would be if we had never had *any* teachers in our lives. Second, it is a world of uncommon, fascinating, and often challenging events, a point that recalls the earlier remarks about the limits of common sense in grasping teaching. Common sense, as that term is usually understood, is necessary but not sufficient for good practice. To teach well implies, at one and the same time, cultivating a moral sensibility, enlarging one's person, and enriching one's conduct. That posture calls to mind the familiar notion that teachers need to be lifelong learners. Third, this new world is a place of meaningful activity. It is a world in which persons can influence others for the good rather than for the bad: to help them learn rather than become more ignorant, to form aims and purposes themselves rather than leaving the task up to others, to develop the skill and talent to accomplish goals rather than being complacent or resigned, and more.

From the point of view of the individual teacher, there are few things more striking, and yet so familiar, than the fact that he or she is a *person*, not a thing, a functionary, or a mere instrument of others' ends. Those who elect to become teachers may become persons, perhaps for the very first time in their lives, who truly understand the meaning of education. This possibility attests to a larger truth embedded in the well-known adage that to learn a subject, one has to teach it. The truth is that in becoming a teacher, a person positions him- or herself to enter and to help sustain a world of human flourishing. That entry, and that ongoing task, will call upon the teacher's person, conduct, and moral sensibility. In turn, the teacher will give shape and substance to the very criteria we can use to judge his or her worthiness to teach society's children.

❧ 3 ❧

An Image of a Growing Person
That Can Guide a Teacher's Work

DEWEY STATES SUCCINCTLY a central thesis that underlies this and the following two chapters: "There is not, in fact, any such thing as the direct influence of one human being on another" (1916/1997, p. 28). Dewey argues that teachers influence students indirectly, through the "use of the physical environment as an intermediary" (p. 28). He explains: "[T]he only way in which adults consciously control the kind of education which the immature get is by controlling the environment in which they act, and hence think and feel. We never educate directly, but indirectly by means of the environment. Whether we permit chance environments to do the work, or whether we design environments for the purpose makes a great difference. And any environment is a chance environment so far as its educative influence is concerned unless it has been deliberately regulated with reference to its educative effect" (pp. 18–19).

Many teachers at all levels of the educational system, and perhaps especially men and women preparing to become teachers, may find Dewey's argument jarring. They cannot educate students directly, or so it seems. They will not, Dewey argues, directly leave a mark on students (which is not to say they cannot leave any mark, as we saw in Chapter 2 and as I will address below). They must "use" the environment as an "intermediary." This conception of teaching and learning contravenes popular notions of the heroic teacher in contemporary culture. Such teachers seem to teach students directly, and they appear to do so entirely through their own will, charisma, and personal vision of education. Moreover, their impact on students appears to unfold *despite* the surrounding environment, not because of it. These heroic teachers actually seem to work against the environment rather than regarding it as what Dewey calls an intermediary. What happens to this picture of educational miracle workers when it is placed alongside the sobering claim Dewey makes that teachers do not educate directly? That claim seems to place the person in the role of teacher off to the side, perhaps like the fellow behind the curtain whom Dorothy and the rest of us in the land of Oz are supposed to ignore.

Talk of characters lurking behind curtains highlights another reason why Dewey's claims may appear unsettling. What are we to make of terms such as "consciously controlling" the education that the young receive, "controlling" or "deliberately regulating" or "designing" the environment in which the young "act," and hence, as Dewey comprehensively puts it, "think and feel"? Such language appears to convert the teacher into an environmental technician who monitors the intellectual, moral, and emotional thermostat of the classroom in order to normalize student growth. But what humane teacher wants to be like the man behind the curtain, masterminding classroom affairs and pulling the strings on student conduct? How does Dewey's language of control and regulation of the environment, in association with his claim about our having only an indirect influence on others, harmonize with ideals educators hold about treating students as ends in themselves with their own agency, autonomy, and outlooks on the world?

Dewey has a response to these questions. My purpose in this and the following two chapters is, in part, to elucidate that response. More broadly, I hope to show why teachers can benefit from pondering the idea of "indirect teaching." For one thing, much of a teacher's influence on students *is* indirect, an outcome I documented in the previous chapter. Teachers may not be aware of this influence. Their students might not be either. They may realize only years after the fact the kind of impact their teachers had on them. Their awareness may surface suddenly, perhaps after they have themselves become teachers or, through some other endeavor, have grasped something about the nature of human influence (cf. Jackson, 1992). From this perspective, teaching "indirectly" comes with the practice. Teachers cannot decide *not* to have an indirect influence of any kind on students. However, they can respond in better or worse ways to this feature of their work. They can become more mindful of their possible impact, and they can take measures to shape their own influence. That process entails, among other things, thinking about their person, conduct, and moral sensibility.

The term *indirect teaching* also highlights how the classroom environment mediates teachers' and students' influence on one another. As I pointed out in Chapter 1, the qualifier *indirect* emphasizes the value to teachers of fashioning a particular kind of environment. The qualifier reminds teachers to attend deliberately to the spatial and temporal aspects of teaching and learning. From this viewpoint, indirect teaching constitutes not so much a method of instruction as it does a component of an overall orientation toward the practice.

My first step in investigating these ideas will be to describe an image of an educated, growing person that can guide how the teacher shapes and organizes an environment. The second step, which I venture in Chapter 4, will be to discuss precedents to Dewey's claim that teachers educate students indirectly. I focus on the dynamics of an environment for teaching and learning. The final step, which follows in Chapter 5, will be to show that terms such as *control* and *regulate*, if understood in a kinetic sense, liberate rather than confine teaching and learning. They shine a light on the generative constraints that give notions of classroom freedom, choice, and autonomy their force and meaning.

AN IMAGE OF A GROWING PERSON

What guides teachers' attempts to fashion an educative environment? What might steer teachers' deliberations in this regard? What helps them develop confidence that they are regulating the classroom environment such that students are benefited rather than harmed intellectually and morally? One answer to these questions resides in the teacher's working image of an educated, growing person. Such an image differs from a formal theory (cf. Joseph & Burnaford, 1994). An image does not constitute a set of propositions, although it is comprised of concepts and ideas, at least in part. It draws on a teacher's entire outlook toward teaching, learning, and human flourishing writ large. That outlook includes memories, often cast in narrative form, and emotion, often bound up with various events and faces. The image does not serve as an interpretive blueprint for a teacher to employ in working with students. Rather, it helps guide perception. It assists the teacher to be alert to incipient signs of student agency and development. As teachers act on these signs, and learn from them, their image of a growing, educated person can broaden and deepen.

I want to compose aspects of such an image. To do so, I will draw on several sources. (1) The first is my reading of tradition in teaching. From Plato, Jean-Jacques Rousseau, and John Dewey, through many contemporary writers, I discern a thread of inquiry and reflection that centers around how teachers can help others cultivate personhood. These writers differ in their politics, their views of society, and their preconceptions. But they bring to bear, or so it seems to me, an insightful passion for education and for how teaching can fuel human flourishing. I will have a great deal to say about tradition in teaching in Chapters 6 and 7. (2) A second, closely related source is a reading of novelists and poets who, like the writers on education mentioned above, also shed light on the unfathomable dimensions of human growth and learning. They show that grasping the meaning and the import of a notion such as "person" draws on philosophical reflection and moral imagination. (3) Finally, the image of a growing, educated person I outline derives from thinking about students I have taught over the years, including those in the secondary teacher preparation program that I currently help direct. Perhaps, like every teacher, I have doubtless been listening *for* certain things in my students' voices. However, I also like to believe I have learned to listen *to* them, and *with* them, in better ways. That process has compelled me to come to grips with images of a growing person that might guide practice.

As I sought to do with concepts of person, conduct, and moral sensibility in the previous chapter, I will try to characterize aspects of a growing person rather than try to define them. I hope to understand these aspects better, not to explain them in some terminal fashion (I am not sure they can or should be). Posed differently, in this chapter and book I do not seek, in Magdalene Lampert's words (1990), "to determine whether general propositions about learning or teaching are true or false" but rather "to further our understanding of the character of these particular kinds of human activity" (p. 37). When serious-minded teachers are impressed, perplexed, troubled, or otherwise affected by students and colleagues, they do not typically seek to "explain" them, as a biologist, for example, might explain the morphology of an organism. They seek to understand them, a process that entails thought, sympathy, patience, and criticism, even if none of that process is made public. In this spirit, the image of a growing person I will sketch focuses on growth as qualitative, not quantitative. Growth can imply letting go of features of the self as much as it can mean cultivating new dispositions, knowledge, attitudes, and outlooks. Immanuel Kant once wrote that a log in water does not grow, it just gets bigger because of absorption. Analogously, a person who, say, merely packs in information and skills may not be growing in the sense I describe here.

Among other things, a growing person is on the way to embodying what Dewey variously calls "traits" of individual method (1916/1997, pp. 173–179), "moral traits" (1916/1997, pp. 356–357), and "personal attitudes" toward thinking and acting in the world (1933, pp. 29–34). These attitudes include what Dewey calls straightforwardness, open-mindedness, integrity of purpose, and responsibility. I examine each of these terms and juxtapose them with remarks on simplicity, spontaneity, na-iveté, open-heartedness, and seriousness. The emerging image of a grow-ing, educated person will not be complete or exhaustive. The latter task would take more than a single chapter—or book. I hope the analysis provides a useful beginning to an image that cuts across differences in personality, age, subject matter, institution, and social background, while also recognizing that, in light of those differences, there would be varying emphases on particular qualities, at particular times and places. There would be different ways of framing and illustrating the qualities and of expressing them in conduct. Yet there would also remain a shared thread of meaning for each quality, so that the overall image retains its coherence. Each quality possesses a form or shape that permits us to talk about it in the first place, while the content will vary (again, not boundlessly) depending upon any number of personal, cultural, institutional, or other local factors. In brief, the image neither presumes nor implies a blueprint for human development. At the same time, I believe the image is true to life or, more pointedly, true to the terms of the practice of teaching as a long-standing, worthwhile human activity.[1]

Straightforwardness

A growing person develops a certain directness or confidence, not to be confused with "self-confidence," as Dewey points out, but rather a kind of "straightforwardness" with which a person pursues what he or she has to do in order to realize an aim or purpose. Straightforwardness, or directness, "denotes not *conscious* trust in the efficacy of one's powers but unconscious faith in the possibilities of the situation. It signifies rising to the needs of the situation" (1916/1997, p. 174). This quality constitutes a striking image of an educated, growing person. It portrays a person who is developing a disposition of faith in possibilities for growth, rather than a stance of pessimism, cynicism, hopelessness, or self-absorption. Such a person learns to "rise" to a situation, not by pulling him- or herself up by the bootstraps but by responding to the scene. To rise to a situation means to engage the possibilities for human flourishing embedded in it rather than to ignore, neglect, or give up on them. The process implies intensifying one's perception. As Dorothy Emmet (1979) puts it, the pro-cess will "call on one to enlarge one's imagination in seeing the situations in which one acts; not only seeing single chains of cause and effect, but ramifications and repercussions" (p. 141). Emmet's terms illuminate what it means to be responsive, rather than closed, to a situation.

Teachers can play a dynamic role in creating conditions that support this quality in students, in their engagement both with subject matter and with one another. But that possibility depends, in part, on whether teachers fuel the very same quality in themselves. Like the other concepts under review here, straightforwardness pertains as much to teachers as it does to students. Teachers who place faith in the possibilities of the situation no longer have to root educational success and failure entirely in themselves, as if students and everything else were satellite or passive factors. Teachers can drop that intimidating burden from their shoulders and concentrate, instead, on fashioning an environment for teaching and learning. I will develop this theme in due course.

Simplicity

A disposition such as straightforwardness materializes if a person has opportunities to throw him- or herself into activities in a way that is "spontaneous, naive, and simple" (Dewey, 1916/1997, p. 173). As I understand Dewey, spontaneity means acting with freshness, with an almost childlike naturalness. Naiveté implies acting in an unguarded way, without looking over one's shoulder. Simplicity denotes acting without pretense or putting on airs. All three terms describe a posture of concentration, focus, and freedom of action.

The terms point to a growing self, to a metamorphosing self, and I want to examine them more fully than does Dewey. For example, to act in a way that is "simple" is not to act simple-mindedly. Nor is it to act in a way that ignores complexity. Simplicity describes an intellectual and emotional disposition or orientation. It calls to mind a form of unencumbered perception that allows for directness or straightforwardness in one's conduct. It suggests a capacity to focus, when appropriate, wholly on the moment, on the people, objects, and tasks that comprise that moment. This capacity is vital to develop. "We always live at the time we live," Dewey disarmingly reminds us, "and not at some other time, and only by extracting at each present time the full meaning of each present experience are we prepared for doing the same in the future" (1938/1963, p. 49). Simplicity becomes a mark of living in the present, which is the only moment in which accomplishments in the past can be carried over to fund prospects in the future. Posed differently, simplicity describes a living person, a person literally alive *in* the moment. This encompasses something other than the functioning of the bodily organs. It highlights the state of the person's spirit, mind, even soul, as some would put it. It mirrors aspects of personhood discussed in the previous chapter: memory, intentionality, will, thought, feeling. Simplicity is an achievement, rather than a quality that can be taken for granted. In a hectic, fast-moving world, simple thoughts and simple emotions may be the most difficult to attain.

Spontaneity

A person who acts spontaneously, as I understand the term, is a person who initiates endeavors and projects. This does not mean acting impulsively or capriciously, both of which are the exact opposite of what I mean (cf. Dewey, 1916/1997, pp. 77–78). Nor does it mean acting mimetically, that is, merely discharging ways of doing things that are culturally or socially sanctioned. Spontaneity highlights a person's agency, his or her ability to imagine possibilities and to act in accordance with them. This need not imply originality, in the sense of breaking new ground or rejecting precedent. Spontaneity captures a person's growing ability to engage directly and actively with the world and its people and things. This ability applies to young and old alike. Dewey (1916/1997) argues that the "child of three who discovers what can be done with blocks, or of six who finds out what he can make by putting five cents and five cents together, is really a discoverer, even though everybody else in the world knows it. There is a genuine increment of experience; not another item mechanically added on, but enrichment by a new quality" (p. 159). A teacher who decides to discuss literature with her students, rather than to lecture them about it, is acting spontaneously. When she realizes students have things to say, and can think for themselves about an author's meaning and design, she is "really a discoverer," to use Dewey's words, despite the fact that many teachers before her already knew such things. Even if all the teachers in the world had exhorted her to try discussion as an instructional approach, their collective advice, while surely valuable, would not have had the same meaning as her own genuine discovery.

This interpretation of spontaneity has a long, historical kinship with the idea of freedom. Kant (cf. 1785/1990, 1788/1993), for example, regarded spontaneity and freedom as conditions for morality, by which he meant, in part, the human capacity to respect and to treat other people as ends in themselves rather than as a means to our own ends. The ability to act spontaneously mirrors the capacity to act freely. It makes it possible for a person to be the cause of his or her own doings. It can take one's actions beyond the causal power of nature—understood as the force of psychological impulse or inclination—and beyond the causal power of culture and society—understood as the force of social expectation and custom. This does not imply breaking with nature or with culture, and it does not mean acting in necessarily novel or radical ways (which might reflect caprice rather than initiative). The idea of spontaneity highlights a person's ability to act on the basis of his own mind, heart, and will, rather than in ways that are determined or scripted by forces not of his own making. To recall the terms of Chapter 2, spontaneity gives rise to what is distinctive about a person's conduct.[2]

Dewey illustrates the particularity I have in mind when he describes a teacher's methods of working. By methods, he means the ways in which a teacher perceives things and how he or she acts in the classroom to realize ends. The term connotes something richer and more variegated than the sorts of instructional formulae which could be listed in a textbook. For Dewey, "methods remain the personal concern, approach, and attack of an individual, and no catalogue can ever exhaust their diversity of form and tint" (1916/1997, p. 173). No catalogue can possibly encompass what spontaneity, or freedom in thought and action, can produce in the classroom, provided that the environment spurs rather than closes down teaching and learning.[3]

Naiveté

The term *naiveté* also yields deeper meanings if we take a second look at it. In everyday parlance, naiveté implies a lack of experience and perhaps also a lack of awareness. In many circumstances, to call someone naive is to render a negative judgment on him or her. However, when coupled with the idea of acting simply and spontaneously, naiveté becomes a desirable condition. It implies a certain innocence, a state of mind not cowed or corrupted by cynicism, greed, or fear. It denotes a freshness of mind brought to bear on issues, problems, and concerns.

Anton Chekhov sheds light on this view of naiveté in his novella *A Boring Story*. Nikolai, the central character, describes his response to the first letters he receives from Katya, a young woman whom he had helped raise and who had now gone out into the world. "I read them," he writes, "and was simply amazed that these small sheets of paper could contain so much youthful enthusiasm, purity of soul, divine naiveté, and at the same time so many subtle and sensible views" (1889/1964, p. 65). Nikolai describes naiveté as "divine" to capture the sense of clear and immediate perceptiveness Katya's letters evoke, as well as their lack of worldliness and self-consciousness. To the somewhat jaded Nikolai, it is almost as if Katya sees the world as it was first made, prior to the explanatory frameworks human beings fashion and which so often, or so Nikolai might say, distort that world and oppress the soul.

However, Nikolai goes on to describe how Katya's letters, within a year, turned angry and bitter as she fell prey to charismatic and manipulative people who took advantage of her. In this light, perhaps Nikolai's qualifier, divine, means that only gods can safely be naive. At the very least, it seems, naiveté should be accompanied by critical awareness and the ability to act intelligently. In stronger terms, there may be times when a person should not be naive and open as characterized here. A person may need to be deliberately guarded. Still, the latter posture presumes the possibility, and the desirability given the right conditions, of what I am associating with simplicity, spontaneity, and naiveté. In Chapter 5, I describe the emergence of a classroom environment that, hopefully, promotes an ethos in which those qualities can develop.

But is it possible to be naive and thoughtful at one and the same time? Aren't the two dispositions contradictory or incommensurable? I do not believe so. Like all the qualities I am examining here, naiveté needs cultivation, at least once persons find themselves in the midst of human society. The ways in which individuals are socialized, what other people expect and ask of them, and the powerful lure of the tried and the known work endlessly to channel their perception. This state of affairs is not necessarily problematic, but it is real. Persons need to act spontaneously, in the sense given the term here, in order (reciprocally) to retain their naiveté. Moreover, their doings can encourage others to act in a comparable spirit. Writing when the Cold War still raged, the Hungarian writer George Konrad urged his readers to "be naive, and catch your friends at their naive best" (1981, p. 49). He sought to evoke images of freshness, of unguarded and unfearful perception. He sought to help others sustain the ability to see the possibilities for growth that lie in front of their very noses—often the hardest things to discern—and he regarded this ability as an expression of freedom.[4]

In Konrad's appeal, we hear the echo of another long-standing idea: the meaningfulness of moral conduct. Annette Baier (1983) examines this theme in her study of why persons might strive to act morally in a world that sometimes appears ravaged by violence and cruelty. In such a world, Baier points out, people may be tempted to abandon scruples and attentiveness to others and, instead, doggedly pursue their own self-interest. They might regard it as pointless to act justly when everything around them appears unjust. Baier responds to these felt concerns by building on Kant's claim that moral conduct, metaphorically speaking, can propagate itself. Kant's entire moral philosophy constitutes, in part, a rebuttal of cynicism and skepticism about the prospects for justice and human good. "One need not be an enemy of virtue," Kant (1785/1990) grants, "but only a cool observer who does not confuse even the liveliest aspiration for the good with its actuality, to be sometimes doubtful whether true virtue can really be found anywhere in the world" (p. 23). Things can feel so unbearable, he adds elsewhere, that the earth can strike us "as a place of atonement for old and forgotten sins" (Kant, 1793/1991, p. 88). But Kant goes on to show that moral conduct is neither a phantom nor a chimera. It is not beyond the bounds of human capability. Quite on the contrary. Moral conduct is not only ubiquitous but also represents one of humanity's most distinctive achievements, despite its fragility and what may often seem like its defeat in human affairs.

Baier (1983) elucidates one of the outcomes of this argument. She writes that if a person acts justly, the person (1) demonstrates the reality of justice to him- or herself, (2) shows others that justice is real and possible, and (3) sustains a tradition of just conduct, of moral continuity across the generations (p. 204). These enactments do not guarantee the emergence of an improved human condition. But they are as real, Baier argues, as the reality of uncertainty about tomorrow's world. Consequently, they point the way to a hopeful rather than cynical posture. Konrad, Baier, and Kant evoke what might be called a naive, critical faith in the moral life.

Naiveté need not be divine. It can be human. To a meaningful degree, persons can shape their perception and conduct rather than have these shaped from without. The poet Rainer Maria Rilke closes one of his most famous poems, "Archaic Torso of Apollo," with a line that comes across like a thunderclap: "You must change your life" (1908/1989, p. 61). Every time a person rereads the poem, he or she will come upon that line again—an obvious point, of course, but what may be less obvious is that the poet intends to challenge the reader on *every* reading, to appeal to or compel the reader to look at the world again, to look anew, to consider every occasion as a chance to grow and, spiritually speaking, to remain alive. Rilke's closing line evokes the quest for a vital, connecting vision of the world, even while engaging the countless social and psychological pulls and pushes that, to be sure, can sometimes bind people against their will. To nourish that quest constitutes an educational aim with a very long history. It is an aim that extends across every level of formal education, from elementary school through advanced graduate programs. Teachers can pursue that aim by creating environments that invite students, and themselves, to act in ways that are spontaneous, naive, and simple.

We can contrast opportunities that foster such conduct with situations that make a person *self*-conscious rather than, as I would like to put it, *object*-conscious. Self-consciousness can mean being divided and dispersed: partly attending to the object, but partly attending to or fretting about the self and/or worrying about what others might think before the task is even completed. "Diverted energy means loss of power and confusion of ideas," Dewey contends. "Taking an attitude is by no means identical with being conscious of one's attitude" (1916/1997, p. 173). To be object-conscious is to "take" or embody an attitude that makes growth possible. It means being attuned directly to *what* it is one is doing, studying, building, enacting. For the teacher, this suggests fueling not a student's self-consciousness but his or her confidence that good things can happen if he or she becomes immersed in an endeavor. Self-confidence, in the substantive sense of that term, emerges not from focusing on self but rather from working out as straightforwardly as possible solutions, answers, and responses to problems, questions, and challenges. In other words, to be object-conscious makes it possible to transform the self, rather than to treat it as ready-made or fixed. To pay attention to the object (person, place, thing) before one is to become a certain kind of self—at the very least, a self that can pay attention to the world rather than ignore or neglect it—or merely read into it whatever one wishes. Persons can become what they learn to see and do, and this seeing and doing can be constantly expanded and enriched.

Open-Minded and Open-Hearted

The qualities of straightforwardness, simplicity, spontaneity, and naiveté harmonize with open-mindedness. Open-mindedness connotes flexibility of mind. It describes a willingness to consider, and even to seek out, contrasting viewpoints and different ways of tackling a task. "The worst thing about stubbornness of mind" and about unexamined biases, Dewey says, with an eye on the capacity to learn, "is that they arrest development; they shut the mind off from new stimuli. Open-mindedness means retention of the childlike attitude; closed-mindedness means premature intellectual old age" (1916/1997, p. 175). The "childlike attitude" calls to mind a sense of curiosity, of adaptability, of receptivity to new suggestions and ways of thinking and acting. It means avoiding a finalized judgment of the world and its people and events. It captures, from another angle, the amalgam of naiveté and thoughtfulness introduced previously.

Open-mindedness comprises a blend of the active and the passive. It describes an interest in exploring the environment and in interacting with others. That means developing the courage and the will to reach out to others, to try the new, to "experiment with the world to find out what it is like" (Dewey, 1916/1997, p. 140). But open-mindedness also connotes the willingness, as Dewey puts it, "to let experiences accumulate and sink in and ripen" (p. 176), and this entails a certain passivity. However, the passivity presupposes activity. In a hectic and often distracting world, the person may have to *act* to position him- or herself to "let" experience "sink in and ripen." In this light, patience constitutes an active, outward-looking disposition rather than a state of resigned endurance. Teachers might be the first to say that it often requires effort and practice to learn how to be patient with students, to remain poised and ready to capitalize on what they say and do in response to subject matter. Such a posture recalls the idea of having faith in the possibilities in a situation, of being open to what the situation might disclose, rather than insisting on finding in it only what one already knows or expects.

Open-mindedness does not come cost-free. By this I mean more than the effort and the discipline entailed in keeping the mind open to the new, indispensable as they are. I mean that being open to particular persons, interests, concerns, and events implies not being open to others, at least for a time. Persons are not sponges. They cannot absorb everything in a given setting. A classroom of 25 students discussing a text contains more doings, thoughts, feelings, and anticipations than could ever be enumerated, much less attended to. Open-mindedness cannot mean being open to just anything or anyone, anytime or anywhere. Dewey would describe such a state as empty-minded (1916/1997, pp. 175–176). For a student, open-mindedness accompanies the ability to read and write thoughtfully, to listen attentively and sympathetically to others, and to entertain new ideas, new points of view, new suggestions for thought and action. For a teacher, open-mindedness occurs in the context of a pedagogical vision and direction. It coheres with a set of aims for learning, that is, for human flourishing. The teacher remains open to whatever may advance learning and development. She or he is closed, metaphorically speaking, to whatever may hamper or hamstring learning and growth. As teachers would be the first to say, it is not always clear what might and what might not help students progress. Consequently, open-mindedness embodies a critical dimension.[5]

In the previous chapter, I described a teacher's moral sensibility as a disposition of mind and feeling centered around attentiveness to students and their learning. That notion fused intellectual, emotional, and moral aspects of practice. This fusion suggests that open-mindedness yields fruitful human conduct when allied with open-heartedness. Open-heartedness is neither sentimental nor Pollyannaish. Where open-mindedness signals intellectual receptivity, open-heartedness emphasizes emotional receptivity. Both qualities augment human connection and understanding, because intellectual receptivity may depend upon emotional openness, and vice versa. Students may have a hard time with a new subject, a new idea, or a new classmate unless they come to grips with their emotional, not just intellectual, posture. Teachers attuned to such matters can help students make the transition. Teachers may have an equally difficult time with new ideas, new outlooks, and new people. Their students often come to the rescue in unanticipated ways (and often without knowing it). Open-mindedness and open-heartedness keep teaching and learning dynamic.

Integrity of Purpose

The qualities analyzed thus far merge with what Dewey calls integrity of purpose. Dewey also describes this disposition as whole-heartedness, meaning literally a matter of giving one's heart and mind over to the endeavor at hand rather than, say, doing the deed but thinking of something else while doing it. The latter tendency, which many observers perceive as endemic in modern life, gives rise to what Dewey calls "double-mindedness." That term denotes giving or, better, surrendering the mind over to too many things at once. It implies letting go of one's own agency and capacity for independent thought and conduct. As suggested previously, this creates the conditions for becoming a divided or dispersed self, rather than for becoming an integrated person who truly attends to others and to the opportunities that life affords. If people allow divided or dispersed mental habits to continue unchecked—or if teachers and other adults allow this to happen to them—this ultimately diminishes the quality of their lives as well as what they can contribute to the improvement of other peoples' lives.

The disposition of integrity of purpose allows for personal and social integrity. Integrity of purpose (Dewey also calls this "single-mindedness" to contrast it with double-mindedness) connotes "*completeness* of interest" and "unity of purpose." It means "[a]bsorption, engrossment, full concern" with the endeavor at hand (Dewey, 1916/1997, pp. 176–177). This disposition allows a person to become a fuller self, literally full of the substance of the world, of its people, places, and objects, with all their diverse intellectual, moral, aesthetic, and emotional qualities. Integrity of purpose carries a person beyond the more evanescent material produced by mere egocentricity or caprice.

Responsibility

In Dewey's terms, responsibility is the propensity "to see something through." It is the predilection "to consider in advance the probable consequences of any projected step and deliberately to accept them: to accept them in the sense of taking them into account, acknowledging them in action, not yielding a mere verbal assent" (1916/1997, p. 178). We can contrast responsibility with the quality of mind that leads a person to defend, in word, a whole host of ideas—or at least attempt to do so—but not live by them or respect them in actual conduct. The outcome of that state of affairs can be either a shallow person or self, easily blown from one viewpoint to another because he or she lacks roots, or a dogmatic self who adheres to possibly disabling beliefs and ideas.

Dewey contends that much of what transpires both in- and outside of school works to divide thought from action, and vice versa. Summarizing his conception of what responsibility means, Dewey writes:

> It would be much better to have fewer facts and truths in instruction—that is, fewer things supposedly accepted,—if a smaller number of situations could be intellectually worked out to the point where conviction meant something real—some identification of the self with the type of conduct demanded by facts and foresight of results. The most permanent bad results of undue complication of school subjects and congestion of school studies and lessons are not the worry, nervous strain, and superficial acquaintance that follow (serious as these are), but the failure to make clear what is involved in really knowing and believing a thing. Intellectual responsibility means severe standards in this regard. These standards can be built up only through practice in following up and acting upon the meaning of what is acquired. (1916/1997, pp. 178–179)

To understand what it means to really know and believe something constitutes yet another striking image of an educated and growing human being. The image is of a person who not only knows and believes things— all persons already do that—but who understands what it *means* to know and believe something. That condition implies a person with direction and purpose in life. It describes a person who is not buffeted about like a rudderless sailboat, but who knows her or his way and can pursue the course. The image calls to mind a person who is intellectually and morally conscious of the world around her or him, and who, given all that has been said above about qualities of a growing person, seeks to deepen and to broaden that consciousness.

Seriousness

John Wilson (1998) suggests that reasoning plays a crucial role in grasping what is entailed in knowing and believing something. He describes a state of mind that he calls "seriousness," by which he means "a disposition to address and act on the world by the use of reason" (p. 143). According to Wilson, reason facilitates standing back and adopting a critical eye toward ideas and actions. Reason helps persons to "monitor" their views, beliefs, and feelings rather than to cling to them in an ideological and possibly harmful fashion. Wilson describes this orientation toward knowledge and experience as seriousness (a term which does not imply, incidentally, being stern or stone-faced in one's conduct). He contends that schooling typically does not provide circumstances or methods for cultivating seriousness. From his point of view, too much that passes for education constitutes unexamined, unquestioned activities, viewpoints, and masses of material. In terms that echo Dewey's support for promoting responsibility, Wilson claims that many educators "do not properly *understand* seriousness or the need for it, and hence do not really take it on board" (p. 153). Most educators would endorse seriousness, or so Wilson suggests. But rather than esteem and support it, he implies that they fail to keep it front and center, either because they ill-advisedly take it for granted or because they have not come to grips with its meaning and promise.

Dewey and Wilson emphasize the intellectual dimensions of, respectively, responsibility and seriousness. I would append moral responsibility and moral seriousness to their claims, a move I believe both authors would accept (they might find it redundant). The qualifier *moral* expands their terms to encompass a concern for the impact on others of one's beliefs and knowledge. It is one thing to live a life according to reason. It is something more to live according to reasoned feeling as well, to be receptive to other people's ideas, concerns, needs, and so forth. It is one thing to commit oneself to embrace the consequences of knowing, believing, and understanding. It is something more to accept, at the same time, the consequences of sympathy, respect, and mutual regard.

The opposite of responsibility and seriousness is treating the things of this world, including ourselves, casually, flippantly, and carelessly. That posture expresses itself in acts as simple as failing to listen to someone or to reciprocate a gesture. George Eliot captures the moral tragedy that can slowly accumulate from such negligent acts—and how much of life is filled with them—when she writes, in her novel *Middlemarch*: "It is in these acts called trivialities that the seeds of joy are for ever wasted, until men and women look round with haggard faces at the devastation their own waste has made, and say, the earth bears no harvest of sweetness— calling their denial knowledge" (1871–72/1985, p. 462). If persons come to grips with what it means to know and believe things, they can overcome this neglect of life. They can reach beyond forms of life predicated on cynicism or heedlessness. They can, instead, partake of the hopefulness embedded in the idea of understanding what it means to know and believe.

As I suggested previously, this condition has both intellectual and moral aspects. William Wordsworth illuminates the condition when he writes, in his autobiographical poem *The Prelude*:

It might be told (but wherefore speak of things
Common to all?) that, seeing, I essayed
To give relief, began to deem myself
A moral agent, judging between good
And evil not as for the mind's delight
But for her safety, one who was to *act*—
As sometimes to the best of my weak means
I did, by human sympathy impelled,
And through dislike and most offensive pain
Was to the truth conducted—of this faith
Never forsaken, that by acting well,
And understanding, I should learn to love
The end of life and every thing we know. (1805 text, 8.665–677)

Like the poet Wordsworth, persons may discover that a sense of responsibility makes it possible to realize their agency. A sense of responsibility positions them to act well and to feel and to understand something about that process. It enables a person, as the poet says, "to love the end of life and every thing we know." For Wordsworth, the "end" or purpose of life is, in part, to embrace the idea of purpose itself, which means treating with respect, and even love, what it is—"every thing"—we can know and do.

A person who really knows and believes something understands it and lives by it. The person takes it into the self, makes it part of the self's orientation to the world. He or she treats it as constitutive, rather than as an outlook to be put aside when it creates difficulties, inconveniences, or "dislike and most offensive pain," as Wordsworth describes the effort of overcoming his pride and stubbornness. A teacher who "really knows and believes" that teaching is worthwhile will likely conduct him- or herself differently from a teacher who has lost faith in the endeavor or who resorts to expediency in the face of challenge rather than considering alternative approaches, consulting with others, and so forth. I do not mean that a teacher genuinely engaged in the work understands it fully. On the contrary, such a teacher doubtless discovers time and again how much there is to learn about successful practice and also experiences his or her share of failure and frustration. The idea of responsibility, as outlined here, points to a harmony of word and deed, thought and action, belief and conduct. Because that harmony is difficult to achieve, educators might take the time and the trouble to work out situations in which students, and they themselves, can perceive what it means. As I discuss in the next two chapters, doing so necessitates sustained attention to the environment that obtains in the classroom.

CONCLUSION: THE PLACE OF IMAGES OF LEARNING
AND GROWTH IN TEACHING

The image of a growing, educated person I have sketched in this chapter is not complete or exhaustive. It is a beginning. I hope it is an acceptable point of departure, if for no other reason than that it is troubling to imagine a world in which educators refused, as a matter of principle, to fuel and support students' open-mindedness, sympathy, seriousness, spontaneity, and so forth. It seems to me that in such circumstances the very idea of education would disappear. One aspect of the qualities I touched on is their plasticity, to make use of another of Dewey's terms (1916/1997, pp. 44–45). The qualities can be extended, reconfigured, re-fined, in light of the actual circumstances, backgrounds, and hopes persons bring to the table. There is no single, right way to cultivate naiveté or simplicity, nor is there a single, right way to express in conduct straightfor-wardness or whole-heartedness. The verb *cultivate* attests to the fact that students do not come to the classroom as empty moral cells awaiting filling from without. Like adults, they are already on the road to personhood, understood in the rich sense I have tried to provide. Like adults, they can broaden and deepen the persons they are. Teachers can nurture that process in uncountable ways, in part through thinking about the qualities I have highlighted in this chapter.

The analysis I have undertaken provides a form to the qualities: a sense of their meaning, contours, distinctiveness, and value. It does not prescribe their actual content in everyday teaching and learning. That content will vary depending on factors such as age, personal experience, setting, and the subject matter at hand. But the content will not vary so much that we lose the ability to communicate about the qualities and their place in the achievement of a human life.

Moreover, the image of a growing, educated person informs what it means, to recall Dewey's terms, to "control" and "regulate" an environ-ment for teaching and learning. The image can play this role, in part, because it is not arbitrary. It does not spring from nowhere, nor from a dogmatic standpoint. It emerges, if not in the exact terms I have used, from tradition in teaching. The qualities I have described have a long history in human reflection and wonder about who and what people can become and how education can advance their hopes and yearnings. The idea of controlling and regulating a classroom environment is not arbitrary either. The control resides, in part, in the vision and the aims that teachers bring to bear in their work. They can guide their work not according to popular fashions or their own whims, but by a thoughtful, broad, dynamic image of a growing, educated person. That image pertains as much to themselves, albeit with differing emphases, as it does to students. Consequently, the control also resides in teachers' receptiveness, in their ability to "rise" to the situations of teaching and learning.

Before turning to the environment for teaching and learning, I want in these concluding remarks to address several questions that may have arisen. A sympathetic reader might contend that the notion of really knowing and believing something, which is embedded in the quality of responsibility I discussed, begs the question of worthy knowledge and belief. In other words, what if the knowledge and beliefs in question are those of, say, a Nazi ideologue? A Nazi might have a very determined sense of what it means to "know and believe" that some people are inferior or lesser as persons and therefore deserve to be treated as such. How does the analysis here respond to this concern? Posed differently, can the analysis respond to it?

The answer to this last question is "yes," but not completely. A full-blown response would emphasize that all the qualities of a growing person I have addressed are embedded in a broad conception of human flourishing. In that conception, the opportunity and the support for flourishing are comprehensive, not reserved for a few. From this perspective, a person who really knows and believes something conceives its moral significance or, at least, is on the road to doing so. As I touched on earlier in referring to moral responsibility, the person tries to understand how knowledge and belief shape ways of being and interacting with others, and whether and how they help meliorate rather than worsen the prospects of others. Responsibility, simplicity, naiveté, and the other qualities discussed equip persons to contribute, however modestly, to general human flourishing. Those qualities do not support a world, such as that represented by Nazism, in which only some are allowed to flourish or are treated as persons in the first place. Posed differently, the qualities I have examined assist persons in confronting and criticizing harmful beliefs rather than buying into them willfully or blindly. The qualities cannot be merged, at least if they are to remain recognizable, with the posture of a person evil in thought and deed. As I comprehend the terms, it would be an oxymoron to talk about an open-minded, serious, or naive Nazi. In contrast, it would be apt to speak of a Nazi, however clever he or she might otherwise be, as closed-minded, fanatical, and corrupt.[6]

What about Wordsworth's notion of loving "every thing we know"? Could that come to mean "loving" such things as intolerance and the willful harming of other human beings? The answer is no. When Wordsworth writes of loving "every thing we know," he has in mind, as I understand his poem, what might be called moral knowledge. This term describes knowledge of people, places, and events that is informed by a moral consciousness and by a moral commitment to the expansion, not contraction, of human possibility and meaning. Wordsworth anticipates Dewey's claim that "the important thing about knowledge in its moral aspect is not its actual extent so much as it is the *will* to know—the active desire to examine conduct in its bearing upon the general good" (1932/1989, p. 281). Dewey argues that the "attitude of *seeking* for what is good may be cultivated under any conditions of race, class, and state of civilization. Persons who are ignorant in the conventional sense of education may display an interest in discovering and considering what is good which is absent in the highly literate and polished. From the standpoint of this interest, class divisions vanish" (p. 282). The moral quality of knowledge lies not in its "possession," Dewey contends, but in how it can foster a widening consciousness and mindfulness. Echoing Wordsworth's call for connection and participation, Dewey concludes that "the need for constant revision and expansion of moral knowledge is one great reason why there is no gulf dividing non-moral knowledge from that which is truly moral" (p. 282).

To love everything we know is to love human prospects, both large and small, as much as it is to love human accomplishments, both large and small. For a teacher, this outlook could be described as a creedal posture toward knowledge. As Paul Smeyers (1995) writes: "Instead of being technicians, teachers pre-eminently have to care about what they convey. . . . They more than anyone else have to be representatives of what they believe in, and therefore they first of all have to be those who love what they teach, the principal advocates of the curriculum" (p. 410; see also Wilson, 1993, p. 133). As we will see in the next two chapters, this kind of love entails developing in themselves the very qualities they aspire to cultivate in students.

Oakeshott (1989) provides another perspective on the understanding of knowledge and belief that underlies the image I have outlined of a growing, educated person. According to Oakeshott, teachers initiate students into what he calls "inheritances" and "achievements" of humanity (pp. 22, 29–30, 41). He also calls them "languages" in which human beings have historically sought to understand themselves: who they are, why they are here, how to conduct themselves, how to realize whatever possibilities the human condition makes available. For Oakeshott, the languages of poetry, art, philosophy, science, history, and so forth constitute something other than prespecified bodies of fact and information, although the latter play an indispensable role in helping students make their way into the world. Rather, to enter these languages is to enter a field of human adventures (pp. 23, 26–28), one that features questions of meaning, understanding, and purpose rather than hardened answers or conclusions.

This view of the curriculum carries us beyond narrow claims about "canons." Such claims presuppose that the curriculum is purely a matter of adopting or supporting preexistent understandings rather than, for example, a matter of helping students grasp what it means to understand something in the first place. To be sure, many teachers and administrators, from preschool through university, have acted as if the curriculum was supposed to dictate beliefs and outlooks, just as many teachers and administrators have failed to be attentive, thoughtful, and mindful of the significance of their work. But these failures underscore, among other things, the very real challenges in teaching well and in bringing curriculum alive. As we will see in Chapters 6 and 7, tradition in teaching sheds light on why many teachers, at all levels of education, have succeeded in helping students join the "adventure" of making themselves something more than what nature or nurture (or social custom) may, at times, seem to be predetermining for them. The qualities I have examined here support persons in engaging the adventure.

Straightforwardness, simplicity, spontaneity, naiveté, open-mindedness, open-heartedness, integrity of purpose, responsibility, and seriousness: These concepts help provide an image of a growing, educated person. Such a person is becoming someone who can act in the world rather than merely being acted upon. This implies a person who not only can think and judge but who also connects or embeds thought and judgment in actual conduct. In this respect, all the dispositions touched on are not only intellectually significant but also morally important. They provide constituents of what I called, in the previous chapter, a moral sensibility. They help dispose an individual to move into, rather than out of, the social and moral complexity of dwelling in genuine community with other people. If Oakeshott is right (1989, pp. 44, 46–47) that the idea of a teacher always implies the idea of a student, then a central aspect of the practice of teaching is harboring an image of a growing, educated person that can help keep the teacher tethered to the challenging dynamics of teaching and learning.

❧ 4 ❧

Teaching Indirectly and the Dynamics
of an Educative Environment

DEWEY SUMS UP his views about some of the attitudes of mind and heart I examined in the previous chapter by speaking of "readiness." "No one can think about everything," he writes, and

> no one can think about *any*thing without experience and information about it. Nevertheless, there is such a thing as *readiness* to consider in a thoughtful way the subjects that do come within the range of experience—a readiness that contrasts strongly with the disposition to pass judgment on the basis of mere custom, tradition, prejudice, etc., and thus shun the task of thinking. The personal attitudes that have been named are essential constituents of this general readiness. (1933, p. 34)

According to Dewey, persons have to cultivate throughout their lives a posture of readiness to engage the world. The propensity to close down thought prematurely remains ever-present, despite people's best intentions. Readiness does not mean ready-made or that which can be taken for granted.

However, Dewey also cautions that teachers and other adults cannot directly inculcate in the young dispositions such as open-mindedness. He claims that teachers cannot educate students directly at all. This standpoint renders the very term *inculcate* out of place. Dewey does not presume that the young *lack* the traits of individual method or personal attitudes he examines. Rather, he argues that they need, and deserve, support, guidance, and encouragement in developing them. Consequently, the claim that teachers cannot educate students directly does not mean that teachers should throw up their hands in the face of an apparently indeterminate endeavor. Quite on the contrary. It is precisely because teachers cannot force learning to happen that they need to attend with care to the kind of environment emergent in the classroom. The person in the role of teacher will become crucial in this process, an emphasis that has marked the previous two chapters. The process depends, in part, on the teacher's willingness to communicate with students and to cultivate trusting relations with them (cf. Applebaum, 1995).

Dewey emphasizes that the young "live in some environment whether we intend it or not, and this environment is constantly interacting with what children and youth bring to it, and the result is the shaping of their interests, minds and character—either educatively or mis-educatively" (1934/1974a, p. 9). For Dewey, an environment that is left up to chance is as likely as not to cultivate the exact opposite of qualities such as spontaneity and responsibility. A chance environment is a random environment, a casual environment, and, in many respects, a thoughtless environment. Such an environment renders human outcomes a toss-up between the better and the worse, the helpful and the harmful, and the good and the bad.

Dewey's argument does not imply paternalism. The opposite of a chance or random environment is neither a predictable environment nor one in which conduct is prescribed. The right response to the very real dangers of leaving the environment entirely up to fate is not to go to the opposite extreme of trying to devise a blueprint for each and every aspect of classroom interaction. How could such a programmed setting invite students to develop the qualities discussed in the previous chapter? How could it impel students to learn to think for themselves, to take intellectual risks, to discover the new and the unfamiliar, to heed others' concerns, and to do so in a spirit of unfettered inquiry?

Moreover, any attempt to create a blueprint for a classroom environment overlooks the rationale behind the claim that teachers cannot educate students directly. The claim highlights the fact that teachers cannot literally reach inside students' minds and hearts and either implant knowledge or, metaphorically speaking, rearrange the internal wiring such that students see the world in a new way. There can be no such direct, mechanistic impact of a teacher on a student—and thank heavens for that—at least if we are talking about experience and learning, rather than about brute behavior. The environment constitutes the intermediary, the medium, the means of educative influence. The environment, not the teacher unmediatedly, generates the stimuli that provoke the human responses and actions that Dewey characterizes as learning and growth. The environment supports, or hinders, the cultivation of qualities of seriousness, open-heartedness, responsibility, and so forth.[1]

In sum, when Dewey speaks of controlling, regulating, and designing an environment, he means something other than leaving it to chance, on the one hand, or employing top-down prescriptions and blueprints, on the other hand. What does he mean? More broadly, What does it mean to teach indirectly, to teach in a mode that acknowledges that teachers cannot dictate or force learning? To respond to the question, I will examine the origins of what can be called, for short, indirect teaching. I highlight Jean-Jacques Rousseau's path-breaking conception and then show how Dewey reconstructed it. In the next chapter, I illustrate the analysis through a detailed look at a course I teach in which I try to act on the premise that teachers educate through the intermediary of the environment.

A "WELL-REGULATED FREEDOM"

Dewey did not originate the view that teachers cannot educate students directly, unmediated by context or setting. His precursors include, as I understand their work, figures as diverse as Plato, Confucius, St. Augustine, and Erasmus. In Plato's writings, set down 2400 years ago, Socrates conducts himself as if the terms of dialogue, rather than individual will or personality alone, constitute the intermediary for whatever positive influence participants might have on one another. Time and again, Socrates takes pains to build or rebuild a conversation, as if doing so were as necessary to learning as breathing is to living. In the *Analects*, written some five centuries B.C.E., Confucius interacts with students in a structured setting that shapes the impact of his counsel and commentary. He, too, seems ever-mindful of the environment in which he is speaking. St. Augustine values conversation as a medium for genuine communication. His *The Teacher*, written in 389 C.E., presents a stylized dialogue between him and his son (who had died at the age of 16). The form and the substance of the piece embody the idea that persons do not share understanding and love unmediatedly, without an environment or medium that buoys those human values. Erasmus, in his educational work penned in the sixteenth century, refers explicitly to the influence of the environment on human development. Drawing analogies with gardening and farming, Erasmus advocates learning conditions in which children can grow "guided by the invisible hand" of their teachers (Bushnell, 1996, p. 93).

Rousseau can be credited, more formally, with fleshing out an initial version of the idea of teaching indirectly. He introduces it in *Émile*, a book which has had an incalculable influence on educational thought and practice since its publication in 1762. The book ranks with Plato's *The*

Republic and Dewey's *Democracy and Education* as one of most ambitious and wide-ranging educational projects ever conceived. Rousseau's text—which he began, he tells us, because childhood remains "unknown" to educators (1762/1979, p. 33)—is a kind of omni-inquiry (cf. Hendel, 1934, p. 75). It investigates social, historical, philosophical, psychological, and spiritual conditions of human development. Rousseau was one of the first writers anywhere to think systematically about childhood through an educational lens. His fictional but unforgettable account of how he educated the boy Émile has inspired countless readers. Many educators have discerned in *Émile* a powerful argument that formal education can improve human lives and societies (A. O. Rorty, 1998, p. 238). Other critics, or in some cases the very same ones, have found Rousseau's image of the teacher authoritarian and manipulative (Cranston, 1991; Peters, 1981; Rosenow, 1980), his conception of learning narrow (Winch, 1996), his attitude toward women backward (Martin, 1985; A. O. Rorty, 1998), his view of the individual and society dualistic (Dewey, 1916/1997), and his political ideas dangerously utopian (cf. Berlin, 1992)—to name only a few of the criticisms. All these viewpoints of his work are matters of continued debate and interpretation (Graubard, 1978; Wokler, 1995). In my view, however right- or wrong-headed some of Rousseau's conclusions may be—and I do not embrace them all, at least as far as I understand them—the originality and the force of the questions he raises, the intellectual and moral courage with which he comes to grips with the idea of education, his willingness to criticize both custom and his own argument—all shed light on the worthwhileness of teaching and of thinking deeply about the practice. To read Rousseau with care is to learn about straightforwardness, open-heartedness, spontaneity, responsibility, and the other qualities I examined in Chapter 3, while also appreciating that even the most experienced of persons still have much to learn about those very qualities.

Such a reading also highlights what it might mean, to recall Dewey's terms, to control or regulate an environment for learning. At the center of Rousseau's approach to education, at least in the phases before adulthood, is what he calls the "indirect method" of teaching (1762/1979, p. 117). This conception is rooted, in part, in Rousseau's ideas about "negative education," by which he meant an education that does not interfere with those aspects of development he viewed as "natural" (on this point, see, e.g., Iheoma, 1997; Rosenow, 1980). Dewey (1916/1997) suggests that, for Rousseau, the "interference by social arrangements with Nature . . . is the primary source of corruption in individuals. Rousseau's passionate assertion of the intrinsic goodness of all natural tendencies was a reaction against the prevalent notion of the total depravity of innate human nature, and has had a powerful influence in modifying the attitude toward children's interests" (pp. 114–115). One could argue that Dewey felt this influence as much as any reader of Rousseau.

Rousseau (1762/1979) calls his indirect method "a difficult art . . . , that of governing without precepts and doing everything by doing nothing" (p. 119). As readers of *Émile* come to see, Rousseau's method is truly an art, in the sense of artifice—something created by a human being. It is an art to keep the child's learning front and center, rather than, on the one hand, calling attention to oneself as an educator or, on the other hand, kowtowing to current social expectations. According to Rousseau, a teacher is more than an acculturator or socializer. A teacher works in the spirit of human possibility, of what human beings can become rather than solely in the name of what they have been. But a teacher is not a preacher or a politician. In Rousseau's educational plan, the teacher must remain in the background. He or she must manipulate the environment, in the root sense of the term, meaning to organize and structure it.

In Rousseau's account, the teacher concentrates on creating conditions that capitalize on the child's natural curiosity. Those conditions should, at the same time, enable the child to cultivate a steadily developing sense of reality, of what he or she can accomplish at a given phase or moment. As a general rule of thumb, the teacher should not issue commands or dictate to children but rather should regulate the surroundings in such a way that children gain a sense of their powers as well as their limitations. Children should not order people about as if they were objects of their pleasure, nor conduct themselves as if they had the godlike strength to grasp the moon. For Rousseau, however, it is crucial that children learn these things not because of an adult's exhortations but because the force of environmental conditions, in the educational setting, teaches them that there are limits to their powers. "It is necessary that [Émile] feel his weakness," writes Rousseau (1762/1979), "and not that he suffer from it" (p. 85). Émile should become mindful of what he knows but may not know he knows, and he should understand what he does not know and, crucially, may not know he does not know. Rousseau hopes Émile will discover that he can learn and that he can take initiative in learning—that is, he can be spontaneous—rather than being a passive recipient of whatever comes his way. Moreover, this entire educational process is about becoming, as Rousseau puts it, a "moral being" (p. 78), a being destined to dwell in human society. Thus, to feel one's "weakness" is not to dissolve one's confidence. On the contrary, it is to perceive how central other people and the things of the world are in the scheme of human life.

According to Amelie Rorty's (1998) interpretation, Émile "is to learn from experience, by the consequences of his actions rather than from persons or books. If he were directly taught by the Tutor, the complex relations of power and dependence would be set in motion. He would become passive, anxious to please, secretly rebellious, biding his turn for tyranny" (p. 248). To educate the young in Rousseau's terms calls forth the teacher's patience and tact. The teacher constructs an environment that should, in Rousseau's view, generate what he describes as a well-regulated freedom. Those terms are not an oxymoron. They crystallize his conception of the indirect method of teaching. The teacher regulates the environment, and does so "well" rather than thoughtlessly, in order to cultivate dispositions and skills that will serve the child's present and future freedom. Rousseau makes plain that freedom cannot mean license to do as one pleases. To recall the discussion in the previous chapter, such a posture describes caprice, not acting spontaneously. Freedom has meaning when juxtaposed with a boundary or limit, just as a boundary or limit is enabling when it facilitates freedom. Rousseau's example of indirect teaching shows that people can recognize humanizing boundaries rather than leave the matter up to chance, fate, or expected custom. They can convert caprice into initiative or spontaneity. They can give themselves boundaries in order, paradoxically perhaps, to make possible broader forms of learning and growth. They can intentionally channel their energy and their focus rather than disperse them aimlessly or expend them in fruitless modes of life. In other words, human beings can influence the environment in which they live. They can fashion stimuli that draw out and develop their best qualities. They can let themselves, in turn, fall under the environment's influence. They can deliberately allow themselves to be influenced, indirectly, by the world they strive to create. They can trust in that world, in its people and its activities.

Kant was deeply influenced by Rousseau's writing. Kant's biographer, the philosopher Ernst Cassirer (1945), argues that Kant learned from Rousseau that "what is truly permanent in human nature is not any condition *in which* it once existed and *from which* it has fallen; rather it is the goal *for which* and toward which it moves" (p. 20). What Kant saw as "permanent" in human nature was its capacity for and movement toward freedom—toward deepening the ability to act spontaneously and, thus, to act freely and morally. Kant was taken with humanity's potential to cultivate its own goodness, which he equated with freedom. He was equally impressed, if not also depressed, by humanity's obvious potential to do harm. His project, in part, was to examine how the potential for good could be realized in the face of the propensity to evil and, one day perhaps, even overcome it (Kant, 1786/1963, 1793/1991). Like Rousseau and others before him, and Dewey and others after him, Kant appreciated the value of education in propelling human beings closer to rather than further from their potential freedom. His outlook might be called an article of rational faith (Kant, 1785/1990, p. 81). The world a teacher and his or her students create in a classroom, at any level of the educational system, can become a microcosm of a larger world in which people bring to life their potential. Their educational work together can have a ripple effect into an untold number of other settings.

According to Rousseau, several factors figure into the art of teaching indirectly. For one thing, teachers must pay close attention to the physical setting. They should do so to facilitate student exploration, albeit within bounds and limits set by students' current capabilities and by the teacher's understanding of them. In this regard, Rousseau (1762/1979) argues that being a teacher means becoming a permanent student of students. "Begin, then, by studying your pupils better," he exhorted the educators of his day, "[f]or most assuredly you do not know them at all" (p. 34). To be a student of students means developing the skills of moral perception, insight, and understanding that help the teacher fashion on educative environment. It does not mean pigeonholing, labeling, or classifying students according to predefined categories, which, as Bernadette Baker (1998) shows, is how the idea of studying students has sometimes been institutionalized.

Rousseau illustrates the fact that the environment includes the objects, materials, and resources a teacher selects. In principle, the source of materials is boundless. A class might examine visible entities such as an ant colony, a poem, a painting, or the starry heavens above. They might address apparently less visible entities such as the nature or existence of a deity, the meaning of love, our grasp of death, and more (cf. Noddings, 1993). All such materials should spark and support what can be called inquiry. However, for Rousseau, as Eugene Iheoma (1997) underscores, the form of the activities in which these materials are taken up should also fuel dispositions such as sympathy for humanity, as well as sentiments of awe and wonder about the sheer fact of being alive.

According to Rousseau, teachers should also employ time wisely, which means, among other things, developing a sense of timing. Rousseau (1762/1979) considers throughout *Émile* the question of when to undertake a particular pedagogical activity. He talks about when to "lose time" (pp. 93, 107; see Hendel, 1934, pp. 90–91), that is, when to hold back, to be patient, to not force the issue. He examines when to "gain" or "use time" (cf. pp. 165–166), that is, when to seize the day and intervene actively. He illustrates when to slow down time (p. 232) or, in other words, when to draw out an endeavor or inquiry.

Rousseau's requirements of the teacher constitute a tall order. Among other things, to teach indirectly entails considerable knowledge of students, of processes of human development, of the nature and place of materials, time, and planning in pedagogy, and more. Dewey seconds all of these points:

> The immediate and direct concern of an educator is . . . with the situations in which interaction takes place. The individual, who enters as a factor into it, is what he is at a given time. It is the other factor, that of objective conditions, which lies to some extent within the possibility of regulation by the educator. . . . [T]he phrase "objective conditions" covers a wide range. It includes what is done by the educator and the way in which it is done, not only words spoken but the tone of the voice in which they are spoken. It includes equipment, books, apparatus, toys, games played. It includes the materials with which an individual interacts, and, most important of all, the total *social* set-up of the situations in which a person is engaged. (1938/1963, p. 45)

Like Rousseau, Dewey highlights the interaction between teacher and students, what he calls the "total social setup" of the situations that unfold in the environment. Because that setup is dynamic, the environment itself is ever-changing. It is never established in a terminal way. As we will see in the next chapter, the educational environment changes along with the persons embedded in it.

DEWEY'S RECONSTRUCTION OF ROUSSEAU'S METHOD

However, both Rousseau and Dewey contend that the educational environment should retain several characteristics. The content of the characteristics may evolve and shift, especially as teachers and students mature in their intellectual and moral outlooks. But the form that the characteristics take endures. Dewey (1916/1997) captures their form in arguing that the educational environment should be simplified, purified, balanced, and steadying (pp. 20–22; here he focuses on the school, but I believe the analysis pertains as much to his view of the classroom).

A "simplified" environment, not to be confused with a simplistic one, features objects "which are fairly fundamental and capable of being responded to by the young" (p. 20). By fundamental, Dewey has in mind, for example, drawing students into an experiment on how to convert a liquid into gas and allowing them to think out loud about such concepts as "solid," "liquid," and "gas," rather than restricting them to a diet of extended, abstract lectures on the topic. A simplified environment embodies respect for students' present capacities and present powers, albeit with an eye on extending them.

A "purified" environment, not to be confused with a pure one, calls forth participants' best thinking, feeling, and conduct, rather than encouraging them to intensify their biases, intolerance, dogmatism, and the like. It draws out students' open-mindedness rather than stubbornness, their willingness to listen to others rather than to rush to judgment, and so forth. A purified environment features activities and exchanges that foster the emergence of moral dispositions, understandings, and outlooks supporting, rather than threatening or undermining, human flourishing.

A "balanced" educational environment sponsors individual development while also fueling a social and moral consciousness. Rousseau hopes that Émile's education will allow him to develop as an integrated, unique, irreproducible person, while also cultivating his identity as a "moral being" (1762/1979, p. 78) who seeks to live justly with others. Dewey parts company with Rousseau on how to cultivate "moral being." Rousseau treats much of human sociality as unnatural and as generating customs and institutions that suppress human flourishing. He isolates Émile from society for much of the boy's early educational life, so that "Nature" can operate uncorrupted. Dewey casts a critical eye on harmful social practices, too, but he regards sociality as fundamental to human being and personhood. He conceives Rousseau's perspective toward the social as unbalanced. Rather than looking to something called "Nature," Dewey emphasizes human capabilities for fashioning just, democratic relations, with "democratic" understood as a form of associated life rather than as a set of governmental institutions or laws (cf. Dewey, 1916/1997, pp. 83–88). In Dewey's writing, democracy is a name for a mode of life in which persons habitually keep in view the interests, the concerns, and the aspirations of others, even as they attend to their own. Dewey believes the environment in the school and classroom should promote such a mode of life by enabling teachers and students to enact it day by day, even moment by moment.

In surveying the educational scene in urban America, Dewey (1916/1997) writes that the "intermingling in the school [and classroom] of youth of different races, differing religions, and unlike customs creates for all a new and broader environment" (p. 21). That environment can balance students' individual interests, as well as their family-centered and community-centered outlooks, with what Dewey calls an emerging "horizon" that also takes seriously the perspectives, knowledge, and activities of others. With teachers' guidance and insight, individuals can pursue their own educational adventures while also interacting with others in ways that widen and deepen social sympathies (1916/1997, pp. 121, 148).

Finally, a "steadying" environment invites students to harmonize their knowledge, insight, feeling, and viewpoints, rather than assuming that life is supposed to be divided up into domains (education, family, work, play) that have nothing to do with one another. Posed differently, from Dewey's perspective the educational environment should help students to "coordinate" (1916/1997, p. 22) their understandings and dispositions. To recall terms from Chapter 2, that coordination fuels the making of a narrative unity in a life. A steadying environment assists the young in seeing their lives as a whole, against the broadest possible backdrop of human activity and aspiration.

According to Dewey and, in some respects, to Rousseau before him, a simplified, purified, balanced, and steadying environment helps constitute conditions in which a teacher can best educate others. But the teacher educates indirectly, or so these authors argue. They suggest that without a supportive environment, teaching cannot take place at all. This claim resides at the heart of Rousseau's indirect method, and it accounts for much of the influence on education he has had since the publication of *Émile*. I will come back to his legacy in the conclusion to this chapter.

In my view, Dewey extends and reconstructs Rousseau's account of indirect teaching in a number of useful ways (I am leaving aside other differences in their philosophies of education). These ways center around the person in the role of teacher.

Redirecting Pedagogical Focus

Dewey's argument implies that if teachers work directly on creating the proper environment, they can place faith in it to help them teach students. They can disperse with the feeling that they have to be heroic miracle workers, which is sometimes how Émile's teacher comes across. They can release the presumption that they, and they alone, are the center of the classroom universe and that any and all learning emanates solely from their direct engagement with students. Teachers continue to play the most decisive role in the classroom. Dewey's conception does not, any more than Rousseau's, eliminate the complexity and the very real demands good teaching makes on the people who occupy the position (Greene, 1989; Schwab, 1978b). However, Dewey's perspective helps turn the teacher's gaze away from him- or herself and toward the classroom environment and the diverse factors that figure into its emergence. Teaching indirectly helps the teacher become object- rather than self-conscious (see Chapter 3), and it helps the teacher identify the objects worth attending to in the first place.

The Teacher *in* the Environment

A second way in which Dewey extends Rousseau's account is his insistence that the teacher be seen as one of the dynamic factors that make up the environment. This point is not to imply that Émile's teacher operates like the proverbial person behind the curtain, although some critics, as I suggested previously, have claimed this to be the case. The point is that Rousseau (1762/1979) expects anyone who would teach to be unusually well educated, experienced, and morally sensitive. "Remember that before daring to undertake the formation of a man," he writes, "one must have made oneself a man. One must find within oneself the example the pupil ought to take for his own" (p. 95). Rousseau appeals to the heart and the soul of the would-be teacher: "It is your time, your care, your affection, it is you yourself that must be given. . . . Loudly proclaim yourself the protector of the unfortunate. Be just, humane, and beneficent. . . . Love others, and they will love you. Serve them, and they will serve you. . . . [B]e humane. This is your first duty. Be humane with every station, every age, everything which is not alien to man. What wisdom is there for you, save humanity?" (pp. 95, 79). This soupçon of Rousseau's rhetoric, so striking for its time, and so beloved to many readers over the last several centuries, soars beyond talk of indirect teaching, although he eventually pulls it back to pedagogical practice. These and many similar claims in *Émile* suggest that, for Rousseau, any person who would teach must exemplify goodness, thoughtfulness, learning, determination, and compassion. Those are qualities that any parent would like to see in a son's or daughter's teachers. However, the question is *when* should we expect teachers to embody them—before they so much as set foot in the classroom or along the road itself of learning to teach, which means while they are in the classroom working with other people's children?

Dewey (1904/1974b) argues that we cannot expect pedagogical ability and insight to materialize on the basis of formal education and of theory alone, crucial as they are. He implies that what we can and should expect, in both teacher candidates and teachers, is *movement* toward wisdom-in-practice, to use David Schultz's (1997) term. More strikingly, with respect to my argument here, Dewey suggests that if teachers regulate or control the environment in the manner he articulates, they will be educating themselves. They, too, will be influenced indirectly by the very environment they strive to bring into being. They will be influenced by their students, whose minds and spirits, ideally, will be energized by the environment. They will be influenced by all the many steps that are part of shaping a meaningful environment, because taking those steps calls on teachers to be thoughtful, resourceful, perceptive, attentive, and more. *But that means continuously developing and extending those very qualities in themselves.* We come full circle and perceive, once again, that to shape a good environment calls on teachers to cultivate in themselves the qualities examined in Chapter 3: straightforwardness, spontaneity, simplicity, naiveté, open-mindedness, open-heartedness, integrity of purpose, responsibility, and seriousness.

Dewey illuminates this outcome when he writes: "Few grown-up persons retain all of the flexible and sensitive ability of children to vibrate sympathetically with the attitudes and doings of those about them. . . . With respect to sympathetic curiosity, unbiased responsiveness, and openness of mind, we may say that the adult should be growing in childlikeness" (1916/1997, pp. 43, 50). To teach means to engage in a practice that can lead to self-improvement, with a corresponding increase in one's capacity to be a good influence on others. It would be unrealistic, even nonhuman, to expect teachers to be complete moral beings (whatever that is) before they so much as set foot in the classroom. It is realistic, and it seems deeply human, to expect teachers to progress toward the qualities addressed throughout this and the previous chapter. As mentioned, this outlook obliges the teacher to regard him- or herself as a dynamic element in the environment. The teacher does not stand apart from the process, as if he or she operated from an Olympian source of knowledge and insight. At one and the same time, the teacher is a technician skilled in the arts that help shape an environment, a participant in that very process who learns continually from students and from their interactions with subject matter and with one another, and a being-in-the-making influenced morally and intellectually by the environment.

Environment and Surroundings

Teachers can contribute further to their own growth, and to that of their students, by making use of Dewey's distinction between environment and what he calls "surroundings." This distinction allows Dewey to reconstruct further Rousseau's portrait of indirect teaching. According to Dewey, we are surrounded by a veritable infinity of things: sunshine, blue sky, night, clouds, insects, buildings, rooms, trees, street litter, electrical outlets, windows, cars, shops, and so forth. But these surroundings do not constitute the *environment* that serves as the medium of influence of one person on another. Rather, the environment pertains to what Dewey (1916/1997) calls the "continuity" between the surroundings and what he calls peoples' "active tendencies" (p. 11). It is not everything around us but rather the things with which we "vary" that form our "genuine environment" (p. 11). The color I have painted my apartment walls, the interactions I have with my neighborhood dry cleaner, and the shape of my dentist's chair do not form part of the environment emergent in my classroom, even though they are always part of my larger surroundings. They are best understood, perhaps, as part of the environment in my home, at the dry cleaner's, or in my dentist's office. The environment in the classroom has to do with its physical features, with the materials employed in it, with the use of time, and, above all, with the innumerable contacts among the classroom's occupants. Those are the things with which teacher and students, taken as a whole, "vary." They make it possible to form, as Alan Ryan (1998) puts it, a "network of meanings" (p. 399). We might say that a good teacher makes explicit in his thinking, in his planning, and in his conduct as many features of the environment as possible. A poor or unsuccessful teacher perhaps lets too many features, interactions, and more, recede into the category of surroundings, with the result that the classroom environment becomes unnecessarily impoverished.

What about individual meetings between a teacher and student else-where—say, in the school hallway, on a playground, at a social gathering, in a faculty office, at a conference, or on an airplane? Teachers cannot control or regulate the environment at a conference in a far-distant town, nor the environment on an airplane, nor the environment at a school celebration, in a school hallway, or in a school cafeteria. And yet we know that such contacts are often influential on students, and indeed can become memorable. Do these facts challenge the notion that educators do not influence their students apart from the medium of the environment?

Two responses come to mind. First, all the out-of-classroom settings described above feature environments. A teacher may have limited power to control or regulate them, but a case could be made that such environments influence the teacher's impact on students when in those settings. They variously shape, constrain, or facilitate particular kinds of communication. Many teachers, for example, alter their talk in some way or another, however subtly, when standing together with students in a museum as contrasted with discussing a poem or a scientific experiment in the classroom. That fact calls to mind why all of us, whether as children or as adults, say things such as "Let's sit down here" or "Is this a good time to talk?" or "Let's wait until we won't be distracted." We want to create the right kind of environment. The point is that the environment remains an ever-present intermediary or medium for one person's influence on another.

A second and perhaps more compelling response centers on the emergent quality of an environment. Consider the following scenario, which I base on what I have experienced time and again and which anticipates the next chapter's discussion. I coordinate a graduate secondary teacher education program at my university. As part of my duties, I chair our admissions to the program. One day in June, I meet for the first time a recently admitted teacher candidate. This is 2 months before she will start taking courses with us, including a course that I teach. In normal parlance, one would say that we do not know each other when we first meet. We are starting from scratch, so to speak. However, an environment that will condition our interaction has already begun to take shape even before she first walks through my office door. She does not walk in cold. She has read and perhaps heard various things about our program, including about its faculty. She has taken the time and the trouble to fill out and send in an application, and then to accept our offer of admission. And these steps may presuppose a great deal of thought on her part about becoming a teacher. Moreover, perhaps she has tutored, coached, or in other ways worked with adolescents. All of this gives her a certain character, a certain sensibility, aspects of which she might not be aware.

On my part, I have read her application. I have seen her grade transcripts, her letters of reference that have talked about her as a person, and her goal statement about why she wants to become a high school teacher. In reading these materials, I form a picture of her, one juxtaposed with the aims of the course she will be taking with me soon as well as with the aims of the teacher preparation program in which that course is embedded. My reading comes on top of my own career as an educator. These factors contribute to the layers of expectation, curiosity, and hope that I bring to reading her application. In short, an environment, in Dewey's sense of that term, has begun to take shape even before the candidate and I meet in person. This environment is generated by a particular set of acts and intentions that pivot, in one way or another, around teaching. It is the intermediary or medium for whatever impact I might have on the candidate, and vice versa, at our first meeting.

Four months go by. The course I teach has met half a dozen times. The candidate, now a student in the class, has heard a great deal from me, and I have heard a great deal from her. Our class has begun to form an environment. One afternoon, the candidate comes to my office to discuss a paper she turned in on which I wrote some comments and questions. A half-hour later she leaves, while stating "I'm clearer now about what I was trying to say." In everyday terms, one might say (speaking generously) that I had a good influence on the student. But it was not a direct, unmediated influence of one context-less mind upon another. Whatever help I rendered the candidate was predicated on everything we had done in our class up to then, and before as well, as I argued in the previous paragraphs. The environment has been the medium. That environment has taken shape as the consequence of a series of events through which meaning has been accruing. And the environment, I hope, has not been a chance or random one. I have brought to it whatever initiative and thought I am capable of mustering. The teacher candidate has brought to it her own initiative and thought, for she has clearly not been passive or merely reactive. These points show that while the environment serves as an intermediary of influence, the environment depends on the agency, intentions, and actions of individual persons. The example also illustrates why teachers might ponder the impact on the *classroom* environment of individual meetings they hold with students in hallways, offices, homes, over electronic mail, or on the telephone. All such meetings can be perceived as parts of a whole rather than as unrelated to the formation of a classroom environment supportive of teaching and learning.

An Emphasis on Activity, Not on Learning

A related consequence of regarding the environment as the intermediary of influence is that teachers should be chary about focusing directly on student learning. Dewey (1916/1997, p. 160) writes of teachers providing conditions for learning, of adopting a sympathetic attitude toward students, and of participating actively in classroom life. He says nothing about their instigating learning in a direct, head-on manner. He regards student engagement, involvement, engrossment, but not learning per se, as the *immediate* aim of teaching. If teachers cultivate and support conditions that engage students in an activity, whether it be interpreting a poem, conducting an experiment, or debating the causes of a historical event, learning will more likely be the outcome, or so Dewey suggests. But if they try to force learning without taking steps to engender meaningful involvement, they may frustrate students and themselves. "Under normal conditions," Dewey (1916/1997) contends, "learning is a product and reward of occupation with subject matter" (p. 169).

For example, I cannot say that I "learned" at precisely 10:43 A.M. on a September morning in history class that World War I had multiple causes. A teacher may have sent those words into my ears at that time, but learning is not identical with hearing something. If I have truly learned, that learning has emerged over time, however long or short. It has derived from immersing myself, to some meaningful degree, in activities such as reading, talking with others, listening to my teacher, and writing about the war. Good teachers, Dewey (1916/1997) argues, "give the pupils something to do, not something to learn; and the doing is of such a nature as to demand thinking, or the intentional noting of connections; learning naturally results" (p. 154). But if teachers try to focus directly on learning, rather than on the conditions and intentional activities that foster learning, they are liable to make their students and themselves self-conscious rather than object-conscious. "Frontal attacks are even more wasteful in learning than in war," Dewey cautions (p. 169).

The idea of focusing indirectly on learning does not lessen the intensity or the integrity of the focus. It constitutes the mirror image of not focusing directly on oneself, as teacher. From the perspective of teaching indirectly, the teacher need not strain to be the fount of all knowledge and insight. All teachers need excellent preparation in whatever subjects they will teach. However, in an equally vital sense, teachers need to lose themselves as much in the classroom environment as their students hopefully do. That process means, as I emphasized previously, that the environment teachers promote should be the kind that calls out certain responses in them as much as in their students. The environment should direct teachers to work straightforwardly at what they do, to be open-minded in the critical sense of that term, to sustain integrity of purpose even if we are talking about activities of only a minute's duration, and to cultivate their sense of responsibility, of believing in the worth of what they do and standing behind it, albeit in a spirit of learning, as the other qualities suggest. Past successes as a teacher should provoke questions and thought, not complacency. "It is not enough," Dewey reminds us, "that certain materials and methods have proved effective with other individuals at other times. There must be a reason for thinking that they will function in generating an experience that has educative quality with particular individuals at a particular time" (1938/1963, p. 46). When Dewey writes of undertaking steps to "generate" educative experiences for students, he once again turns our attention to the environment.

CONCLUSION: A CONCEPTION OF INDIRECT TEACHING

This chapter has centered on Rousseau's conception of indirect teaching and on Dewey's reconstruction of it. Rousseau's enduring contribution to education derives, in part, both from his focus on the child *as* a child and from his equally powerful account of what kind of person a teacher must be. Rousseau provokes the reader to face the thorny question of who should be allowed to teach—who should be permitted to take hold of the opportunity to have an intellectual and moral influence on the young. In not always comfortable or reassuring ways, Rousseau highlights what might be called an individual's worthiness to teach.[2] These stark terms intensify the significance of concepts I addressed in Chapter 2, such as the teacher's conduct and moral sensibility. The unsettling idea of worthiness to teach, coupled with how one actually goes about the work, dramatizes the importance of a teacher's moral sensibility, or what, following Kant (1793/1960, pp. 41–42), might be called his or her "moral cast of mind." A moral cast of mind embodies, as I interpret Kant, a willingness to honor students' dignity, agency, and autonomy, even while working hard to educate them. It suggests a grasp on why there is no contradiction between teaching students and respecting their individuality.

In a broad sense, a moral cast of mind embodies a commitment to treat other people as ends in themselves rather than as merely a means to our ends. Some might say that such an orientation is the product of a lifetime. It is certainly not easy to cultivate, at least for many people. Wordsworth attests to that fact (see Chapter 3) when he writes about the "dislike" and "offensive pain" he felt in doing the hard thinking and compromising sometimes involved in being a moral agent.

Some critics argue that the teacher Rousseau created in *Émile* fails to conduct himself in the spirit Rousseau advances (see, e.g., Cranston, 1991; Peters, 1981; Rosenow, 1980). Moreover, to recall the familiar image of the figure behind the curtain, other critics question what they characterize as "the invisible controls of child-centered education" (Rousmaniere, 1997, p. 128), which they trace directly to Rousseau. For example, James Donald (1992) claims that " 'allowing the child to develop' has instituted an emphasis on surveillance and monitoring; 'liberating the child' has involved stratagems as lovingly manipulative as any of those devised by Émile's tutor" (p. 13). Kate Rousmaniere and her colleagues (Rousmaniere, Dehli, & de Coninck-Smith, 1997) suggest that formal education today "is experienced differently by different individuals, not by some accident or fault of design, but because differentiation and individuation constitute a condition structured into the very organization of modern schools and school systems" (p. 9). That condition, the authors write, involves what they describe as an ongoing process of "moral regulation" designed for "the production of self-disciplined individuals" (p. 3).

The term *moral*, as these authors employ it, takes its meaning from Michel Foucault's argument about how power works subtly but inexorably to regulate or normalize personhood and conduct.[3] I share Foucault's concerns about the weight that the urge to organize and to control has placed on the modern world. All too often, it seems, people use things, time, and ideas, and even use values, other persons, and themselves, as simply a means to an end, but with that end itself becoming merely a means to some other end. Foucault highlights the outcomes of such a way of life. The propensity to account for every step we and others take converts the human habitat into what he calls, in one of his studies, a place of "pure morality" (quoted in Rabinow, 1984, p. 138) in which rationalistic control has come into its own. Erving Goffman (1961) called such a place a "total institution," in which concepts of "freedom," "agency," "spontaneity," and others I have examined in these pages may retain a surface luster but underneath lack the substantive, generative meaning I have associated with them.

This perspective contrasts with the way I have been framing terms such as *regulating, controlling,* and *designing an environment.* They contrast with what I have said about teaching indirectly. None of these terms implies or necessitates the kind of rationalistic control that Foucault, Goffman, and others have usefully characterized. To fashion a particular environment in the classroom does not mean trying to orchestrate every detail, every action, every undertaking. On the contrary, the process involves something closer to *learning* from acts, undertakings, and the details of classroom life. To regulate or control an environment for teaching and learning involves not a totalizing impulse, à la Goffman, but a belief that what teachers and students think, feel, say, and do can matter. It seems to me that a teacher cannot, in good faith, leave the environment up to chance, any more than he or she can, in good faith, simply borrow lock, stock, and barrel the approach of another teacher.

I will have more to say about this outlook in subsequent chapters. Here, I have been examining ideas and examples from Rousseau and Dewey. In my view, both authors were acute observers of educational practices in their societies, and they were trenchant, resolute, and prescient critics. I believe they were deeply mindful of some of the ominous forms that "surveillance and monitoring" can take. They recognized the fact that those forms could accompany, and possibly take over, any deliberate approach to education. But they also show that such an outcome is neither inevitable nor a "structural condition" that teachers and students must simply assume as a driving force underlying their settings and actions. They show that the materialist language of the "production" of individuals is out of place, or at least has no automatic priority, in conceiving what it means to shape an environment for teaching and learning. As with the cultivation of a moral sensibility, or moral cast of mind, both writers recognize the genuine challenges this task presents to the teacher.

As we have seen, Rousseau brings considerable substance to the idea of indirect teaching. He articulates the personal qualities that he regards as necessary to teach in this way. He illustrates in abundant detail that the physical setting, materials and resources, time (as well as timing), and more, all figure into the "art" of teaching indirectly. Dewey extends and reorients Rousseau's formulation. Dewey elucidates features of an environment supportive of teaching and learning, while also illustrating how a teacher can help bring such an environment into being. Like Rousseau,

Dewey highlights the person in the role of teacher. His *Democracy and Education* constitutes, and can provoke in the reader, a sustained meditation on what it means to be a teacher. In the next chapter, I describe an approach to teaching indirectly that pays heed to Rousseau's initial formulation and to Dewey's reconstruction of it, about which I still have more to say. In this approach, I endeavor to take seriously the image of a growing, educated person that I presented in Chapter 3 as well as the argument in the present chapter about the importance of the environment.

✌ 5 ✌

Shaping an Environment for
Teaching and Learning

IN THE COURSE I DESCRIBE in this chapter, I try to enact a pedagogical approach that I call *focused discussion*. As the name implies, the approach centers around discussion as an instructional method. The qualifier *focused* might seem redundant, since a discussion cannot be a discussion unless it is focused. I employ the qualifier to emphasize that the approach to discussion I take extends beyond the classroom, in both spatial and temporal terms. As I anticipated in the last chapter, it encompasses meetings with students in my office, in hallways, and at orientation sessions. It characterizes, ideally, all my contacts with students. Focused discussion is an attempt to promote an ongoing conversation about teaching with students, in which talking, listening, thinking aloud, and questioning constitute the main terms.

I want to examine and illustrate focused discussion for several reasons. First, the approach illuminates what is meant by teaching indirectly. Perhaps most, if not all, formal approaches to classroom discussion constitute indirect teaching. In any case, I believe focused discussion holds a key to why a seasoned and profoundly knowledgeable educator like Dewey (1916/1997) would urge upon us the idea I first quoted in Chapter 3, that "there is not, in fact, any such thing as the direct influence of one human being on another" (p. 28).

Second, focused discussion takes inspiration and form from a long-standing human commitment to dialogue as a medium for learning, as names such as Socrates and Confucius attest. That commitment has endured because people have realized that talking *with*, rather than *at*, one another can yield meaning, knowledge, and, sometimes, even wisdom. People have found that teaching through conversation constitutes a way to regain what I called, in Chapter 3, naiveté: a freshness in outlook and understanding, a peeling off of encrusted beliefs and assumptions that otherwise cling like barnacles on a boat. Conversation can become a recurring invitation to begin again, to become "simple" (another quality I described in Chapter 3), to get to things that matter and to grasp why they matter, and, thus perhaps, to live by them that much more. My students and I have experienced such outcomes through focused discussion, although, as we will see, their emergence cannot be predicted or forced.

Third, the approach complements recent work on the uses of conversation and discussion in the classroom (see, e.g., Burbules, 1993; Dillon, 1994; Haroutunian-Gordon, 1991). Because I esteem the educational benefits of classroom discussion, I want to support this body of work and contribute to it. I hope to do so critically, in the sense of working through the prejudice I have in favor of discussion rather than merely enacting that prejudice here. I acknowledge the worth of good lectures, well-crafted small-group activities, well-designed individual projects, well-organized fieldwork, and the like. I also perceive limitations in discussion as an instructional strategy. I believe it is important to question the values in discussion, if only to resist converting its use into a dogma or blueprint for pedagogical conduct.

However, I have developed and employed focused discussion (or aspects of it) for many years—with children, with doctoral students, and with age groups in between. While any teacher's testimony is limited and partial, I have judged it warranted to refer to my own work because Dewey's talk of controlling and regulating the classroom environment, which I introduced in the previous chapters, can appear, at first glance, heavy-handed, if not authoritarian. In my experience, focused discussion does not imply a top-down or dictatorial method of instruction. There is no contradiction between regulating a learning environment, as I understand the terms, and fostering edifying conversation within it. Meaningful, educative discussion cannot emerge unless the teacher takes steps to organize the environment, which can include trying not to suffocate exchanges between participants. In the pages to come, I outline the steps I take, some of which I have witnessed school-based teachers implement in their classrooms.

Finally, the example of focused discussion I present centers on a course I teach in which students and I devote considerable time and energy to Dewey's *Democracy and Education*, a book whose ideas I will draw upon in this chapter, just as I have in previous ones. I hope the example will show that teaching indirectly is both a viable and less novel idea than it might initially seem.

BACKGROUND TO FOCUSED DISCUSSION

Several recent studies support the hope I just expressed. For instance, Harriet Cuffaro (1995) takes a detailed look at the early childhood classroom. She weaves together concrete classroom doings, including interaction between teachers and students, with an inquiry into Dewey's conception of learning. She is especially interested in his view of what she calls the "social individual," that is, how persons become social beings through cooperation and communication with others. In the course of her analysis, Cuffaro makes extensive use of Dewey's arguments about the importance of the environment, or what she usually terms the educational "setting." She examines factors that Rousseau brought to our attention, including the physical aspects of the setting, the kind of materials and resources to be employed, and the temporal aspects of teaching and learning (see also Yamamoto, 1979). She adds further factors such as scheduling, which includes lesson planning as this is understood at the middle and high school level. Although Cuffaro does not discuss indirect teaching per se, her study sheds light on the influence the classroom environment can have on its occupants. For example, she illustrates how physical space can function "to create those conditions that will evoke each child's potential and capacity, and, further, will facilitate interactions that promote and encourage the communication necessary to create community" (pp. 32–33).

Cuffaro and Dewey emphasize that teaching and learning in the classroom constitute a social undertaking. The process is not one of isolated minds operating in isolation from other minds. From this point of view, teaching and learning in the classroom constitute an intellectual and moral experience. Teaching and learning reveal and influence mind and person through the interplay of participants with one another and with the materials and objects people have fashioned, such as books, ideas, arts, and experiments.

If mind is connected to the world, however, it is not necessarily always public. Cuffaro's and Dewey's perspective does not downplay an individual's contemplation, reflection, or wonder, even if it does not emphasize them. Nor does their view denigrate the notion that these "inner" activities, as Iris Murdoch (1970) conceives them, have their own integrity. Murdoch argues that these inner activities are neither determined by nor are mere shadows of public events and practices. They can dramatically influence how a person conducts him- or herself. Moreover, persons can communicate, or attempt to do so, much of what they contemplate, reflect on, and wonder about. The inner can be made outer, the private public, and vice versa, although Dewey (1916/1997) contends that the process entails transformation:

> To be a recipient of a communication is to have an enlarged and changed experience. One shares in what another has thought and felt and in so far, meagerly or amply, has his own attitude modified. Nor is the one who communicates left unaffected. Try the experiment of communicating, with fullness and accuracy, some experience to another, especially if it be somewhat complicated, and you will find your own attitude toward your experience changing; otherwise you resort to expletives and ejaculations. The experience has to be formulated in order to be communicated. To formulate requires getting outside of it, seeing it as another would see it, considering what points of contact it has with the life of another so that it may be got into such form that he can appreciate its meaning. Except in dealing with commonplaces and catch phrases one has to assimilate, imaginatively, something of another's experience in order to tell him intelligently of one's own experience. All communication is like art. (pp. 5–6)

Focused discussion contributes to an environment conducive to communication. It spurs participants to formulate, to cultivate, and to heed ideas, interpretations, knowledge, emotion, insight, questions, and more.

Stephen Fishman and Lucille McCarthy's (1998) project complements Cuffaro's fine-grained classroom study. They present a version of indirect teaching in the context of Fishman's Introduction to Philosophy course for undergraduates at a large public university. Teaching indirectly, in their view, differs from "presenting" already established truths through lecture or other direct instructional methods. Rather, to teach indirectly means "to structure classes so that [teachers] and their pupils identify genuine problems, use the curriculum to investigate and discover solutions to these problems, and, as a result, establish connections with course subject matter" (p. 20). The approach is indirect because rather than zeroing in squarely on curricular matter, teachers and students first articulate questions and concerns they care about, and then study and resolve them through employing the ideas, the logic, the methods, and the materials of the curriculum. The authors' extended look at Fishman's teaching demonstrates how the approach makes possible what Dewey calls "continuities and connections" between student and world. It spurs students to broaden their horizons by starting, but not ending, with personal interest and experience, something they can learn to do by connecting with the curriculum. For Fishman and McCarthy, indirect teaching enables teachers to attain a happy medium between focusing too much on students' personal interests, at the sacrifice of subject matter, or privileging subject matter, at the expense of any consideration of its place in students' lives. Both extremes, in their view, diminish meaningful teaching and learning.

The analysis of my own teaching that follows will corroborate much of what Cuffaro (1995), Fishman and McCarthy (1998), and others have to say about the influence of the educational environment. At the same time, I believe that attending to the environment can figure more centrally in teaching than these studies reveal. I also hope to show why teachers need not presume an inherent gulf between students' interests and subject matter. John Zahorik (1996) demonstrates that some teachers who take this gulf as a given search for ways to make their subjects "fun." Zahorik shows that many of the methods they turn to are not rooted in the subjects they teach, but constitute gimmicks, tricks, or games. Some teachers in his study regard the academic subjects they teach as inherently uninteresting (!), thereby creating problems for themselves that otherwise might not exist. However, teachers need not regard students as fixed or frozen selves with fixed or frozen "interests" that they must somehow engage. According to Dewey (1916/1997, p. 126), interest constitutes a dynamic, evolving human quality.

Moreover, teachers can also benefit from considering subject matter in expansive terms. For example, subject matter can be understood as what Oakeshott (1989) calls "languages"—poetry, history, science, literature, and others—in which people, over the generations, have contemplated and questioned who they are, what they know, what they have done, how to lead a humane and flourishing life, and more. For Oakeshott, an education means, in part, entering these languages, expanding one's horizons, and participating in what he conceives as an ongoing human conversation. Focused discussion, as an approach to tackling subject matter, coheres with Oakeshott's view.

The approach also shares terrain with what have been called transactional theories of subject matter. For instance, Louise Rosenblatt (e.g., 1978) locates the meaning of a text (poem, short story, novel) in the transaction between reader and text, "in the personal lived-through quality of a literary experience" (Connell, 1996, p. 395). As I understand this approach, readers do not invent, create, or construct meaning, nor does the text embody a single, predetermined meaning. Rather, meaning emerges in their "transaction," in which an inert text comes to life (literally speaking, Rosenblatt suggests) in the hands and voices of readers, even as the text influences or substantiates (literally, gives substance to) readers' outlooks, understandings, emotions, and more. According to Rosenblatt, neither the reader nor the text remains quite the same as a result of their encounter.[1]

Rosenblatt's approach is rooted, in part, in Dewey's view of experience and growth. She argues that the "work" of literature, understood as something more than just the words on the printed page, reflects both an author's and a reader's efforts. Dewey (1934/1980) describes a "work" of art as comprising both the artist's endeavor and the interpretive response of a viewer of (or, better, participant in) that work. In other words, the work of art constitutes an always living process, not an inert object hanging on a wall or residing between a book cover.

This outlook does not presume a dogmatic equality of insight or understanding on the part of reader and text. Quite on the contrary. It accords with a remark Harold Bloom (1998) makes about Shakespeare's plays, that they "know more" about the human condition than any individual reader or listener (p. 719). The notion of transaction emphasizes that a reader cannot gain access to the insight and sensibility in Shakespeare's plays without engaging them and, moreover, that the reader's insight can bring to life, sustain, and extend our sense of the plays' power and meanings. Posed differently, what those plays "know," to use Bloom's way of speaking, is not stable in scope or content, anymore than a thoughtful reader of them is locked into a fixed self with a congealed understanding of human affairs. Shakespeare's plays live on and shine because of their readers, and vice versa.

Dewey suggests that with regard to the classroom world, the subject matter of teaching and learning describes an interactive, or transactive, process. It does not feature an immobile body of material on the one side and a body of terminally formed persons on the other, which somehow have to be brought into contact. Subject matter and instructional method do not necessarily exist apart from one another either, despite the fact that they are often presented that way in the educational literature. Subject matter can constitute what teachers and students *do*. The term describes aspects of *activity* intended to cultivate learning and growth. This activity depends heavily on the environment, which becomes yet another reason that the environment figures so centrally in the account of indirect teaching I present. I clarify and illustrate these points in the pages ahead.

I begin by describing the initial actions, all of them embedded in what I call focused discussion, that help bring an environment into being in my classroom. Then I turn to the main business of the course, which is to assist students in beginning, or continuing, the long process of crafting a sound philosophy of teaching. Given my purposes here, I emphasize my designs as teacher more than I do students' aims and intentions, although toward the conclusion I present students' testimony. I hope the spotlight on my purposes and actions as teacher does not convey a one-sided, teacher-centered image of teaching. That outcome would be ironic, to say the least, given the analysis thus far of the educative influence of the environment and given my view that focused discussion can translate into a genuine, sustained form of paying attention to students. I also hope the account addresses not just teacher educators but also teachers elsewhere in schools and universities. The promise in focused discussion is not limited to teachers at any particular level of the educational system.

INSIDE THE CLASSROOM

Beginnings

The class I describe is an introductory course on teaching and curriculum for master's degree students who are preparing to become high school teachers. I have taught the course at my university for the past 5 years. I draw the examples I cite, with a few exceptions I employ for expositional purposes, from the version I taught in the fall of 1997. What I am calling focused discussion takes shape before the course meets. It begins in all the deliberations that go into the construction of the course. These encompass an internal dialogue, in which I consider how students might respond to certain readings and activities, and a systematic review of the previous years' versions, including students' many comments about them. Focused discussion also begins in the work I do as chair of our admissions committee in our secondary teacher education program and as a program adviser. It comes into play in interviews I conduct with some of the students as part of the admissions process. It emerges in my first meetings with students in my office, when I ask them to talk about themselves, their backgrounds, and why they want to teach. I try to respond to their questions, concerns, and aspirations. I am conscious of wanting to talk with them in a way that can carry over into the classroom. I describe the introductory course on teaching and curriculum I will be teaching in which they and all newly admitted students enroll. I characterize it as, among other things, an opportunity for them to begin to craft a philosophy of teaching in the company of others also engaged in the same endeavor.

On the first day of class, I attempt to draw students into talking about certain issues and into doing so in a certain spirit. I ask them each to pair off with someone in the class whom they do not know. I instruct them to take 5 minutes or so to ask their peer about such things as their educational background, their work experience, and why they want to teach high school as well as why they want to teach their particular discipline. After 5 minutes, the two reverse roles. Then, we go around the room and each student introduces his or her peer and shares the information just gathered. However, before doing so, I tell students to take out a large sheet of paper and make a seating chart as we proceed so that everyone can begin to learn one another's names. I should add that I always go down to the classroom an hour or so before class starts to rearrange the tables and chairs to form a rectangle so that everybody can see and address everyone else. (There are usually about 30 students in the course.) For the next 5 or 6 weeks—the class meets once a week for 3 hours—we begin each session by going around the room and repeating names, while making a seating chart, until students and I have learned them. This practice facilitates whole- and small-group discussion. I also believe that using names regularly in classroom talk supports the emergence of a humane environment or, phrased differently, an environment that humanizes.

The mundane, all-too-familiar act of setting up the classroom in advance is part of teaching indirectly, even though it takes place before students have arrived on the scene. When students walk through the classroom door, they will encounter a setting organized in a deliberate way. I envision two benefits for learning. The first is the sheer fact that the setting displays an intention rather than none. It is not a random setting and thus, hopefully, does not promote random thought. The second benefit resides in the message emitted by the classroom layout. My hope is that the physical setting expresses the idea of valuing what is about to take place: namely, shared inquiry into the practice of teaching rather than, say, the distribution of information about teaching over a transom. I hope that as students enter the room and settle in their seats, they will orient themselves, however subtly or unselfconsciously, toward our reasons for being together in the first place. Cuffaro (1995) implies that arranging a physical setting in advance has an indirect influence on the teacher. As she notes, for a teacher to "articulate how space is to be used, that is, to state the kind of living to be encouraged among the people who use it, anchors thoughts and feelings in reality" (p. 32). The act of manipulating a physical setting moves the teacher's thoughts and feelings in a particular direction. It "anchors" the teacher in a purpose, an aim, an ongoing educational practice. To set up a classroom in a way that allows students to see and address one another spurs the teacher to consider more seriously *what* students might actually say and do once they are there. It helps prime the teacher to attend to students. Consequently, to work on the environment is to work on one's potential self, or sensibility, as teacher (cf. Garrison, 1997, p. 73).

My purpose for opening the course in the way I have described is to invite students not just to begin talking and getting to know one another, but to begin talking publicly about teaching and about becoming a teacher. I have learned from experience that students bring to the program different depths of commitment to and understanding of teaching. Some students have taught before and have been planning to enroll in a program like ours for some time. Because of their sense of purpose, they are often extraordinarily enthusiastic and their interest is irrepressible. Other students have a vaguer feel for what teaching is about—they may never have taught before—and have applied to the program out of a mixture of curiosity about the practice and the wish to discover and test their own commitment. These are students who tend to sit on the fence sometimes and who often hold back from participation because they are not sure what to say or how to contribute. They are not sure on what basis they have anything to say. A few appear to be intimidated by the teaching experience others have had, as well as by the course curriculum. Consequently, they find it hard to be naive and spontaneous, in the sense of those terms developed in Chapter 3.

I am reluctant to let students sit on the fence, in part because our program is only 2 years long and more generally because of how significant it is to take on the role of teacher. In this respect, there is not a whole lot of time for students to make up their minds about their commitment. However, the kind of resolution I am looking for is not to have them throw down their reserve and come charging forth carrying the banner of teaching. Rather, I encourage them to begin thinking seriously about teaching itself: to commit themselves to *that* object or aim, to give themselves over to the task of investigating it wholeheartedly in the spirit in which they can best test their commitment and understanding by "trying it on for size." For some students, it takes considerable time before they begin to climb off the fence. As I will show, the course readings, discussions, and their peers' enthusiasm and insight contribute to an environment that makes a transformation possible. (These same factors perhaps convince the small number of students who drop out of the program each year that teaching is not right for them, and/or vice versa.)

Some students who have taught before are more dogmatic and testy in their outlooks than those with no formal experience. In a few cases, they enter the program in a hurry to obtain a state license, thinking that they have little more to learn about pedagogy. I urge students who have taught before, or who are currently teaching, to bracket their experience. I ask them to place their background to the side, metaphorically speaking, and to open themselves to potentially new perspectives and knowledge. Those understandings can help them criticize what they have learned from experience. A recurrent theme of our work is that teaching is a career-long learning process for teachers, a theme that helps place those with and those without formal experience on shared ground.

Cultivating that shared ground begins in our first meeting. In the second half of our first class, after the introductions and a preview of the course, I ask students a series of questions, giving them a few minutes between each to write down a response. In my most recent course, the questions were (1) What is teaching? (2) What, if anything, makes teaching distinct from parenting? (3) What, if anything, makes teaching distinct from being a doctor? (4) What, if anything, makes teaching distinct from being a politician? Finally, I repeat the question "What is teaching?" and ask them to write down any additions or changes to their initial response to the question, having gone through the crucible of comparing teaching to these other practices. Then, I open things up for discussion until the class ends. In the course of that discussion I try to call on every student at least once, by name, making use of the seating chart I referred to before. My intent is not to put quieter students on the spot. It is to bring their voice further into the conversation (each has already spoken up in introducing a peer to the class). It is to help the more reserved and uncertain students begin to climb off the fence.

Dewey (1916/1997) states in the quotation we have seen before that "the only way in which adults consciously control the kind of education which the immature get is by controlling the environment in which they act, and hence think and feel" (pp. 18–19). I make the assumption that my students are themselves "immature," as are, ideally, all persons, at least in Dewey's sense of the word. Immaturity, according to Dewey, does not denote a lack, a gap, or a deficiency. It constitutes a potentially lifelong force that he calls "the ability to develop" or "the power to grow" (p. 42). It is a positive "potentiality" and capacity, embodying what he describes as "plasticity," or the power to learn from experience (p. 44). It incorporates notions of simplicity, naiveté, and spontaneity, which I described in Chapter 3. I assume that my students are immature in these terms. I assume that they are not hardened in their views or in the persons they have become. Even when I am disabused of this assumption, I try to sustain it as an article of faith so that as best as possible my views of students do not harden. Thus, to take up Dewey's final words in the line I have repeated, I try to engage students and myself during our first meeting in certain actions—talking out loud and publicly about teaching and about becoming a teacher—in the hope that these actions will indeed provoke a certain direction in both thought and feeling, namely, about what it means to be a teacher.

First Half of the Course

Focused discussion remains the modus operandi for the entire course. This is a 15-week, semester-long course. As mentioned, we meet once a week for a 3-hour session. For the first eight or nine sessions, we read a variety of books and articles that address teaching from both a philosophical and empirical point of view. I select these readings for their potential to generate meaningful discussion while also illuminating the contemporary world of urban high school classrooms and the many elements that comprise that world: teachers, students, administrators, curricula, educational policies, community settings, social and cultural factors, and much more. We devote the last six or seven sessions of the course to Dewey's *Democracy and Education*. I have followed this curricular sequence, in part, because by the time we arrive at Dewey students have a context for appreciating his arguments about education. They have developed certain ways of working together that facilitate their coming to grips with and, above all, profiting from Dewey's demanding book. And they have spoken and written at length about their evolving philosophies of teaching, which is a major theme of the course—to bring their nascent conceptions of teaching out of the shadows and to begin the challenging, career-long task of articulating a philosophy of teaching. This curricular arrangement also positions me, as teacher, to better appreciate my students' ideas and reactions both to Dewey and to the educational questions our inquiry generates.

Focused discussion begins not only in the meetings that lead up to the course and in our interaction the first day of class. It also takes shape in my syllabus for the course, which addresses how to prepare for, participate in, and evaluate a discussion as well as one's contributions to it. A number of the articles and book chapters we read in the initial weeks illustrate and raise questions about discussion, especially with high school students (e.g., Grant, 1996; Haroutunian-Gordon, 1991). I ask students during the first few weeks to talk about their previous experiences with class discussion, both good and bad. I share my own view that students and teachers can benefit from an approach that stays close to the object at hand (book, article, painting, musical piece, etc.) and thereby engages that object as a source of questions and perspectives for them to examine.

I describe this approach to reading and discussion as pivoting around three core questions: What does it [the reading] say? What does it mean? and What difference does it make?[2] The questions call on the class to read with discipline, to interpret the reading, and to draw lessons from their engagement with it for their own outlook and action. The questions presume that our readings provide more than information (which is all some candidates expect from them, at least at the start). Rather, in metaphorical terms the readings address us. They ask questions, and they invite us into possibly broader ways of thinking and acting. There is a logic to the sequence of questions, in that it is hard to know what difference a book like Dewey's *Democracy and Education* can make for teaching until one has studied it and generated an interpretation of it. My students and I do not follow the sequence in a wooden, mechanistic fashion. But I call it to students' attention from time to time throughout the semester in order, for example, to draw a connection between the theory and practice of discussion. In my view, the sequence positions students to form an enlightened standpoint. After coming to grips with the questions "What does it say?" and "What does it mean?" students can turn to questions such as "Am I willing to conduct myself in this way? Do I believe this?" "And do I believe," adds Eva Brann (1999), "—or reject it—because *I* want to or because the *matter* compels me?" (p. 162). Brann means that shared inquiry can lead persons beyond uncritical opinion, including the opinion that their own outlooks possess automatic validity or truth.

As part of this process, I make plain to students that I welcome mention of personal experience, but I ask students, and I agree to this term myself, to try to connect that personal experience to the reading and to our discussions. During these initial sessions we also address nuts-and-bolts items, such as why raising hands can be useful (even if it sometimes feels stilted), how to break into the queue gracefully if an idea cannot wait, how to try to connect what one says to something said previously, and other aspects of conducting a conversation as opposed to a series of monologues. We discuss the value of reading the assigned material at least twice before class, the first time to get the gist of what is being said, the second time to plumb deeper for meaning and to write down questions and concerns that I urge students to bring to class. I emphasize the importance of carving out regular, undisturbed time for reading and reflection, something that experience has taught me is important to discuss with students. Some work part or full time and are parents, and some have forgotten or, to judge from their testimony as well as my own observations, have never really learned how to study. I underscore the value of both attendance and punctuality, not for decorum's sake but for the sake of building a learning community in our classroom in which each person, not just the teacher, plays a constitutive role. Moreover, we engage in activities in which students play leadership roles (see below), so that it becomes important to know if they will not be able to attend. I ask students to call me if they will be absent or late, and I begin each class by announcing who will not be there or who will be late and why.

Briefly, discussions during the first eight to nine weeks of the semester proceed as follows. For an hour and a half, I lead a whole-group discussion centered around a particular reading. I may base the entire discussion on a single question, such as "Why does the author (Jackson, 1986) argue that teaching can mean transforming individuals as well as imparting skills and information?" or "What does this author's (Peshkin, 1991) argument about adolescent views of family, culture, politics, and society imply about approaches to teaching in the urban setting?" In the second half of the session, I may continue to lead the discussion on the same or a different reading. On other occasions, we may devote the first hour and a half to a small-group activity in which groups of, say, four students examine issues raised by the reading. I preface our first engagement with small-group work by asking students to share their experiences, pro and con, with this kind of classroom activity. The upshot of the discussion is a protocol, subject to continued revision, for how to make the activity productive; for example, having one of the four serve as a chair to ensure that all get a chance to participate (and do in fact participate) and having another serve as official note-taker or recorder. In the second half of the session, we have a whole-group discussion in the course of which each recorder shares what his or her group concluded with respect to the guiding issues or questions. Each group's conclusions constitute a kind of text open for question and comment. Finally, some evenings feature a mix of my leading the whole class interspersed with small-group work.

I limit my lecturing to brief summary remarks at the end of each discussion and to a 15- to 20-minute review of the previous week's class at the start of each session. I devote a great deal of time to preparing these reviews and to ensuring that I deliver them in class as clearly as possible. Students have told me they find the reviews helpful, particularly given the amount of time we devote to discussion. As I will elucidate in due course, focused discussion is unwieldy and unpredictable. It calls on participants' intellectual and moral stamina, first and foremost the teacher's, but also students', perhaps especially those who have had few experiences with discussion. It is not always easy to listen carefully to others or to give them their due, and it is not always easy to keep hold of the thread of inquiry. Consequently, I make a point in my reviews of including comments on our procedures, not just on their outcomes: "I thought it was good last week that you were beginning to use each other's names in discussion," "I want to highlight the fact that you seemed to go to the text a great deal to support your ideas," "I think we saw last time how hard it can be to have to wait your turn in discussion, so let me urge you again to take notes as we go along, including about your own ideas," and so forth. I encourage students not to abandon an idea because they think it has already been said. I try to point out examples in which a participant felt he or she was being redundant but, in fact, added a valuable nuance or even a quite different idea.

Self and Interest

I share these details, many of which will be familiar to teachers, because I believe they are the sort of factors that Dewey has in mind when he talks about "controlling" and "regulating" the environment. These factors make certain kinds of interaction possible (e.g., whole-group discussion) while ruling out or discouraging others (e.g., uncritical monologues on my or the students' part). I have left out many details that, in my view, also inform the environment: the numerous individual contacts students and I have during the semester in which some crucial intellectual, moral, and emotional business sometimes gets addressed (see below), the perspectives students introduce from their other courses and from their experience writ large, and much more. The outcome of the actions I have described—all of which, according to Dewey, induce certain kinds of thinking and feeling—is that by the time we reach Dewey's *Democracy and Education* in the eighth or ninth week of the term, an environment has emerged through which students have come to know things about teaching, about participation as the engine that can generate and drive the subject matter of teaching and learning, and about each other and me.

This last point should be stated carefully. We do not, in fact, know each other as the selves we may have been before this class began. Rather, for 3 hours 1 day a week, and more if one includes meetings outside of class, we are in an environment that I hope invites students and myself to become selves constituted in a particular way. Hopefully, that way centers around or comprises an interest in teaching. I hope students will become selves ready, poised, and positioned to express this kind of interest, which in my view will ultimately benefit their own future students. In the terms I examined in Chapter 3, I hope our work fosters qualities of straightforwardness, open-mindedness, integrity of purpose, and responsibility. I do not spell out such hopes at the start, for fear that students will become self-conscious rather than object-conscious. Posed differently, *becoming* open-minded about teaching is not the same thing as treating open-mindedness as a lesson or fact to be acquired or studied as part of a course. Open-mindedness is a state of mind that comes into being slowly, fitfully, unevenly, and it has to be more or less constantly cultivated. Moreover, pleading with students to be open-minded tends to fall flat and sounds contradictory, as compared with triggering activities that engender the disposition (Dewey, 1909/1975, pp. 1–4; 1916/1997, p. 354). I let students come upon these ideas themselves, and when they do, I try to highlight them.

Students often comment on how what we are reading and discussing reflects what we are actually doing. We read about discussing readings with students, and we discuss those very readings ourselves. This process calls to mind what I referred to earlier as the subject matter of teaching and learning, which I believe Dewey urges us to consider as a single concept. With respect to texts, people, and the world writ large, we become, in metaphorical terms, not just *what* we read but also *how* we read. This claim mirrors a core idea from Chapter 2, that a teacher's moral sensibility embodies not just what she says, but the ways in which she thinks, regards others, and conducts herself.

The language of self I have turned to here suggests that part of regulating or controlling an environment is an element of self-regulation and self-control. That is, there is a sense in which environment and self emerge together in a reciprocal, dynamic fashion. It is a deeply social process that depends on the energies and engagement of everyone in the classroom, although the teacher remains a central catalyst. The teacher has to initiate the process of forming an environment and has to support it continuously. Among other things, this often means learning how to step aside and provide students opportunities to play a leadership role (Nicholls & Hazzard, 1993; Oyler, 1996). Along the way, teachers give themselves over to the many tasks of teaching, from planning to grading. They do so literally, at least as I am employing the terms. Just as students (ideally) find themselves in the issues they take up, so teachers give themselves over to the work of teaching when in the presence of students and, consequently, become something they were not before.

Integrating Writing with Focused Discussion

Students write several papers in the first half of the course. The assignments and my evaluation of the papers illustrate the points I have been making about change and growth in the self. For the second or third meeting, I ask students to write a 2- to 3-page, double-spaced paper in response to a quote about teaching. Because this first written assignment asks students, in a sense, to open themselves up and put some cards on the table, I try to respond in kind. I return the papers the following week, with penciled comments and questions in the margins and in a concluding paragraph. I often include personalized notes: "The kind of thinking you reveal here is going to help you develop a sound philosophy of teaching," "These strike me as the right questions to be asking at this stage in your formal preparation," and "Your comments in class discussion have been helpful; I hope you will keep making them." The second paper is an 8- to 10-page essay due at the midpoint of the course, before we turn to Dewey's book. Students choose their own topics on teaching; I require them to draw on our readings and discussions. I provide a list of possible topics, which some students choose not to look at until they have deliberated on their own. Students also write a 10- to 12-page essay, due at the end of the course, in which they again choose the topic and make use of our reading and discussion of Dewey. I respond to both papers by writing a page or two of comments, on the computer, which I staple to their papers. The only writing I do on their actual papers are marks indicating errors in spelling and grammar.

In sum, my written evaluation starts on a personalized note, literally writing on the students' papers, but turns increasingly formal (which should not be equated with distant). The approach coheres with my hope that as the course proceeds, students and I will become object-centered, in the sense of deepening our understanding of teaching and of broadening rather than merely replicating the persons we are. The process is dynamic and unpredictable. For example, every time I teach the course I learn more about what qualities such as simplicity and naiveté mean for teaching. While I have consistently employed focused discussion in teaching this course, its enactment has evolved.

This evolutionary process involves difficulties in grading students' work that are built into focused discussion. In the syllabus to the course, I include a one-page rubric that outlines criteria for evaluating written work. The criteria are subject to amendment in light of our discussions in class. I ask students to talk about their experiences with evaluation, especially about approaches they found effective and fair. The rubric I employ pivots around the idea of readiness to teach. That idea emphasizes that teacher candidates must be active in their learning rather than expecting me, the readings, or other sources to hand out what they need to know. Consequently, participation in class discussion is required. I explain to students that for the purposes of evaluation, the quality of participation matters more than the quantity. Quality has to do with showing that one is coming to grips with the readings and with the ideas and issues about teaching that arise in class. It can manifest itself in posing questions and in sharing doubts, just as it can in offering interpretations or background information. It reflects the energy and the preparation students devote to their formal opportunities to lead classroom activities. As I address later in the chapter, this approach to evaluation raises the question of how and whether to provide students opportunities to participate that take forms other than speaking up in class. All these aspects of evaluation comprise a permanent challenge with which I wrestle each year.

Second Half of the Course

After our first eight or nine weeks together, students and I devote the rest of the semester to Dewey's *Democracy and Education*. While the acts described thus far have helped set the stage for tackling the book, this should not be taken to mean that the environment in the class is set, finished, or complete. One of the greatest challenges I have felt in teaching has been learning how to cultivate evolution and growth with a group of students, an issue also taken up by Cuffaro (1995), Fishman and McCarthy (1998), and many others, and an issue deeply familiar to teachers. The question for me is, How can a teacher promote an environment that itself promotes improvement in that very environment?

I add some new wrinkles, while continuing to operate in the spirit of focused discussion. For one thing, the week before we discuss the first chapters in Dewey I give a two-part lecture, the only true lecture in the whole course. The first part includes a line-by-line discussion of the book's preface, in which I touch on Dewey's meaning and how he will flesh out his ideas in the chapters to come. I discuss the subtitle (the original title) of the book: An Introduction to the Philosophy of Education. I remind the class that we have been doing philosophy of education, or at least a form of it, since our opening night's treatment of the question "What is teaching?" I comment on the titles of the first chapters and speculate about Dewey's decision to use the conjunction *as* rather than the verb *is* in those titles (for example, Education as a Necessity of Life).

The second part of the lecture focuses on how to read Dewey. These comments reprise some of what the class has been doing since the first week of the course. Moreover, by then we have also read and discussed several articles that examine reading as a human experience (e.g., A. O. Rorty, 1997), and I remind the class of our discussions of them. I provide a set of questions as a kind of working guide to getting a handle on the chapters: What is Dewey saying? Why is he making the arguments he makes? Why does he present them in the order or sequence he does? How do his arguments illuminate teaching and learning? I also invite students not to start off skeptical of the book because it was written early in the century, before our current idiom of national standards for teachers, constructivism, multiculturalism, whole language, and so forth. I suggest that the adventure of tackling this book can shed invaluable light on how to identify and criticize assumptions about teaching and learning that underlie contemporary educational passions, including those we have been addressing up to then and which we may have embraced. I extend some comments I made at the start of the course in introducing the readings, to the effect that we are studying Dewey's book not because he is "right" or infallible but because he provides an unusually comprehensive and thoughtful view of education. I urge students to compare or contrast what they see in Dewey with theories of teaching and learning we read earlier as well as those they may have encountered elsewhere.

Finally, I also comment on Dewey's writing style. I point out, for example, that his style may take some time to get used to. I suggest that because he employs familiar terms—*control, regulate, experience, interest, subject matter*—in unfamiliar ways, they need to be ready to reconsider some of their initial impressions.[3] In addition, I mention that some of his terms, at first glance, may jar or offend our sensibilities. For example, he employs the term *savages* at a number of points. Again, I urge students to attend with care to the context in which Dewey uses his terms, rather than merely reading into his language our contemporary meanings and concerns. I encourage them to neither reject nor to approve of any concept or term uncritically.

In a subsequent discussion, several students interpreted the word "savage" as reflecting racist attitudes on Dewey's part. They objected to his contrasting it with the term "civilized." We examined several contexts in which he employs the terms. Eventually, the same students who had raised the issue came to see, in part because of other students' comments, that Dewey's use of the term "savage" describes a state of mind he is trying to picture, not an actual or historical part of humanity. Moreover, it is a state of mind he is as quick to apply, and forcefully so, to present-day, supposedly civilized circumstances and outlooks as to those that obtained in the past. Later in the term, one of our discussions evolved into a consideration of Dewey's optimism and apparent faith in human progress, which goes against the grain of some contemporary orientations. One of the great values in discussing the book, in my view, lies in how the process can help us surface our own doubts and troubles, even our perhaps unsuspected cynicism and jadedness. I have come to regard the latter states of mind as a very real challenge to teaching in today's world. This challenge attests, once more, to the significance of the qualities of a growing person, such as naiveté, that I sought to flesh out in Chapter 3.

End of lecture, and end of all of these phases of regulatory work on the environment. Now we're into week 1 centered on Dewey's book. We spend the first hour and a half in a whole-group discussion I lead centered around a question such as "Why does Dewey argue that growth does not *have* an end but rather *is* an end?" I prepare notes for use while leading the discussion. They include several subquestions whose investigation might shed light on the main topic (e.g., Why does Dewey emphasize that growth pertains to adults as much as to children? Why does Dewey highlight the concept "growth" more than the concept "learning?"). I also list, on my notes for class, key terms and ideas in the chapters that, in my view, can shed light on the issue. I append page numbers after each term or idea so that I can quickly refer to the text while in the midst of class. If I judge that Dewey's own words will fuel, or challenge, an interpretation the class is building, I take students to a passage and ask someone to read it aloud. Many of my notes and page references remain untapped. Their use depends on the turn of conversation.

At the start of discussion, I ask students to write down the central question and to take a few minutes to write out a response to it. This technique gives students some quiet moments to compose themselves intellectually. It also allows me to call on every student during the discussion, if appropriate, knowing that they will have something to say in answer to the guiding question. I stay close to the question, bringing discussion back to it whenever I feel we are wandering fruitlessly or whenever I sense we have been developing an insightful response to the question. However, there is no blueprint here, and discussion invariably takes surprising and unanticipated turns. In part because of our previous eight or nine weeks' worth of work, most students are reasonably adept at participating in a discussion. They go to the book for evidence to support their views, they frequently read passages out loud without being prompted to do so, they ask each other on what page a particular claim can be found, they refer to each other's ideas while developing their own, they make use of personal experience to illuminate their viewpoints, they sometimes interrupt to say they have something to contribute that will help the group, and they bite their tongue when they see others have been waiting to speak. They are familiar with each other by now, and good-natured teasing and laughter are common.

Students sometimes disagree vehemently with one another. Early in the course, their disagreements can take an unpleasant turn. For example, I have witnessed students employ a tone of scorn or dismissal in criticizing a peer's comment. Such acts create difficult moments for me and the students. How should we respond? Whenever I deem it necessary, especially early in the course before we have learned what conversation can mean in our context, I intervene and ask the class how they want to address each other over differences of opinion and outlook. Depending on the situation, I do so on the spot by temporarily suspending the discussion, or I raise the issue at the end of class or at the beginning of the next one. I might ask students to share previous experiences with classroom conflict and how it was handled. On other occasions, I ask a student (or students) to meet with me privately to discuss the particular event that caused hurt or anger.

Moreover, when I judge the moment propitious, I talk with students about what Richard Rorty (1983, pp. 165–170) calls moral and epistemic privilege. According to Rorty, every person has the moral privilege to speak about and to interpret his or her own life and outlook. That privilege comes with being a person rather than a thing or, as Kant would put it, merely a means to other people's ends. But moral privilege, Rorty goes on to argue, does not imply epistemic privilege. For example, my interpretation of a reading is not automatically true, warranted, or cause for action simply because it is my interpretation. My knowledge, or what I think I know, does not have the same status as my personhood. As a person, I am always worthy of respect (presuming, one might add, that I do not go around harming other people). However, Rorty tells us, my claims to knowledge are not automatically worthy of respect. Those must be talked out, examined or tested, considered in a public way.

As teachers would be among the first to point out, human beings differ widely in their willingness to question or reconsider their claims. Certainly, persons may have excellent reasons for adhering to a standpoint. But teachers are well positioned to help students—and, thereby, to help themselves as well—understand the limitations and seductions of what Joseph Schwab (1978a) calls "self-measured judgment of self-held opinion" (p. 131). I make use of Rorty's argument to help my students appreciate that in classroom discussions such as ours, the aim is not to attack others as persons nor to cling doggedly to entrenched opinions. The aim is to articulate ideas, to think hard and seriously about them, to listen intently and patiently to others, and to learn how to agree or to disagree in intellectual and moral terms.

As a rule, by the time we reach the midpoint of the course students have learned to speak their minds in a way that does not pigeonhole other people's views or cast others as unworthy partners in a dialogue. I have mentioned some factors that contribute to this state of affairs: We often discuss discussion itself, we read articles on the meaning of discussion and dialogue, and I hold individual meetings with many of the students before the beginning of the course as well as during the semester. As mentioned previously, I try to set a conversational tone in the meetings.

These practices are not always successful. For example, one teacher candidate in the group was prone to lengthy monologues and to interrupting others. I met with him several times in my office to ask if there were other ways he could channel his energy. I invited him to think of ways to raise questions rather than just offering his own viewpoint. I suggested he write about his views, and I volunteered to read his work. I asked him to imagine himself as a teacher and to ask himself if he intended to talk all the time and to cut short students who were groping their way toward their own ideas. My efforts and those of the class—some of his peers, in their own ways, alerted him to his habits—kept matters in hand, but barely.

In contrast, during the same semester several of the quieter students in class came to see me because they were enthused about the idea of discussion as an instructional approach and wanted to learn, as a first step, how to become more active participants. One of the students explained that she had been reticent in her classes since childhood. She shed tears while asking me for help in how to change, because she wanted to participate. She said she appreciated how important it is for a teacher to be able to speak publicly, both in the classroom and in the school (another theme of our course). I volunteered to meet with her before the next few classes to discuss the readings, so that I would have a sense, during discussion, of when she might have a comment to share. I also raised the idea that I could call on her to read passages. I recommended she take advantage of our small-group work to think out loud. The upshot was that she began to speak up in discussion, although modestly in comparison with most other students, and also performed well when she took over a leadership role in discussion (see below).

At the end of our initial hour-and-a-half discussion of Dewey, I call on a number of students to recall any responses to the central question they remember. After doing so I supplement their recall with notes I have taken during the course of discussion. One reason I do this is to demonstrate for students how much progress they have made. They often spontaneously reveal their surprise and delight at what they have accomplished, especially given how challenging Dewey's book truly is. A second reason for doing so is that given the difficulty and value of the book, I believe it is helpful to keep reminding ourselves of what we have said and understood about it.

After our break, we take up additional questions and issues students raise about the chapters we have read—a practice we follow for the rest of the semester. These questions and issues center around how to realize or implement, in a contemporary urban high school classroom, what Dewey and we ourselves have been talking about. Several students take the lead here, whom I ask to read some recent articles or chapters (e.g., Hostetler, 1997; Seixas, 1993; Zahorik, 1996) that shed light on, or help us better grasp, the particular aspects of teaching and learning addressed in the chapters assigned for the session. These readings, students' background experiences, our earlier readings and discussions, what students are learning in other courses, and more—all work their way into the development of examples of what it might mean, for instance, to create the conditions for meaningful discussion in a tenth-grade history class. We are usually able to compose a realistic and even exciting scenario. We discuss how to bring to life specific ideas Dewey raises, for example, his view of why subject matter and method are organically related.

During one of our sessions we examined why, in a high school literature class dealing with poetry, the subject matter comprises not just the poems but also the teacher's and students' responses to them. We pointed out that, according to Dewey, the subject matter of teaching and learning is not inert materials or texts. It is the material at hand *and* everyone's response to it, perceived as a dynamic whole. Consequently, the method the high school class would follow is embedded in the subject. That is, *discussing* both the poem and each other's responses to it is the vehicle, the method, for bringing the subject to life, for animating it. Questions such as "Why does the poet employ that word? Why does it come where it does in the poem? Why do you think he meant to convey a sense of loss here?" are embedded in the very act of engaging with the poem. They instantiate how the poem, metaphorically speaking, calls out to be read, listened to, taken in, pondered. Such questions do not constitute a method that stands apart from the poem, anymore than the poem stands apart from human responses to it. In a literal sense, the poem is nothing to teacher and students without their engagement; it is lifeless. In an equally literal sense, teacher and students cannot extend their horizons of thought, of feeling, of knowledge, and of questioning without poetry, not to mention a good deal more that comprises the curriculum. From Dewey's perspective, subject matter is something teachers and students do, not something inert that the one "teaches" and the other "learns."[4]

Student Leadership

In subsequent weeks, I add some further wrinkles to our proceedings. For one thing, starting in week 2, on Dewey, it is students, rather than me, who lead the initial hour-and-a-half discussion on the chapters from the book. To prepare for this moment, early in the semester I ask students to fill out a written form asking them to rank their preferences for what kind of formal pedagogical roles they would like to try out in this class: chair of a small group, recorder, co-presenter to the class of a report based on additional reading, or co-leader of a whole-class discussion. As soon as I collect these forms, I place all the students into particular roles and slots for the activities that comprise the course, so that each student will have at least one formal opportunity to lead the class. I pay particular attention to who has listed "co-lead a whole-class discussion" as their first (or at least second) choice, and I identify a group of ten or twelve students, to work in teams of two, for when we get to Dewey's book.

Here is how things work with the student discussion leaders. Two or three days before class, I meet for about 2 hours with the two students who will be responsible for leading a whole-class discussion on some of the chapters. I ask them to bring to our meeting questions they have about the book: questions about words, phrases, ideas, or about the broad gist of one or more of the chapters. The students begin the conversation. I take notes while listening to them talk about their reactions to the chapters. I ask them many questions, mostly for clarification, and I interject conjectures of my own while also turning us to passages in the book (students also do this spontaneously). As the meeting progresses, I assist them in forming a single question that captures what most interests and puzzles them about Dewey's meaning, while also being sufficiently broad in scope to generate a sustained discussion. Our purpose, which they appreciate when they come to my office, is to create a question that they will place at the center of the discussion they are going to lead with the class in a few days' time. Usually, we end a meeting with a question they are happy with. Sometimes, we have to use the phone, e-mail, or another meeting to settle the matter. We also discuss strategies for how to lead a focused discussion that will likely last more than an hour. Most students have a good idea of how to proceed, since both discussion and talking about discussion have been a mainstay of the course up to now. Each successive pair also has the benefit of learning from the previous pairs' successes and mistakes; I make a point of highlighting aspects of what the previous leaders have done. We review useful practices such as re-membering to call on people who have not had a chance to speak. (In class itself, I offer remarks at the close of a discussion led by students on effective and less effective actions they undertook. I emphasize that all such comments are intended for everyone rather than just for the two co-leaders.) At the start of a new class, I begin with my usual review of the previous week's session. Then, the team of student discussion leaders takes over. The typical procedure is for them to write the question on the board and give the class time to write down a response. After that, they are off into unknown territory.

Here is a sample of the guiding questions students have developed and used:

- Why does Dewey examine theories of learning, including his own, before he addresses democracy?
- According to Dewey, how can a teacher help students cultivate how to think?
- What kind of a person does Dewey expect the teacher to be?
- Why does Dewey think teachers should treat subject matter and method as inseparable?
- Why does Dewey conclude the book by focusing on the moral dimensions of education?

Things do not always proceed smoothly during these challenging weeks. The pace and substance of discussion sometimes become wooden or stilted. The leaders become self- rather than object-conscious, they fall into short monologues rather than soliciting the views of the class, they forget to ask people to clarify their ideas and to relate them both to the book and to their evolving philosophies of teaching, they allow unrelated comments to pile up, and so forth. The student leaders experience the same problems I encounter, year after year, in trying to balance equitable participation with hammering out the best interpretation of a passage or argument. The student leaders sometimes ease off on developing a particular line of thinking because they want to allow more voices into the conversation, voices that are not always attuned to the issue at hand. At times, the leaders neglect to help the class appreciate critically which interpretations and views have been shown to be untenable or just plain wrong-headed. They sometimes permit the most articulate participants to dominate the floor.

In addition, they are sometimes thrown, as am I, by students who interject, often in heartfelt terms, their fears about whether public school teachers today can actually teach in the spirit and terms we are describing. The student leaders and I are often unsure how to respond at such moments. On the one hand, we cannot meaningfully address the question whether teachers can "really" perform the things we are describing until we understand the things themselves. That understanding can only issue from serious-minded reading, writing, listening, thinking, speaking, imagining, and so forth. On the other hand, such pressing questions constitute the raison d'être of this course: to assist candidates in articulating a philosophy of teaching that can be realized in classroom practice. Some student leaders appreciate these matters and attempt to relate the questions directly to our discussion and reading, including that from previous weeks of the course. They draw on what students have learned elsewhere, including from personal experience, about teaching in the urban setting. They seize the opportunity to help the class, if not in so many words, to wed idealism with a sense of reality (an issue I return to in Chapter 8). Other leaders throw up their hands and leave the course of action up to their peers, not always with helpful results. For example, the class may drift into a sudden bull session about education today in which everything we have examined suddenly seems to go out the window. Unless the leaders show some gumption, matters can degenerate into a fruitless cacophony rather than into an inquiry.

Later in the class, or in a subsequent session, I highlight some of these predicaments—if students do not do so themselves—and discuss them with an eye to how the students can respond to them when they have classrooms of their own. I refer to previous instances in the course when we examined the very same issues. I share my own knowledge, and that of my peers in universities and schools, about local high schools. I remind students that they are just beginning their program of study.

They will have more time and more opportunities for thinking through their questions and concerns, which, fortunately in my view, they have at least had the chance to put on the table.[5]

In general, the teams of discussion leaders perform well, assisted by many of their peers, who, as I have said, by this point in the course know some things about how to read and how to discuss ideas in a public setting. Stated differently, the leaders teach indirectly. They lead a discussion whose outcome is as uncertain and unpredictable to them as it is to their peers. But it is a focused discussion that aims to generate the best thinking we can do centered around educational concerns. The leaders endeavor to stay true to the approach. As a rule, most refrain from lapsing into lecturing. When stuck, they remember that they can repeat the opening question or can find out what those who have not had a chance to speak might have to contribute. They learn how to show respect for ideas, not by offering bland comments such as "Good" or "I agree" but by questioning ideas and connecting them to the reading and to what has been said thus far. There have been discussions, lasting well over an hour, in the course of which I have not said a word and have not felt the need to say a word except to want to share an idea of my own on Dewey and education. I have learned to raise my hand to do so.

Consider a session centered on the question of why Dewey examines conceptions of learning, including his own, before introducing his view of democracy. Among the many interpretations the class developed (without my participation) were: (1) Dewey places political life within a vision of what promotes human growth, which is why he starts with the nature of learning first, (2) by the time he turns to democracy, he has already demonstrated his message by making readers think for themselves rather than trying to tell them what to think, which is not democratic conduct, (3) what he says about democracy is another way of characterizing what he has said about the necessary conditions for human growth, understood as growing in capacity and inclination to grow (this illustrates, some students added, how Dewey keeps making passes at the same idea, circling back again and again as his argument develops), and (4) Dewey is not pursuing politics directly but rather wants to provoke us to think about the kinds of persons we are and how we can become persons who can shape educational and political life rather than merely being shaped by it.

"An ideally perfect knowledge," Dewey (1916/1997) writes, "would represent such a network of interconnections that any past experience would offer a point of advantage from which to get at the problem presented in a new experience" (p. 340). Students in the course learn to make connections between past experiences and present ones. They learn to draw comparisons and contrasts between our earlier readings and discussions and our ongoing work with Dewey. However, I believe students are learning to do more than make connections between ideas, or between theory and practice, important as these processes are. I see them learning the lesson embedded in a remark a student offered in the middle of a discussion, that by the time one has "gotten into it," almost any sentence in *Democracy and Education* can become a springboard into Dewey's philosophy of education—and, at the same time, into one's own. Dewey (1916/1997) echoes the student's observation when he writes: "An experience, a very humble experience, is capable of generating and carrying any amount of theory (or intellectual content), but a theory apart from an experience cannot be definitely grasped even as theory" (p. 144).

To appreciate the educational potential in even "humble" experiences is to learn something more than just how to make connections. It is to understand the primary fact of interconnectedness: that we become persons, in part, through the agency of interconnection with others and the world (as represented, for example, in the curriculum). These are powerful lessons for teacher candidates to learn, even if they may learn them indirectly at this stage in their development and may appreciate them only after they have taught for some time. Dewey's remark also attests to why I regard it as worthwhile to undertake the kind of regulatory work on the environment I have described. That work assists or positions students to grasp, as Dewey puts it, Dewey's own philosophy. I believe it helps students come to grips with what it means to really know and believe something, rather than to settle for superficial acquaintance. It attunes them to, or at least affirms, the simplicity, the naiveté, the spontaneity, the open-mindedness that can characterize shared classroom inquiry.

Student Views

On the basis of students' comments, including those in formal course evaluations, as well as on my own judgment, there always appear to be several students who remain disengaged, despite my efforts and those of their peers. I mention this last point because students tend to become deeply involved in how their peers are doing, to the extent, for example, of shedding tears publicly when a classmate had to drop out of the program for medical reasons. I can rarely predict who might remain on the sidelines. Most of my students are in their mid to late 20s. Most are women, and most are White. They appear to be committed to thinking about teaching as best as they can. Most minority students, students who have immigrated to the United States, and men also tend to absorb themselves in our proceedings. I always end up coaching some students outside of classtime on their reading, writing, and/or participating, but these needs seem to cut across gender, ethnic, racial, and age lines, and they cut across disciplinary lines, too.

I can never predict who will find discussion uncongenial. While almost all students end up participating, at least to a degree, some complain that we feature discussion too much. They ask for more lecturing, small-group projects, outside visitors, and so forth. In recent years, I have tried to emphasize even more explicitly the value in talking with high school students, regardless of whether the discipline is art, physical education, or physics. I reiterate that while we will highlight talk and discussion in this course, it is but one course in their degree program. And, whenever the moment seems right, I emphasize that participating in and, above all, leading a discussion requires intellectual and moral stamina. I urge students to develop such stamina now, rather than presuming they will magically turn it on in a year or two when they find themselves with five classes a day and more than a hundred students.

I can also never predict who is not going to buy into the idea of employing Dewey in a course like ours. Some students would prefer to focus on more contemporary writers who use a more contemporary idiom.[6] Others appear, at least at the start, to want the expected fare of teacher preparation courses, such as strategies and techniques of teaching and classroom management, offered to them in expected ways. I point out to the class that we will be creating our own "methods course," given our highlighting and practicing focused discussion as well as other enterprises such as small-group work. More centrally, I add that a basic premise of our work is that instructional methods, considered in themselves, may be ineffective or possibly damaging if they are not guided by a sound philosophy of teaching.

Nonetheless, some students appear not to accept or understand these premises, and in a few cases they object to what they call "too much time" on Dewey. I was disappointed by this reaction when I first taught *Democracy and Education,* as any teacher would be, perhaps, whose passions are not echoed by all of her or his students. Schwab (1978a) writes of the yearning of a teacher who wants his students "to possess a knowledge or skill in the same way that he possesses it, as a part of his best-beloved self" (p. 124). But the complaint has forced me to examine further my motives for including the book in a teacher education course. It has helped me to work through my predilections toward using Dewey's work, rather than just to bull my way forward. The process has also led me to question more critically some of Dewey's arguments and perspectives (see Chapter 7).

My approach to teaching indirectly is not a sure-fire way to engage all students, an outcome that Fishman and McCarthy (1998) report from their work as well. The approach has to be continuously evaluated and refined. However, I am confident that the benefits of the approach are real and warrant its use. In the course I have described, most students wrestle in a serious-minded way with the question of what it means to teach. They play an energetic leadership role in our proceedings. Their responses to the readings, to the questions raised in class, and to each other provide the trajectory for our discussions. Here is some of their written testimony: "Because of every student's contributions, so many of my ideas were challenged and I liked this. . . . The class was very helpful in making me think and develop and refine my philosophy of teaching. . . . We learned by making connections with each other. . . . I particularly enjoyed reading Dewey. I felt like it was an exciting journey that took us deeper and deeper into the world of education. . . . The best part of the course was really thinking about what being a teacher means. This was a recurring theme throughout the course. . . . I learned a lot about classroom instructing and what teachers should be striving to attain. It helped me clarify my role as a teacher. It also helped me understand the important role of students. . . . I liked the philosophical inquiry directed at practical experience. . . . After every single class, I felt inspired, renewed in my convictions, bolstered by the passion shown by my peers. . . . I learned how to discuss, how to read, how to listen."

Such comments support my sense that more than a mere change in behavior takes place in this class. Rather, students develop ways of thinking and conducting themselves as educators.[7] In my view, most leave the course feeling more prepared and interested in teaching. They depart with a deepened sense of how challenging and rewarding teaching can be. They gain a horizon, a perspective, the beginnings of a philosophy that can serve them in becoming teachers who stay the course through difficulty.

CONCLUSION: THE PROMISE IN TEACHING INDIRECTLY

In Chapter 3, I quoted Dewey's (1916/1997) claim that "[t]here is not, in fact, any such thing as the direct influence of one human being on another" (p. 28). In light of the analysis in the present chapter, we should now repeat the rest of Dewey's sentence: "apart from use of the physical environment as an intermediary." According to Dewey, there are no environment-free transactions between teachers and students. They are always in an environment of one kind or another. The educational question is: What kind of environment? Dewey's thesis, as we have seen, is that teachers can take action to shape the environment so that it promotes teaching and learning. They can try to control, regulate, and design the environment. Those terms attest to human influence and agency, not to nonhuman mechanics. The idea of control Dewey evokes is neither authoritarian nor implemented by dictate, nor is it in any sense complete. Rather, control describes a dynamic quality of participation and of relationship, centered around educational purposes. Those purposes are the controlling magnets.

With respect to focused discussion, authority and control come to reside, in part, in the activity itself, in the complicated, developing process of reading, listening, speaking, forming and changing minds, working through emotions, and more. Ideally, the approach allows better arguments and broader understandings to emerge, rather than ceding the terrain to the opinion of any one person, including the teacher. But the teacher must play the leading role in making possible this displacement of authority. In a sense, the teacher never relinquishes his or her authority. Rather, he or she employs it to foster an environment for teaching and learning. That process obliges the teacher to attend to students' ideas, conjectures, emotions, uncertainties, and interpersonal dynamics. The teacher serves as guide, facilitator, director, sounding board, role model, arbiter, source of knowledge, source of comfort, source of unsettlement, and more—terms that, considered separately, may contradict one another but that find a place in the often unwieldy, unpredictable process of inquiry through discussion.

I have sought to illustrate in this chapter what it can look like to operate on the principle that educators teach indirectly by means of the environment. I try to realize that principle by centering our work around focused discussion. I allow our weekly discussions to take their own course, albeit tethered most of the time to a guiding problem or question. I do not concern myself with trying to cover all the material, for example, giving equal weight to all Dewey's core concepts or to the full range of arguments our other authors present. It would take far more than a single course that meets 3 hours a week for only 15 weeks to perform such tasks. Moreover, Dewey and the other authors we read might be dubbed, in metaphorical terms, experienced participants (or perhaps well-traveled elders) rather than dogmatic authorities. They raise telling questions, they offer timely insights, and they force us to come to grips with central aspects of teaching. They invite us to question their arguments and to examine our own.

In short, I accept the fact that there is much in and about *Democracy and Education* that we will never discuss, at least directly. I usually have students who point this fact out, sometimes in worried tones, as if they might be missing out on something. And so they are. It remains unfathomable how much valuable work can be done with this book, and with focused discussion, that neither my students nor I come close to imagining. My hope is that the spirit in which we conduct our work constitutes a worthy model, or projection, of the spirit in which they might teach in the future. The day will soon come when they will have classrooms of their own in which they must, if they do not wish to leave it to chance, regulate and control an environment for teaching and learning.

POSTSCRIPT: QUESTIONING PARTICIPATION

In this postscript, I want to examine in greater detail the complicated issue of participation in discussion. Some of my students report having had few courses during their educational lives that have featured classroom discussion, a fact I always find sobering (if not disheartening). Others recall negative experiences, in which discussion dissipated into unprincipled debate, bull sessions, monologues by the teacher, and the like, a fact I find equally troubling, if less surprising, given how challenging it is to lead meaningful discussions. Moreover, some students appear to feel a tension between their desire to retain their sense of identity and the requirement to participate in the public life of the classroom. Children and adults alike, it seems, can sometimes regard participation as problematic, or possibly even as a threat. From their point of view, participation might connote conformity, as they strain, or so they may feel, to fit themselves to the temper, mood, and orientation of a particular discussion. In such circumstances, the need to participate might deaden rather than fuel open-mindedness, responsibility, naiveté, spontaneity, and simplicity, as I have described those terms.

Elizabeth Ellsworth (1997) offers a spirited criticism of the use of dialogue in classrooms. She does not advocate eliminating conversation out of hand but rather seeks to uncover what she regards as dialogue's power to coerce and to privilege particular political interests. Dialogue, she argues, "is not just a neutral conduit of insights, discoveries, understandings, agreements, or disagreements. It has a constitutive force. It is a tool, it is *for* something" (p. 15). According to Ellsworth, dialogue can conceal a "striving for power. . . . If dialogue is continuous, unbroken, and everyone is participating in dialogue, they aren't doing something else. That's power" (p. 105). She adds that "no matter what her conscious critical or political affiliation, every participant [in discussion] is constituted as an effect of the desire to persuade to participate" (p. 105). Ellsworth's conviction that some, perhaps even all, forms of dialogue mask aspirations for power and nondemocratic control leads her to use the ironic term "dialogism" (p. 110) to describe the perspective she criticizes.

I want to respond to Ellsworth's criticism, although I will do so in attenuated form, given the scope of this chapter. From a certain point of view, what I call focused discussion is clearly "for" something. This entire book presumes that teaching is for qualities such as open-mindedness, spontaneity, and a spirit of questioning, meaning that it is ipso facto "against" such things as closed-mindedness, fanaticism, and indoctrination. But to presume that this posture constitutes an "-ism," as in dialogism, would be a mistake. The stark and polarizing language of "for" or "against" does not capture other, more generative ways of thinking about teaching and conversation. For one thing, such language distorts what persons mean by political standpoints, positions, or interests. In other words, if qualities such as naiveté and spontaneity, as I presented them in Chapter 3, are presumed to be harboring or supporting a political ideology (an "-ism"), then we will need to create new terms for describing such things as the standpoint of the Democratic party, the actions of the National Rifle Association, and the aims of Planned Parenthood. Ruth Grant (1996) argues, convincingly in my view, that discussion differs from debate. She shows that discussion need not presume partisan or ideological standpoints on the part of participants, even if some enter the process thinking that is the case. Grant argues that it is dogmatic and misguided to presume that every discussion is determined by a conscious or subconscious striving for power or is motivated by competing interests.

For another thing, while I commend Ellsworth's brief against heavy-handed or uncritical views of dialogue, her notion that "every participant" in discussion becomes an "effect" of power's "desire to persuade to participate" (p. 105) strikes me as ceding too much authority to a theoretical standpoint (one informed, in part, by her interpretation of Foucault). The breadth and variety of human activity in dialogue far exceeds, and seems far more complicated than, what can be captured by any theoretical point of view, including any that I might call upon here. Moreover, the deterministic language of persons as "effects," while without doubt emerging from genuine questions about participation in dialogue, unjustifiably and unnecessarily strips away persons' agency, character, and spontaneity (or freedom). It threatens to convert those qualities into chimeras. The perspective overlooks the fact that individuals can shape the course of discussion just as much as they may be shaped by it. Discussion can be understood as an "effect" of human agency as much as vice versa. "Nothing is more habitual or customary than our ways of speech," observes

Oakeshott, "and nothing is more continuously invaded by change" (1991, p. 471).

Ellsworth's criticism reflects, in part, a broader concern with issues of authority and conformity in classrooms. Such terms describe some of the issues I have sought to illuminate. My students and I examine them throughout the course I have described. We also link them to larger social forces, not of an individual's making, that often bear down on him or her and that constrain the scope of imagination and conduct. One outcome of this inquiry is the recognition that some forms of talking can be harmful to students—and to teachers as well. Some forms can lead teachers to suppress their own knowledge, insight, and questions. Some can intimidate students. Such talk can coerce persons, breed homogeneity, and shut down important lines of investigation and thought.

However, these facts do not render suspect all discussion and dialogue per se. Rather, they raise the question whether the harmful practices we have in mind should be called discussions in the first place, rather than something else. At the very least, they suggest the need to attend to local context. Some forms of discussion do not necessarily lead to harmful outcomes or have negative "effects." Some forms of discussion are not "tools," as Ellsworth too hastily asserts about dialogue, but rather mirror modes of human life and development that emerge and evolve over extended periods of time, including in classrooms. "'Participation' is a strange word," Gadamer (1984) writes.

> Its dialectic consists of the fact that participation is not taking parts, but in a way taking the whole. Everybody who participates in something does not take something away, so that the others cannot have it. The opposite is true: by sharing, by our participating in the things in which we are participating, we enrich them; they do not become smaller, but larger. The whole life of tradition consists exactly in this enrichment so that life is our culture and our past: the whole inner store of our lives is always extended by participating. (p. 64)

Dewey would argue that the substance of our lives depends upon communication and participation with others. To be sure, the threat of unjust, coercive relations remains ever-present. But the forms of participation Dewey and Gadamer have in view constitute a concrete medium for respecting persons and for pursuing the long-standing human quest for meaning. Focused discussion is one such form.

Teachers who employ discussion, rather than solely lecture or adopt some other method, can discover why participation does not necessarily threaten individuality. Participation can *substantiate* individuality. It can literally generate human substance in the form of deepened insight, en-hanced sensitivity, wider knowledge, greater breadth of understanding, and more. The process cannot be forced, anymore than learning can be accomplished by fiat. That fact complements the argument in previous chapters about the slow, uneven, and unpredictable process through which human beings become capable of spontaneous, integrated, respon-sible conduct.

Although I have featured discussion in this chapter, it constitutes but one approach to teaching and learning. It is not the only legitimate method. Moreover, while genuine discussion in the classroom and else-where can help form democratic dispositions and fuel democratic conduct (cf. Garrison, 1996; Grant, 1996; Green, 1994; Haroutunian-Gordon, 1991), it is not a recipe for solving all societal ills. In this respect, Ellsworth's (1997) criticism serves as a cautionary note to those educators who might make overweening claims about what dialogue can accomplish and who, in the process, might become morally obtuse. David Simpson (1997) con-tends that "there is an enormous potential for self-deception among even the most well-intentioned apologists for the conversational mode when that mode is made a model for resolving social conflict: a potential for assuming that because 'we' can talk to each other then those who cannot talk to 'us' are not playing by the rules and do not therefore have the right to a hearing" (p. 78). Simpson's remarks echo Ellsworth's (1997) conclusion that dialogue cannot, in itself, solve problems of injustice, bigotry, environmental degradation, and the like (p. 114). Neither focused discussion nor any other conversational approach to teaching of which I am aware can accomplish such things by themselves.

But that is not their purpose. Focused discussion can help cultivate person, conduct, and moral sensibility, and it can deepen qualities such as responsibility, open-heartedness, and seriousness. It can fund people's moral knowledge, understood as knowledge graced by the light of a moral consciousness, by a sensitivity to the significance and impact of knowledge in human affairs. Focused discussion can help equip persons with what it takes to tackle problems in respectful, thoughtful, and non–for-or-against ways. That is, it can spotlight the dangers in presuming to take the moral high ground on an issue, rather than conceiving the task as clearing moral ground. It seems to me that teachers are well placed to lead children, youth, and other adults in meaningful, sustained discussion devoted to intellectual and moral learning.

One of the pressing questions for teachers concerns what kind of discussion, and what degree of participation, they might expect from students, as well as from themselves. The working answers to that ques-tion will evolve as the teacher and his or her students grow and learn.

As they sort this issue out, teachers might want to have options available for allowing students who do not take to discussion (at least initially) to express their learning, for example, through giving presentations, contributing in small-group activities, completing individual projects, and the like. Teachers might also hold onto the fact that edifying conversation is not a means to an end. Rather, it enacts educational ends. Phrased differently, meaningful discussion is not so much a *precondition* for mutual understanding and appreciation of persons and subject matter as it is the *reward* of genuine attempts to speak, to listen, to read, to think (cf. Simpson, 1997, p. 82). In the course I have described, my students and I have to work our way toward meaningful discussion. Our initial successes can be misleading. The novelty, for many, of talking together about teaching wears off. Participants discover they have to cultivate their seriousness, their responsibility, their integrity of purpose, and more. As I have emphasized, focused discussion takes time, effort, persistence, and faith in the possibility of purposeful, trustworthy human relations.

◈ 6 ◈

Teaching and the Sense of Tradition

SOME FOUR HUNDRED YEARS ago, John Donne penned these now-familiar lines: "No man is an island, entire of itself; every man is a piece of the continent, a part of the main . . . any man's death diminishes me, because I am involved in mankind; and therefore never send to know for whom the bell tolls; it tolls for thee" (*Devotions*, quoted in Abrams et al., 1962, p. 384). Donne's beloved words, somewhat revised, introduce the theme of these next two chapters: No teacher is an island unto herself. Notwithstanding the familiar image of teachers working behind closed classroom doors, no teacher can isolate herself from the world. Nor does any teacher have to invent teaching from scratch. Every teacher's work is saturated with tradition—that is to say, with what has come before, whether in the guise of teachers she had, in the formal preparation she received, or in the models of those who taught or are still teaching in the teacher's present setting.

The mere mention of tradition in teaching, however, can trigger strong, politicized reactions. On the one hand, it may attract the heart of conservative-minded educators who believe we can, or already have, arrived at the one best definition of teaching. From their perspective, most of what is being written and said about the practice today smacks of opportunism, group politics, bandwagonism, political correctness, or any number of other contemporary impulses. They might say: Enough cacophony; tradition shows the way back to the basics. On the other hand, talk of tradition in teaching might alarm progressive and reform-minded educators who believe the educational past constitutes a burden that we cannot too hastily overcome. From their point of view, the idea that teaching is a practice with a lengthy tradition behind it may tip the scales in favor of the past. It may appear more backward- than forward-looking.

It imparts a certain sanctity to ideas, concepts, and methods from days of yore, which we supposedly inherit and to which we must adhere. Roy Rappaport (1971) describes sanctity as "the quality of unquestionable truthfulness imputed by the faithful to unverifiable propositions" (p. 69). That definition mirrors why some educators may equate tradition with traditionalism. The latter term denotes an uncritical, even slavish, obedience to the past, a past that many regard, moreover, as marked by injustice and evil. Consequently, to heed tradition can be perceived as immoral or, at the very least, as unenlightened. Reform-minded educators confronted with the idea of tradition in teaching might say: Not sanctity and a return to the past, but critique and hope for the future.

In contrast with both of these outlooks, I want to suggest that a sense of tradition can deepen and intensify a teacher's connections with and commitment to the present. Rather than turning a teacher's gaze backward, with an eye on regaining a lost world, a sense of tradition encourages a teacher to see her- or himself as a being in time, as a person responsible for ensuring that things of value—knowledge, understandings, outlooks—endure in a dynamic way for future generations. This orientation, which I will examine in detail, explains why tradition and traditionalism are not the same. Tradition in teaching can be understood as a way of steering clear of "-isms," with their often polarizing, alienating connotations. A sense of tradition equips teachers to be wary of axe-grinding, conservative, and progressive approaches to pedagogy that are more dogmatic than self-critical. At the same time, a sense of tradition provides teachers with a means for standing back, in a thoughtful spirit, from the immediacies of teaching and from the public debates about what they should be doing in the classroom. The sense of tradition helps teachers fashion an identity that can help them to keep in view the service dimensions that are built into the practice. It can encourage them to stay the course in the face of political, social, or psychological forces that push them to accept predetermined, rather than responsive, educational answers to the challenges in teaching.

To substantiate these claims, I examine two aspects of the idea of tradition and address how they pertain to teaching. They are (1) what it means to speak of a "living" tradition and (2) how tradition influences a person engaged in a particular practice such as teaching. This inquiry will shed light on the idea of a "sense" of tradition in teaching. As we will see, the sense of tradition means something other than enacting a particular version of tradition. Rather, it describes an overall orientation or outlook on teaching. This outlook both draws teachers into the practice and, at the same time, provides them critical distance from the work. It discloses shared intellectual and moral ground that allows teachers to talk with and learn from one another despite differences in their institutional settings, the age level of their students, and the subjects they teach.

In Chapter 7, I develop these ideas further by showing how the sense of tradition in teaching differs from mere knowledge of past practice and of the conditions in which it took place, valuable as that knowledge may be. A person well versed in history does not necessarily have a sense of tradition. I illustrate this argument with an extended look at one teacher/ scholar's encounter with the past (Bushnell, 1996). I provide suggestions for teachers and teacher candidates on how to cultivate a sense of tradition.

All in all, I hope these two chapters will show why the themes I have taken up previously—person, conduct, and moral sensibility in teaching, an image of a growing, educated person that can guide the work, and attentiveness to the environment for teaching and learning—find their enduring moral and intellectual warrant in human time and tradition. The idea of a living tradition provides a backdrop, or horizon of significance, for appreciating the terms of the practice of teaching.

A LIVING TRADITION

Anthony Cua (1998) suggests that the idea of tradition makes sense, or is "intelligible" only if one presumes a "community of adherents" rather than a mere collection or aggregate of individuals thrown together (pp. 243–245). In other words, to speak of tradition in teaching presupposes a community of practitioners, of men and women who, through the generations, have perceived themselves as teachers and who have sought to enact the terms of the work. But tradition, as contrasted with traditionalism, also presupposes ongoing discussion about "the present significance of the tradition" (p. 243). It presumes continued conversation about the terms of the work and how to realize them in practice. Thus the "community of adherents" is also, at the same time, a "community of interpretation." Quoting J. G. A. Pocock (1968, p. 210), Cua writes: "The concepts we form from, and feed back into, tradition have a capacity to modify the content and character of the tradition conceptualized and even the extent to which it is conceived and regarded as a tradition" (p. 247).

Serious-minded teachers routinely ponder, characterize, and question the everyday work they and their peers perform. They are constantly interpreting both the significance and the terms of teaching, even if not in so many words. Moreover, they interpret the work from the inside of the practice. They are not mere spectators of teaching and learning. In short, they *participate* in tradition. And they perpetuate tradition in teaching precisely by enacting it, by reflecting on it, and by discussing with peers how best to achieve it.

The idea of a "living" tradition illuminates these claims. A living tradition undergoes more or less constant modification and adjustment. Since no tradition of practice, be it teaching or poetry, exists in a social or historical vacuum, its practitioners are permanently subject to any number of broad social influences. For example, teachers work in an ethos characterized by diverse, often competing, conceptions of what teaching is for. As I outlined in Chapter 1, some educators and members of the public claim that the aims of teaching are academic in nature, while others argue that they are social, cultural, political, religious, or economic. A living tradition responds to this kind of ethos through the agency of its practitioners: what they believe, how they conduct themselves, and what they bequeath to those who come after them (in their role as "precursors," a term I return to below). In a living tradition, practitioners do not simply sail with the prevailing wind. Instead, they chart a course that takes them toward the highest possibilities embedded in their practice. They cannot chart that course from nowhere. They need tradition. A practice and a tradition go hand-in-hand.

According to MacIntyre (1984), the activities that characterize a particular practice distinguish it from other practices. For example, "helping young people" is not a practice. An adult can be helpful as a parent, a minister, a nurse, a counselor, or a teacher. But teaching, as a set of activities and as a purposeful endeavor in its own right, is not the same thing as parenting, ministering, nursing, or counseling. The differences between them do not imply that practices are hermetically sealed off from one another, as if social life were a matter of discrete games that have no effect on one another (consider how the rules of chess, for example, are safely immune from problems or predicaments associated with the rules of basketball [cf. Hoy, 1978, p. 78]). There can be overlap between practices, and the joys and pains experienced in one domain (e.g., the family) can spill over into another. Nonetheless, although social practices can and do overlap in some respects, each features its own constellation of activities, purposes, satisfactions, and histories.

Moreover, a practice is distinct from the institutions or occupational strata in which it is carried out. Practicing medicine or law is not identical with working in a hospital or a law firm. Teaching is not the same thing as being employed by a school, district, or university, despite the fact that most teaching takes place within such institutions. Phrased differently, teaching is not identical with schooling. Practices such as teaching have distinctive shapes, concerns, and activities that differentiate them from institutions. A practice forms an "intermediate place" (cf. Popper, 1963, p. 133) between individuals, or the one hand, and an institution, on the other.

According to MacIntyre's (1984) analysis, institutions often privilege what he calls "external" over "internal" rewards (pp. 188–196). In both formal and tacit ways, an institution may push for better salaries, increased benefits, heightened prestige and status, a good reputation, and so forth. All these rewards have their value. But in many respects they are generic; they are prized by institutions everywhere. They are only contingently associated with a practice. A person could pursue money, reputation, security, and status by partaking in any number of endeavors without ever truly becoming engaged in a practice.

In contrast, the internal rewards of teaching reflect what renders the work important, distinctive, and irreproducible. To help a group of students learn to read, to write, to interpret literature and historical events, to understand nature, to think for themselves, to take delight in learning—to comprehend such things, and to know that one has helped bring them about, captures the fulfillment that teaching can yield. These internal rewards derive from having a positive influence on the growth of students. They cannot as easily be measured or categorized as external rewards. They do not have an exchange value. Nor are they limited or scarce, as tends to be the case with external rewards. Internal rewards are potentially unlimited, and they are accessible to any serious-minded teacher.

A person can pursue external rewards directly (indeed, their pursuit can become all-consuming). But internal rewards cannot be sought directly. A sense of meaningfulness cannot be purchased over the counter. Internal rewards derive from committing oneself to the terms of the practice, from giving oneself over to them, so to speak. Teachers who plan good lessons, who listen to students, who devote thought and care to evaluation, and who think about the environment in the classroom and school open the door to the fulfillment and satisfaction that can accompany helping students flourish. And that fulfillment can motivate teachers to greater heights of effort and imagination, thereby positioning them for that much deeper a sense of internal reward from teaching.

Studies have shown that many teachers stay in the field precisely because of its internal rewards (see, e.g., Foster, 1997; Johnson, 1990; Lortie, 1975). Other studies have illuminated why we can think of teaching as a practice (see, e.g., Arnold, 1997; Buchmann, 1989; W. Carr, 1995; Hansen, 1995, 1998; Hostetler, 1997; Olson, 1992; van Manen, 1991). One way to summarize the lessons from this body of work is to say that teaching is steeped in presuppositions that help describe the substance of a flourishing life. Teaching has to do with cultivating students' minds and spirits. Phrased differently, teaching pursues changes in students that are broadening, deepening, and enriching. These terms suggest that teaching has to do with intellectual and moral growth. Teaching is a continuous activity of encouraging and fueling attitudes, orientations, and understandings that allow students to progress rather than to regress as human beings, to grow rather than to become narrow in their outlook and range of capabilities. In order to perform this kind of work, teachers themselves must grow intellectually and morally. This familiar claim dramatizes, once again, the internal rewards that can accrue from engrossing oneself in the practice. The rewards can include increasing insight into the splendors, the ambiguities, and the unfathomableness of human development.

At this juncture, the idea that a practice such as teaching has a tradition comes into play. The practice of teaching is older than the current institutions in which much of it is housed. To judge from its tradition, whose roots go back at least as far as the likes of Socrates and Confucius, teaching is typically a publicly conducted endeavor involving an adult working with other people's children or with adults. What do teachers do? They draw students into worlds of knowledge, experience, and outlook that extend beyond what the family or local community can normally provide alone. Teachers lead or guide others to know what they did not know before, to articulate or apprehend what they did not know they knew, to do things they could not do before, and to embrace potentially better or more warranted attitudes and ideas than previously held ones. Such notions suggest an intellectual and moral ascension. They imply expanding rather than contracting the horizons of thought and conduct. They often involve questioning contemporary values and beliefs, not necessarily with the aim of rejecting them but rather to hold them up against a larger backdrop than those values and beliefs can themselves provide. These notions of what the work is about call attention to the fact that tradition in teaching is not something determinate. Tradition and its voice alter, if ever so slightly, with the entrance onto the scene of each new teacher who brings to bear a distinctive, if still evolving, intellectual and moral sensibility.

This argument underscores the point that tradition is not traditionalism. The latter term describes what might be called a dead tradition, an inert, fixed set of activities and ideas oblivious to the animated world, including to the perhaps legitimate purposes that originally gave the tradition its impetus.[1] "Tradition is the living faith of the dead," Pelikan (1984) writes, while "traditionalism is the dead faith of the living" (p. 65). In a living tradition, ideas and conduct are in motion. Philosophy and practice remain dynamic. As I argue in subsequent sections, individuals can shape the nature and the outcomes of the practice even as they remain under its nurturing and steadfast influence. I suggested previously that teaching means broadening, deepening, and enriching students' lives. But as the embodiment of a living tradition, teaching declares no preset limitation or boundary on such changes. That fact is why the sense of tradition can propel teachers to strive for the highest possibilities embedded in the practice. Part of being a teacher is learning to identify just those possibilities. As members of a practice informed by a tradition of helping students learn and develop, teachers constitute a "community of hope" (Cua, 1998, p. 244).

THE INFLUENCE OF TRADITION

Harold Bloom (1975) illuminates the interplay between person and tradition in a study of how artists and writers, and especially poets, respond to their precursors. Bloom's analysis will help me show how teachers can grow into the role precisely by engaging tradition.

According to Bloom, a poet cannot "choose" whether to take his precursors seriously or not. He cannot choose whether to regard poetry as having a tradition behind it. "Do we choose a tradition," Bloom writes,

> or does it choose us, and why is it necessary that a choosing take place, or a being chosen? What happens if one tries to write, or to teach, or to think, or even to read without the sense of a tradition? (p. 32)

He answers his own question:

> Why, nothing at all happens, just nothing. You cannot write or teach or think or even read without imitation, and what you imitate is what another person has done, that person's writing or teaching or thinking or reading. Your relation to what informs that person *is* tradition, for tradition is influence that extends past one generation, a carrying-over of influence. (p. 32)

According to Bloom, without tradition and the precursors who have generated it, a person cannot become a poet—or teacher, thinker, reader, and so forth. MacIntyre (1984) makes a similar point: "What I am . . . is in key part what I inherit, a specific past that is present to some degree in my present. I find myself part of a history and that is generally to say, whether I like it or not, whether I recognize it or not, one of the bearers of a tradition" (p. 221).

But tradition serves as more than the source of a beginning. Phrased differently, tradition is more than that which is imitated. As Bloom notes, it has to do with what "informs" those whom a person (initially) imitates. Tradition comprises a background set of commitments, activities, questions, concerns, and aspirations that continuously evolve as individuals in one generation respond to the efforts and projects of those who preceded them in the particular practice. Langford (1985) clarifies this view. "Without tradition," he writes, "there would be nothing *to* change and no scope for creativity" (p. 9). "Creative individuality of one sort or another," he argues, "is made possible by the relevant tradition rather than being ruled out by it. . . . The individual does decide what to do and how to do it, but the opportunity of doing is provided by the tradition" (pp. 21–22; see also Allan, 1993, p. 27). As Luise Prior McCarty (1997) notes in discussing the art of drawing: "Shading and stippling are techniques that are tradition-objects; the young artist who learns them must reproduce—if only by violation—the tradition in drawing that the pencil as tool represents" (p. 394).

The creative process is complicated and difficult. Bloom (1975) describes the influence of tradition as "the giving that famishes the taker" (p. 18). Poetry and its influence beckon the person to write, they "give" him a trajectory without which he could not begin at all. But they also "famish" him, for how is he to create anything when he confronts a "sea of poetry, of poems already written" (p. 16)? How can the poet become more than merely an imitator? How can he obtain critical distance from the ocean of poetry that precedes and now surrounds him? How can there be any "new" poems at all?

According to Bloom, a sense of tradition provides a response to these intimidating questions. It does so, in part, by turning the poet to his own origins as a reader and listener, as a person who responded to tradition in the first place and to whom poetry became real. In Bloom's words: "Trying to write a poem takes the poet back to the origins of what a poem *first was for him,* and so takes the poet back beyond the pleasure principle to the decisive initial encounter and response that began him" (p. 18). The turn to origins goes "beyond" the pleasure principle because those origins reside in an exchange *in* the world rather than in some inner psychological impulse. That is, the "decisive initial encounter" that "began" the poet was when poetry first came into his orbit—or, better perhaps, when poetry first drew him into its orbit and thereby changed what the world was for him. Phrased differently, he did not grasp poetry as merely another object to consume or to satiate a restless ego. Poetry grasped him. The sense of tradition propels the person out of the realm of mere impulse and ego, and positions him to discern what Oakeshott (1991) calls "the voice of poetry" in the conversation of humanity. The poet writes because he wants to respond to that voice, because of his engagement with poetry and his hope to say something himself. If he heeds this beckoning and persists, he may, in turn, alter the tradition and its future by becoming himself a precursor to as yet unformed poets.

The sense of tradition both connects *and* distances the poet from the vast ocean of poetry that precedes him. He creates critical distance from previous poetry precisely by understanding how tradition affected, continues to affect, and will always affect him *as* a poet. As Bloom claims, without tradition there can be no poetry. But without possible entrants into the world of poetry, there will soon be no tradition. Tradition means simultaneously conserving a form of life—in this case, reading, reciting, pondering, and writing poetry—and transforming that form of life as each new person enters and responds in his or her own way. As Bloom contends, a newcomer may actually need to "misread" tradition as embodied in percursors. That is, "to avoid over-determination," the newcomer may at times have to "forsake correct perception" of the poems he or she most values, whose magnetic power can constrain as well as inspire (Bloom, 1973, p. 71). But this possibility itself depends on tradition, and it also advances tradition. "The reception of tradition," Edward Shils (1958) emphasizes, "is aided by resistance to it" (p. 159).

The bottom line is that, to make use of Bloom's words, nobody has the very same "initial encounter" with poetry, and nobody's subsequent history as a poet will ever be identical with another's. Thus, tradition does not describe that which remains identical or frozen or that which should be blindly accepted. Tradition, once again, is not traditionalism. Everyone in a practice begins as an imitator, but what they imitate and, with effort and luck, grow beyond is always on the move, whether subtly or dramatically. In this light, the sense of tradition funds human freedom, understood as the capacity to offer a positive answer to the earlier question, Can there ever be anything new in a practice like poetry?[2]

This argument holds in an analogous fashion for a person who feels pulled or drawn toward a life in teaching. By developing a sense of tradition, such a person makes it that much more possible to craft, in his or her distinctive way, a positive answer to the questions, Can teachers do anything new? Can they do more than merely imitate and replicate? Can teaching become more than just socializing the young into expected custom and belief? The sense of tradition both invites and provokes teachers to take themselves seriously. The poet Rilke captures how hard this can be, at least at first. Tradition and the past can feel so weighty, Rilke writes, that one sometimes feels that "it takes a great, fully ripened power to create something individual where good, even glorious, traditions exist in abundance" (1908/1986, p. 7). In his own poetic career, Rilke discovered that time and experience were necessary for him to fashion a distinctive, "individual" way of going about the practice of poetry. As with poets, so with teachers. New teachers often feel both inspired and intimidated by the example that previous teachers, including their own, have set. It takes perseverance, experiment, self-criticism, talking with peers, and seasoning to create a pedagogical style and signature. That style and signature gain their identity against a backdrop of tradition in the practice.

As I posed the matter in Chapter 1, teachers can learn to respond imaginatively to the moral and intellectual terms they discover are embedded in the practice of teaching. Those terms remind us that teaching and poetry, for all the suggestive analogies one might draw between them (I will make several more below), are not identical undertakings. Teaching is a deliberate and typically public affair of fostering knowledge, insight, understanding, and more. I have suggested that through engrossing themselves in the practice, thinking about their precursors, and talking with their peers, teachers make tradition into a partner in a generative transaction. Tradition provides them the opportunity to teach in the first place. They, in turn, vitalize tradition as they take on and shape the role. Their encounter with tradition in teaching need not become a monologue in which, metaphorically speaking, either they act as lords of the classroom realm—more likely, as emperors without clothes—or past practice issues edicts to which they and their students bewilderingly try to respond. Instead, the sense of tradition keeps teachers tethered to the terms of the practice, just as their efforts keep tradition tethered to human creativity, insight, imagination, and hope.

MORAL CONTOURS OF THE SENSE OF TRADITION

The sense of tradition constitutes an orientation or outlook toward the practice. As such, it reaches beyond adherence to a particular set of pedagogical methods or curricular materials. The sense of tradition attests to a person's feeling *for* human time, as well as to his or her feeling for being *in* human time. The person feels him- or herself to be part of the human story and also grasps his or her agency in continuing that very story. For a teacher, a sense of tradition generates a feeling for teaching itself, a feeling for the activity of helping others to learn. I mean something more than affection for the work and for students, although many teachers certainly have those sentiments. I also intend to convey something other than mere intuition. The sense of tradition in teaching unifies pedagogical knowledge and commitment. It helps guide thought and emotion. In contrast with states of alienation, anomie, cynicism, or burnout, a teacher with a sense of tradition is buoyed across challenging or dispiriting moments by knowing that he or she is not alone, in the sense that previous forms of those challenges confronted his or her precursors and peers—and many of these persons taught (or are teaching) their way through them. They kept alive the terms of teaching. That is, they continued to broaden, deepen, and enrich their students' learning. If they had not done so, there would be no practice of teaching today. The sense of tradition animates a teacher's consciousness of following on the heels of previous teachers who believed in meaningful education. That consciousness generates solidarity with those now departed from the scene. The teacher sees him- or herself as attempting to live up to their legacy, or inheritance, even while questioning it in the search for his or her own form of expression—and all of this while bequeathing whatever he or she can to those teachers who have yet to make their entry.

This orientation can fund a teacher's moral sensibility. It combats the temptation to create a hard-and-fast hierarchy in which some teachers are perceived as on the side of the angels, while the rest are dismissed as ne'er-do-wells—or worse. The sense of tradition guides me to recognize, however grudgingly, that in my capacity as a teacher, I cannot say that bad or even evil teachers, or evil systems of education in which they worked, have nothing to do with me. I cannot say, Those bad or corrupt educators are over there, but I am over here in the land of the Good. I would like to be in that land, metaphorically speaking, but it is not a separate continent. Those who failed, or who, far worse, harmed human beings while wearing the mantle of teacher are a part of my past. My task is to accept that truth and to act on it by learning to distinguish the moral and the intellectual wheat from the chaff. The sense of tradition issues from, and supports, this unpredictable, unforced, ongoing intertwining of understanding and personal transformation. As I engage in the process, I begin to comprehend the hopefulness in teaching. I discern how the practice contrasts with its countless counterfeits. I realize teaching's enduring commitment to assist rather than to thwart human development, in the very broadest meaning of that term.

According to MacIntyre's (1984) analysis of tradition, this orientation could be described as a virtue. It constitutes "the virtue of having an adequate sense of the traditions to which one belongs or which confront one" (p. 223). MacIntyre describes the willingness to connect with tradition as a virtue because it enables a practitioner to build on past efforts while also looking to the future. "This virtue," he explains,

> is not to be confused with any form of conservative antiquarianism. . . . It is rather the case that an adequate sense of tradition manifests itself in a grasp of those future possibilities which the past has made available to the present.

> Living traditions, just because they continue a not-yet-completed narrative, confront a future whose determinate and determinable character, so far as it possesses any, derives from the past. (p. 223)

The "virtue" of having a sense of tradition forms part of a teacher's moral sensibility because it can influence how he or she regards other people—students, colleagues, parents, administrators, and others. A feeling of critical solidarity with tradition in teaching triggers a deeper concern for those living today, and in whose lives one plays a part, because in that concern hangs the balance for how one affects human flourishing.

This claim takes on added significance because most teachers do not choose with whom they will work or whom they will teach. Especially in public institutions, they must try to work with the colleagues and the students who come their way. That fact means making educational contact with individuals who may, at times, resist their advances or even oppose their efforts. However, a sense of tradition enables teachers to retain an engaged, imaginative, and balanced outlook. It helps them appreciate when to back off or to wait, as well as when to put their foot forward. Ralph Waldo Emerson (1844/1990) captures this posture in his poetic call for how persons might conduct themselves in our often confusing, confounding human world: "Without any shadow of doubt, amidst this vertigo of shows and politics, I settle myself ever the firmer in the creed, that we should not postpone and refer and wish, but do broad justice where we are, by whomsoever we deal with, accepting our actual companions and circumstances, however humble or odious, as the mystic officials to whom the universe has delegated its whole pleasure for us" (p. 223).

As I anticipated in the previous section, teachers can approach such a creed by thinking about their precursors and by talking with serious-minded peers. We witnessed examples of that process in Chapter 2, when I described how Michael Oakeshott and Suzanne Hoover sought to understand their teachers' influence on them. To contemplate one's precursors and peers in this way is to perceive, very quickly, that serious-minded teachers differ widely in their style, their manner, their pedagogical signature.[3] Teachers vary in how they emphasize ideas and meanings embedded in a subject, just as they vary in how they express attentiveness to students' individual development. Tradition in teaching underlies these differences in trademark. Phrased differently, tradition gives them their shared identity as enactments of the practice of teaching in the first place. Tradition provides the backdrop or horizon of significance against which to appreciate their value. One might say that, in an ideal world, every teacher would realize in equal measure the terms of teaching examined here and elsewhere in the book. Every teacher would strive to broaden, deepen, and enrich students' understandings, capabilities, and outlooks. But though we do not dwell in an ideal world, we can and do dwell in living traditions that make it possible to move closer to, rather than farther from, what such an ideal represents. The sense of tradition helps teachers to hold onto this truth and to actualize it in their work.

THE DYNAMICS OF TRADITION IN TEACHING: QUESTIONS AND REPLIES

As we have seen, tradition is a more complicated and challenging concept than it might at first seem. From one point of view, tradition reduces to what people did in the past and how they did it. It is simply a name for the world of yesteryear. To conservative-minded educators, the concept may trigger images of cherished, unchanging values that are beyond criticism. To their reform-minded colleagues, tradition may call to mind worrisome, and burdensome, debris from the past. The concept may spark images of weight and stagnation rather than images of lightness, progress, and liberty of movement.

In this chapter, I have sought to chart a different course. I have argued that tradition and the sense of tradition play central, dynamic roles in the practice of teaching. They provide a background, or source, for capturing the terms and the significance of the work. In technical terms, they generate a principled nonpresentism *and* nontraditionalism. On the one hand, the sense of tradition provides teachers critical distance from contemporary conceptions of teaching, such as those that I touched on in Chapter 1. It allows them to weigh the various claims they hear about the work and to measure them against what the practice itself has bequeathed to them. On the other hand, the sense of tradition propels teachers to self-criticism, to resist an unexamined embrace of past methods and ideas. The sense of tradition offers a place where teachers can stand, metaphorically speaking, when surveying their own classrooms and when responding to the often conflicting public claims made on who and what they are. It positions them to respond respectfully to legitimate public concerns but without abandoning the integrity of their practice.

In the next chapter, I extend the argument by showing why the sense of tradition differs from mere knowledge of past practice. I also address how teachers and teacher candidates can cultivate a sense of tradition. To set the stage for that discussion, I want to respond here to several questions that the analysis thus far may have raised. The questions are: (1) Are there evil traditions and practices, and, if so, does that fact raise problems for my argument? (2) How can people employ a tradition of practice to criticize that very tradition? Don't people require a standpoint outside tradition in order to criticize it? (3) Should we speak of tradition in teaching in the singular or plural?

The Question of Evil Traditions and Practices

I underscored in the previous section that the sense of tradition leads a person, as teacher, to criticize, not to elide, the harms and injustices that have been carried out under the name of teaching. I have emphasized that tradition itself provides grounds for this criticism. That is, a teacher does not have to abandon or step wholly outside the realm of practice in order to pose the right kind of questions (additional perspectives can help, as I show below).

Still, the overall argument in this chapter may seem to imply that, with respect to teaching, concepts of tradition and practice tend to align with truth and goodness. But are there evil traditions and practices? It would take another book to provide an adequate reply. However, one way to approach the issue is to ponder whether evil practices, to the extent that they endure over time, shed more light on traditionalism than tradition. Evil practices, such as making war on others and enslaving them, make me think of constitutional narrowness and rigidity in mind and soul—the very opposite of terms I am associating with tradition, such as *living, open to questioning, hopeful,* and so forth. To be sure, traditions can petrify into traditionalisms and could thereby become a source of harm. Moreover, there is no tradition or practice of which I am aware that is unambiguously pure from a moral point of view. With the possible exception of monastic orders, no tradition or practice can wall itself off from social, cultural, and political influences, which are not always benign in nature. Those influences can potentially sunder any human endeavor. Nor can the members of a practice, if its tradition is alive, simple-mindedly determine which participants will sustain and enrich the practice and which might endanger it.

However, thanks to serious-minded people who take it up, a practice with a living tradition, such as teaching, can be understood as striving toward truth and goodness. In the concrete world of the classroom, those big words stand for supporting rather than for undermining students' learning and growth. This condition holds despite the fact that teachers everywhere (this writer included), from preschool through graduate-level programs, often stumble, stray, fail, and misconceive the work. It holds despite the fact that the practice is recurrently threatened by institutional and other pressures. Through all these vicissitudes, the practice has en-

dured, often wondrously so. I believe this approach to the question of
evil traditions and practices, while in need of an argument to sustain it,
reaches beyond stipulation or a high-flying form of idealism. The approach is more a matter of historical reckoning, of receptivity, and of
critical sympathy, as I have sought to document here.

How Might I Criticize My Own Tradition?

Let me turn to the question of criticism of a tradition from within. "The
desire to criticise," Langford (1985) reminds us, "depends on awareness
of the possibility of doing so" (p. 33). The sense of tradition can trigger
both the desire and the awareness. It widens the lens through which to
ponder the contexts in which teachers work. It provides teachers powerful
grounds for self-criticism and for useful conversation about each other's
work and viewpoints.

Langford (1985) points out that

> to acquire a personal vision is in the first place to acquire the way of seeing
> which a tradition provides and, therefore, to become acquainted with and
> accept for oneself the overall point or purpose of a social practice such as
> painting or teaching. To do that is to acquire a view both of what that purpose
> is and what it ought to be. It is therefore to be in a position to justify or
> criticise what is done in that practice on a particular occasion by reference
> to that view. (pp. 41–42)

As they gain experience, serious-minded teachers learn how to identify
quality teaching. They learn to differentiate the real thing from the bogus.
They discern the potential in new curricula and in new ways of organizing
classroom and school life. Like painters or poets who have learned to
harmonize form and substance—or, at least, to appreciate the meaning
of such a harmony—experienced, thoughtful teachers embody insight
into the subject matter of teaching and learning. If not in so many words,
they grasp how and why teaching is at once both an intellectual and
moral endeavor. They can answer questions that outsiders would be hard-
pressed to address: How does a person know when he or she has become
a teacher? How does a person know when he or she has made the moral
and intellectual turn from being a novice to being a full-fledged practitioner who can contribute to the well-being of students and to the en-
hancement of the practice? From an occupational point of view, a person
becomes a teacher upon receipt of the appropriate degrees or licenses
and upon obtaining a position. But those steps do not represent the
unpredictable process through which the phase of being introduced to
the practice—a phase that can last for an indeterminate amount of time—

gives way (sometimes suddenly) to feeling like a teacher and to doing the real work of teaching. Moreover, the latter experience can continue to come and go, possibly for an entire career, as the person encounters successes and failures. For these and other reasons, it is no surprise that teacher educators, many of them former primary or secondary school teachers, have long advocated developing close professional relations with mentor teachers in the field (cf. McIntyre, Hagger, & Wilkin, 1993). Teachers are, in irreproducible ways, potentially their own best critics. With time and experience, they learn how to educate one another, even as they learn how to respond in a mature way to the demands and needs of parents, administrators, and other public actors.

However, a critic might charge this perspective with insularity. How can teachers, he or she might ask, employ the terms of their practice to criticize and enrich those very terms? Phrased differently, how can teachers respond critically to tradition if they remain cocooned within the tradition? Or, as Langford (1985) puts it, "How can [educators] base their criticism on an appeal to tradition, since it is tradition which they wish to criticize?" (p. 37; also see Will, 1985a, pp. 125–126). I will touch on five ways in which educators can criticize tradition in teaching. These ways complement the analysis in this chapter about how tradition constrains and empowers teachers at one and the same time.

Langford (1985) suggests that there are always at least two elements operative in a tradition: discrete skills and techniques for carrying out the practice and ways of seeing and understanding the work (p. 37). Either element can become a standpoint for criticizing the other in the name of an overall enrichment of the practice. Together, they attest to the fact that there exists "a capacity *in* accepted practice to transcend, oppose, and in other ways modify itself" (Will, 1985b, p. 195; emphasis added). For instance, baseball players have, for generations, refined their individual skills and techniques in ways that have influenced the overall strategies and purposes of the game. At the same time, there have always been participants who have taken a broad view. They have focused on how to shape a successful season or on how to motivate players to excel, rather than just on how to pitch to the next batter. Their vision has generated new insights to improve individual technique and skill. The analogy holds for teaching. For example, as a result of the evolution of tradition in the practice, teachers today agree that it is good to teach the young how to read, write, numerate, and more. They applaud those purposes. But for generations they have disagreed about the appropriate skills and techniques to employ in instruction (cf. Langford, 1985, pp. 37–38). Moreover, they have discussed and criticized the skill with which they and their peers implement particular techniques of teaching reading, writing, or numerating. These forms of internal criticism have been dynamic and fruitful.

A second strategy for criticizing one's tradition is to adopt the vantage point of another practice or tradition. For countless generations, poets have discerned new forms of expression and have deepened their ideas through pondering other arts: painting, sculpture, dance, and more. Teachers can discover new aspects and nuances about their work by comparing and contrasting its terms with those of practices in which they may have participated themselves, such as social work and parenting. They can gain insight into the role of a teacher by considering traditions in educational leadership (e.g., as materialized in the principalship), in nursing, and in counseling. In addition, they can cultivate more efficacious educational relationships with students by considering cultural, religious, and other traditions that may constitute, in part, their students' current horizons. Furthermore, they can gain perspective on their practice by immersing themselves in what Oakeshott (1989) calls the historic "languages"—art, literature, science, history—in which people have sought to understand themselves and their world. These various vantage points do not displace tradition in teaching. Rather, they and others can fuel the work of enhancing both tradition and practice.

A third route to criticizing one's tradition of practice is to take a global point of view. This approach might mean using a variety of sources to contemplate the current political, economic, and social scene nationwide and beyond. It could include examining the history of one's region or society as a whole. Time and again, artists have enriched their work through trying to grasp the concerns, questions, fears, and hopes of people. Their efforts have shed new light on the significance and possibilities in their art. Like art, teaching never operates in a societal or existential vacuum, and filling in that larger backdrop can yield new insight into how best to fulfill its terms. Again, taking this perspective is no substitute for engaging teaching and its terms. It does not mean breaking with practice and tradition. Rather, it provides another, potentially productive spur to criticism.

Fourth, Bloom's (1975) account of how poets become poets reminds us that entrants to a practice bring to it a history of personal experiences, concerns, questions, and aspirations. Teaching is no exception. The practice of teaching may have, metaphorically speaking, called individuals to the work. But they, after all, heeded the call. Something in their personal constitution made them receptive, even eager to join the field. Not every entrant will succeed. To retain the image, many are called, but not all can serve. Nonetheless, every serious-minded teacher can cultivate a distinctive approach to the work. That approach can do justice to the time-honored terms of the work, while also generating new ways of expressing and extending them from which others can learn.

Finally, a fifth way to criticize tradition in teaching returns us to the opening comments in this chapter. In John Donne's words regarding "for whom the bell tolls," we hear an echo of the venerable idea that teachers serve human flourishing, in the broadest sense of the term. They cultivate the persons they and their students can become. This perspective can assist teachers in checking their course by reminding them of their moral solidarity with humanity. As is well known, the historical record discloses multiple instances in which one group denied the status of humanity, or personhood, to members of another and sought to control, dominate, or even crush them. For example, Frederick Douglass, W. E. B. Du Bois, and many others have documented how slavery reduced the terrain in which Black Americans could engage in meaningful conduct. The institution stripped away conditions for cultivating a sense of personhood, although never completely, as these same writers show. They illuminate vividly the depths of human resilience and agency in the face of organized coercion. Tzvetan Todorov (1996), among many others, shows how some individuals in Nazi concentration camps and in the Soviet gulag retained their personhood. They carved out spaces in which they could act morally, rather than merely react to circumstance. As narrow and threatened as that space was, it speaks volumes about the human quest for dignity and meaning. Writers who focus on war and its effects—I am thinking, for example, of Theodor Plievier's trilogy on World War II (e.g., Plievier, 1947/1966) and Simone Weil's (1941/1986) essay on the *Iliad*—further reveal how events and situations can reduce, or eviscerate, personhood and moral agency. The suffering of soldiers and civilians in war is terrible. War annihilates human beings who might otherwise, with perhaps but a slight shift of the world's moral axis, be playing and working with one another.

These recollections intensify the enduring significance of the terms of teaching and of concepts such as person, conduct, and moral sensibility in teaching. The terms and concepts capture central features of what it means to cultivate one's humanity and to contribute to human flourishing. People might not employ such terms in describing their purposes and affairs. Nor must they, since the point is not to strike a pose but to live as fully and humanely as one can. Teachers might not conceive of themselves as "contributing to human flourishing"—and, as Oakeshott (1989, p. 62) cautions, it may be the better part of wisdom to be circumspect in the use of such talk. Such talk can become sentimental, and it ill suits the practice of teaching to picture it as a missionary endeavor. But tradition in teaching shows that fueling human learning and growth has long been a core aim of the practice. Teachers help others learn to read, to write, to numerate, to draw, to dance, to repair machines, to speak publicly, to ponder other people's ideas, emotions, and aspirations, and more. In so doing, teachers help others expand their range of activity and capability. And to expand the horizons of a human being's world, rather than to contract or narrow them, means positioning that individual to flourish that much more. The individual's learning, in turn, enables him or her to engage others and the world that much more. People might not describe teachers of automobile repair as helping others "to enter a broader horizon of experience." But I know of no more encompassing way to capture the act's significance.

In short, teachers make a difference in human lives. A teacher's moral sensibility and grasp of the terms of teaching—perhaps unspoken, yet ever-present—underlie his or her efforts, whether these be in the third-grade reading group, in the tenth-grade history discussion, or in the university biology lab. The concepts of practice and sensibility attest to a moral underpinning, or source, from which the familiar activities of teaching derive much of their long-standing reasons for being. Teachers can gain additional critical insight into those reasons through remembering broad moral solidarities with others. But remembrance, not displacement of tradition in teaching, remains the watchword here. As I discuss in Chapter 8, it is all too easy for ideals of service and mission, as noble as they may sound and feel, to blind a teacher to human realities and to his or her obligations.

I hope these standpoints help clarify why working within a tradition of practice does not, from the point of view of thought and conduct, cocoon or imprison teachers. As I have argued in this chapter, rather than limiting a teacher's critical perspective, the sense of tradition helps substantiate it in the first place.

Tradition or Traditions in Teaching?

The third and last question I want to take up here asks whether we should speak of tradition in teaching in the singular or plural. Talk of tradition may raise moral hackles because it could be taken to imply that there is one, and only one, correct or true way to define teaching and to carry out its terms. I framed the issue in Chapter 1 by asking whether teaching, as a singular concept, implies a singular meaning. I hope I have made clear that that posture, taken by itself, connotes something closer to traditionalism than tradition. In a living tradition, persons characterize the work in which they engage—they articulate its character, its terms, its challenges, and more—but they do not "define" it or "explain" it in some terminal, closed fashion. Practitioners keep the tradition alive and moving precisely by reflecting on and questioning what they do.

A critic could usefully argue that there are many traditions of teaching, each of them deeply informed by a particular culture's customs and beliefs. There are traditions of teaching in China, in India, in Africa, in Europe, in Brazil—in short, so the argument could go, there are traditions of teaching among peoples everywhere (cf. Reagan, 1996). Alternatively, the critic could take a broader, more universal point of view. For example, Philip Jackson (1986) describes two traditions of teaching that he regards as rooted deep in the human past. He calls them, respectively, the mimetic and the transformative traditions. The former captures the long-held view that teaching means transferring knowledge to the young. It means passing on what a community knows. Many regard teaching as a process of handing on knowledge of mathematics, history, science, and so forth, as well as skills such as reading, writing, swimming, dancing, and the like. Jackson argues that method takes on supreme importance in this tradition, because teachers have to figure out how to transmit the knowledge and also how to be sure the young have absorbed it. In contrast, teachers in the transformative tradition seek to do something other than just transfer knowledge. They hope to transform students as persons (and possibly themselves as well, Jackson points out). Rather than *filling* students' minds with material as if they were empty vessels, transformative teachers seek to help students *develop* their minds. They do not think about students strategically, so that knowledge transfer can take place in an orderly manner. Rather, they think of students as moral beings. They ask questions, they express wonder and doubt, and they offer themselves as role models for how students might conduct themselves ethically and rationally through the vicissitudes of life. Jackson suggests that both of these traditions remain viable today, although their popularity waxes and wanes. Moreover, he tells us, their coexistence creates tensions and difficulties for teachers who attempt to be mindful of both.

In response to the pluralist perspective, it is possible to speak of different traditions of teaching, perhaps as many as there are different cultures, school subjects, and levels of education around the globe. A comparable point could be made about poetry. People talk about American poetry, Urdu poetry, Icelandic poetry, medieval poetry. They speak of feminist poetry, postmodern poetry, working-class poetry, gay poetry, war poetry, and more. However, since time immemorial poets have learned a great deal from one another across regional, cultural, and temporal divides. It would be impossible to enumerate all the instances in which they have developed new ideas and stylistic possibilities from peers across space and time. Moreover, poets have ways of communicating with one another that mirror their practice. Just as seasoned teachers are best positioned to answer questions such as "How does one know when one has become a teacher?" so it is with poets. They know poetry. Moreover, their knowledge is not solely a matter of being clear about definitions and theories of poetry or about different modes of expression and their structural properties. It is as much, or more, a matter of their being *inside* the practice, of possessing it and being possessed by it, of being bound up in it, albeit, as I would like to put it, in a manner that does not bind. In a broad sense, poets are conjoined by a shared tradition of form, substance, and beckoning. Phrased differently, poetry is not simply an alternative to prose, dance, or any other art. Rather, it generates its own unique opportunities and requirements. These facts account for why poets deepen and intensify their craft by seeking out peers to talk with and by studying poetic works from the past and present. They do not rely, at least solely, on the views of poetry of their nonpoet neighbors, of artists who work in other media, and so forth.

Obvious as it may be, I will likely learn more about teaching from a serious-minded peer from South Africa or India than I will from my nonteacher loved ones and friends close to home in America (from whom I learn things I cannot learn from colleagues). My fellow teachers and I have concepts, ideas, images, and experiences derived from the practice of teaching that allow us to talk critically and productively. Moreover, we can talk intelligibly with one another because teaching, as I have argued throughout this book, is not identical with socialization or acculturation (nor, for that matter, with indoctrination). There are legitimate, rather than honorific, reasons that educators the world over speak of *teacher education* programs, rather than of socializer or acculturator preparation programs. The fact that some teacher education efforts have amounted to little more than socialization does not eliminate the differences. This claim does not mean the terms are opposed, since teaching and socializing students are often overlapping processes (see below). But the concepts are not interchangeable. They do not describe the same things. According to Oakeshott (1989), socialization constitutes "an apprenticeship to adult life . . . governed by an extrinsic purpose" (p. 84). I have argued that teaching takes its identity, to an important degree, from its *intrinsic* aims and character as a practice with a living tradition. Understood in these terms, teaching may not be as old as human culture, and thus not as old as processes of socialization and acculturation. As I have sought to show in this book, teaching (and I would add teacher education) constitutes an invitation to a practice with rich, and time-honored, moral and intellectual significance.

Teaching as a practice, as compared with teaching as a socializing function, highlights what people can become, not simply what people have been. It invites people to participate in what they could be, not solely in what they are or in what others perceive or want them to be. The practice draws teachers and students alike to make use of their best imagination (their worst imagination can create things we are not yet, too). I refer to states such as being more rather than less knowledgeable, more rather than less thoughtful about other views and outlooks, and more rather than less capable of participating in a quest for meaning and purpose.

As a practice, rather than as merely an instrument of socialization, teaching emerged when people raised questions about what they valued and how they were socializing youth into those values. It emerged when they speculated about the adequacy of their moral and political institutions, when they wondered about their knowledge and understanding, and when they sought a larger backdrop against which to respond to such questions than that provided by existing beliefs and values. I do not mean that teaching arose as a practice in order for people to denounce, much less overthrow, the prevailing customs, values, and modes of socializing the young. Rather, it took shape, in part, because those customs, values, and modes could not in themselves provide adequate perspective for judging their nature and worth. In other words, teaching has to do with helping people attain critical distance, while at the same time cultivating concrete relations with the world. Teaching may not be poetry, but it is a creative rather than merely replicative or socializing act.

Jackson's (1986) analysis helps us appreciate that the creative and replicative dimensions of the work sometimes coexist in tension. But this need not imply that we should speak of two traditions in teaching, which Jackson names the mimetic and the transformative. The mimetic approach to instruction might best be understood as an indispensable phase of all or at least most teaching, but not as a tradition of teaching in its own right.[4] Persons of all ages, when they first encounter a new subject, imitate and absorb what their teachers say. This is how a great deal of learning happens, and should happen. I would hate to learn how to garden, for example, without having somebody experienced around to point out facts to me and to offer tips and insights. New teachers, too, can hardly help but imitate much of what they have learned from others. These teachers' students imitate aspects of what they hear and see in the classroom. In short, passing on information and ways of doing things constitutes a central aspect of teaching. But as a distinctive practice, teaching is more than that. Teaching emerges when teachers assist students in becoming something other than sponges (and not just bigger sponges than when they began). Teaching happens when teachers help students to think about what they are doing and learning, to ask questions, to consider new possibilities, to take seriously their own capacities to grow and learn, and, as Oakeshott (1989) emphasizes, to develop a sense of judgment.

This process is more than a process of imitation. Teaching has to do with helping individuals break new ground in their lives, even if the tilling, like writing poetry, is mostly undramatic and often difficult.[5]

Teaching constitutes a pattern of activity, an idea I discussed in Chapter 2 in examining the meaning of a teacher's conduct. We cannot determine whether a particular classroom act constitutes teaching if it is taken out of context. Classroom work at any level of the educational system is far too complicated to permit that. It always features phases or moments of socialization, acculturation, and mimesis, jumbled together in unpredictable and often implicit ways. The overall pattern of the work remains the key, along with the larger purposes of growth and learning that inform that pattern, which I have sought to elucidate throughout this book. The idea of a practice, and the sense of tradition associated with that idea, helps us grasp both the pattern and its meaning.

The terms of teaching that have emerged from tradition provide the teacher a form, or direction, for thought, feeling, and conduct. They do not, and cannot, prescribe the content of that thought, feeling, and conduct. In this light, the terms of teaching mirror the qualities of a growing, educated person I featured in Chapter 3. Those qualities, too, provide a form but not a prescribed content. They allow teachers to identify and to talk about the meaning of qualities such as open-mindedness and simplicity in the first place—thereby illustrating the value and power of a form—but they do not provide a blueprint of what to think about. Similarly, I know of no formula that can ensure that a teacher will be able to help students broaden, deepen, and enrich their understandings and outlooks. Yet the form itself— that is, the very emphasis on broadening and deepening students' under- standings—helps us recognize when we are talking about teaching, rather than about something else that may go on under that name.

Thus, the sense of tradition does not depend on strict adherence to a particular way of doing things. It extends perception beyond any singular enactment of tradition. *That* we are teachers, not solely *what* we do at a given moment, constitutes part of the equation. The sense of tradition yields insight into, and perhaps even what the poet Wordsworth would call a love for, the opportunity, the privilege, the adventure, and the moral and intellectual responsibility that accompany taking on the mantle of teacher. This standpoint enables teachers to talk productively across what may be perceived as different pedagogical traditions, or as differences about means and ends within the practice. It provides grounds for teachers to learn from one another across differences in institutional setting, in the age level of students, in the subject matter at hand, and so forth. It opens the way to valuable criticism that keeps in view the long-term health of the practice. To recall Cua's (1998) terms, the sense of tradition helps teachers form a community of interpretation as well as a community of hope.

7

Cultivating a Sense of Tradition in Teaching

What you have as heritage
Take now as task;
For thus you will make it your own!
                                    —Goethe

IN THIS CHAPTER, I want to illustrate further the dynamics of a sense of tradition by showing why it differs from knowledge of history, important as that is. The analysis will complement the distinction I made in the previous chapter between cultivating a sense of tradition and adhering to a particular enactment of tradition. I suggested that a person can develop a relationship with the past that differs from mere knowledge of what people have said, thought, and done. The latter posture can lead people to treat the past instrumentally, as a reminder of how things can go awry or succeed, but not as containing questions, insights, and yearnings that may be as important as, or even more so than, how people in the present conceive their concerns and projects. An instrumental view converts the past into a mere encyclopedia. In contrast, the sense of tradition reveals how the past can constitute, metaphorically speaking, a conversational partner in the human quest for understanding, for meaning, and for flourishing.

To make this argument, I examine and contrapose ideas from John Dewey and Hans-Georg Gadamer about how to approach the testimony of the past. I illustrate the argument with an extended look at one scholar/ teacher's engagement with tradition in teaching (Bushnell, 1996). Finally, I shed additional light on how teachers can develop and deepen a sense of tradition in teaching. As the analysis proceeds, I try to provide enough signposts, and commentary, to guide us home to the idea I introduced in the previous chapter: Seeing oneself, when in the role of teacher, as a being in human time, living neither in the present, past, or future alone, but in their continuity.

THE CONVERSATION WITH TRADITION

In his educational writings, Dewey expresses pragmatic doubts about the wisdom of talking about tradition. He does not dismiss the past as a long litany of human folly that is—hurrah!—being overcome in the wonderful present. Dewey is as critical of smug and dogmatic trumpeting of the present as he is of a reactionary embrace of the past. He objects to educational practices that privilege the study of the past or that (worse, in his view) fuel a greater respect or admiration for the past than for the present. Dewey grants that people can benefit from making use of literatures, methods, beliefs, and so forth from the past. However, he argues that "there is an enormous difference between availing ourselves of them as *present* resources and taking them as standards and patterns in their retrospective character" (1916/1997, p. 74). "A knowledge of the past and its heritage," Dewey goes on to say, "is of great significance when it enters into the present, but not otherwise. And the mistake of making the records and remains of the past the main material of education is that it cuts the vital connection of present and past, and tends to make the past a rival of the present and the present a more or less futile imitation of the past" (p. 75).

Only a card-carrying antiquarian would claim that education should focus solely on the past and ignore present circumstances.[1] I have no quarrel with Dewey's pragmatic concerns. However, he does not help teachers when he suggests that the past is "useful" only as it helps people tackle present problems and predicaments. That posture threatens to convert the past, and tradition itself, into mere tools, rather than appreciating them as a source of criticism of the tools we use today and of the ways we use them. By tools, I mean everything from pedagogical methods and curricular materials to the ways teachers organize their classrooms. Dewey's stance can lead, inadvertently, to an instrumental view of the past that drains tradition of its critical power. Such a view emasculates tradition as a standpoint for gaining critical distance from contemporary perceptions, concerns, and aims. It supports the tendency to regard the past as a mere storehouse of lessons we in the present can learn from. In an important sense, history provides just that. But it is one thing to look for lessons in history based on *present* criteria of what will count as a lesson and quite another to learn *from* history what can constitute a lesson in the first place (Mounce, 1973; D. Z. Philips, 1979). The former posture implies that present beliefs, assumptions, and purposes will remain intact, perhaps without being subject to any questioning at all. That result means that the "lessons" derived from the past will merely confirm what people already know and believe. They are not true *lessons*. They do not unsettle, disturb, or challenge present convictions, whether these be dubbed conservative, radical, democratic, liberal, or whatever. They do not assist persons in reconceiving, rediscovering, or reidentifying issues and ideas that might matter.

From the point of view of the practice of teaching, Dewey is right to worry about uncritical adherence to past beliefs and habits. However, to learn *from* history and tradition necessitates treating them as something other than mere tools for laboring at present concerns. To learn from the past requires that persons expose their beliefs and assumptions, however cherished or upright they may seem, to critical scrutiny. This does not mean undermining or destroying those beliefs. The study of past practices, ideas, objects, and events might, in fact, shore them up, but this would be the outcome of thinking, rather than of a nonselfconscious or ideological search for confirmation. Nor does learning from history and tradition imply granting the past moral superiority and deeper wisdom than the present. But it does entail allowing the past a voice, which means denying ourselves automatic moral superiority and keener insight. Such a stance makes possible a conversation with the past rather than, as I pointed out in Chapter 6, a one-sided monologue in which either the past rules as queen or we in the present look down our noses at everything that has gone before. Both of those postures promote intellectual and moral stagnation.[2]

In this light, George Santayana's familiar aphorism about history takes on new meaning. He said that those who cannot remember the past are condemned to repeat it. The "it" could be taken to refer, in part, to stagnant thinking and feeling. If a particular generation fails to let itself be questioned by tradition, its thought and sensibilities may harden, which means its way of life may harden, even as it perceives itself as unusually enlightened or liberated. Alternatively, that generation's practices may become unmoored and its way of life dissipate without a sturdy replacement in view. Thus it will "repeat" what has happened to previous generations, who, inadvertently, brought trouble upon themselves by seeking to remain cocooned within a rigid worldview. Edward Shils (1981) argues that to take away the opportunity to learn from history, or to deny tradition entirely, "confines a person to his own generation" (p. 327). Shils's verb choice aptly captures the danger in treating the present as a sufficient standpoint for thinking about human problems, needs, and prospects.

Present thinking and opinion, if accepted uncritically, oppress genuine questioning, just as does a dogmatic adherence to the past.

Shils's (1958, 1981) work constitutes the most in-depth sociological study of tradition of which I am aware. He examines what he regards as four central features of tradition, some of which we have encountered already. (1) Tradition endures over time, unlike fashions. (2) Every tradition is carried forward and transformed, in part, through the agency of exemplary individuals. For example, Cua (1998) suggests that at the core of the Confucian moral tradition is "the idea of paradigmatic individuals as exemplary embodiments of the spirit and vitality of the tradition" (p. 241). Cua also adds the helpful insight that a tradition persists and animates people because of paradigmatic or exemplary events, scenes, and narratives (a point I return to below). (3) Tradition is an object of ongoing interpretation and dialogue, and thus it is subject to change and modification. Finally, (4) the stock or material of tradition is passed on in selective ways, sometimes as the outcome of specialized debates or inquiries. "The process of tradition," Shils (1981) writes, "is always a process of selection. Parts of the traditional stock drift downward into obscurity so that they are known only to a few people or conceivably to none at all" (p. 26). An example from teaching would be classroom textbooks employed in, say, 1900. Not many educators today know what they contain or are even mindful of their existence. However, textbooks, not to mention a host of other materials with stories behind them, can be found in classrooms everywhere. I will continue to examine aspects of these and other features of tradition throughout this chapter.

Gadamer (1960/1996) elucidates the idea of conversation between past and present. His analysis of tradition sheds helpful light on its critical potential. Where Bloom (1975) addresses tradition and poetry, Gadamer considers the arts more broadly, including poetry, literature, and painting. He examines philosophical writing as well. His fundamental claim is that such works can continue to "speak" today. That is, part of what constitutes them as works of art or philosophy is their capacity to continue to address people in the present. The voices within those works question our beliefs and aims. They illuminate forgotten ideas and possibilities. They point the finger at our various shortcomings. But they also reveal, through their own limitations and character, the distinctiveness of the present, the fact that it is something other than a pale replica of the past.

According to Gadamer's viewpoint, a play by Sophocles, written 2500 years ago, is more than words on printed page. It is more than merely a particular story written by a particular person at a particular time with particular questions and concerns in mind. Thanks to readers who take it up, a Sophoclean drama is a living entity that can genuinely move, disturb, perplex, and capture the imagination of people today. Through a long and elaborate argument, Gadamer seeks to show that a contemporary reader's response to such a drama is a potential *constituent* of that drama as a work of art, that is, as an element of tradition.[3] The drama cuts across differences in time, place, and circumstance, and it "speaks again" in conversation with the present. This means that the play submits itself in turn, metaphorically speaking, to the contemporary reader's questions— for example, about the nature of virtue, or of religious belief, or of justice, or of the best political arrangements, and so forth. For Gadamer, the ideas of tradition and conversation go hand-in-hand.

People can and do treat past works of art and philosophy as lifeless objects. In contrast with Dewey's worry about a slavish devotion to works from the past, people can and do regard them as so many outdated, outmoded curiosities, hardly fit partners for purposes of a genuine conversation. Others stare at or read them through a one-way window formed out of present concerns and aspirations. They pick and choose those aspects that confirm or support their present states of mind, rather than permitting these works to address and question them. Gadamer suggests that these habits result from what he calls human "prejudice," or, more precisely, unexamined prejudice or preconception. People bring to past works of art, literature, and philosophy just what they bring to many of their present projects and relationships: a host of variously harmonizing and conflicting assumptions, aspirations, desires, and more, many of which elude their consciousness. Under such circumstances, it is not surprising that all persons, in one way or another, or at one time or another, find it difficult to be receptive to what is different, including the voice of tradition. "We are always affected," Gadamer (1960/1996) writes, "in hope and fear, by what is nearest to us, and hence we approach the testimony of the past under its influence. Thus it is constantly necessary to guard against overhastily assimilating the past to our own expectations of meaning" (p. 305).

Prejudices are not immutable, and here is where tradition plays its powerful moral role in Gadamer's argument. He shows how the voice of tradition can open the one-way window fashioned by the self. It can bring a person into touch with his or her prejudices and place the person on the road to criticizing and possibly altering them. To expose one's thought and sensibility to a Sophoclean drama, to a classical Japanese rock garden, to a music form from sixteenth-century Jaipur, to a poem by Emily Dickinson can help one engage new ideas and possibilities for human expression and relation. Those ideas and possibilities are not mere echoes of the past. They are not inert or lifeless artifacts of days gone by. They are a dynamic amalgam of what the playwright, sculptor, composer, or poet attempted to do and the questions, concerns, and insight of the contemporary person. For example, Dickinson writes about (among many other human predicaments) the promise and the pain in renouncing present inclinations in favor of something larger. But her ideas spring to life because the reader has taken them seriously, in part by connecting them with his or her own questions, sentiments, and worries about the place of inclination in crafting a life—questions and worries, moreover, the reader may not have hitherto understood, but mostly felt.

The image of a conversation with tradition complements the analysis in the previous chapter. It sheds added light on the meaning of a living tradition, as well as on the influence tradition has on a person in a practice such as poetry or teaching. The image shows how the individual can leave a mark on that very tradition. The conversation with tradition keeps it living and oriented toward human hopes for meaning and flourishing.

How might persons learn to expose their thought to questions from tradition? Why might they pick up a poem by Emily Dickinson or contemplate a classical Japanese rock garden in the first place? Teachers can play a central role in introducing others to the voice of tradition, a process that fuels their own engagement with it. For example, Oakeshott (1989) examines how teachers can initiate students into what he calls "inheritances" and "achievements" of humanity (pp. 22, 29–30, 41). As I pointed out in previous chapters, he also calls these inheritances "languages"—art, science, literature, history, and more—in which human beings have sought to understand themselves. To enter these languages is to enter a field of human possibilities, one characterized by questions of meaning, purpose, and value rather than by prefabricated answers or dogmatic conclusions.

Yael Shalem (1999) argues that this process of initiation and criticism—that is, of conversing with tradition—obliges the teacher to regulate an environment for teaching and learning, a topic I examined in Chapters 4 and 5. She focuses on curricular and instructional design, an ongoing dynamic that she dubs "epistemological labor." Those terms highlight, in part, the teacher's efforts to engage students, through thoughtfully planned activities, with knowledge and understandings for which they may not have language—that is, prior to their exposure to tradition. Shalem argues that such efforts help students come to grips with tradition as incarnated in whatever subject is under study. "Through this epistemological labor," she writes, "a teacher provides a path for the learner to enter into the tradition, to attend to its language and use it to criticize and extend its achievements" (p. 68). The teacher selects works from the tradition—readings, paintings, experiments, many other kinds of objects—and assists students both in studying them and in reflecting on the questions this process can spark. For example, I owe my interest in Dewey's view of education to several teachers I have had, as well as to work on Dewey that I continue to read. Through their curricular and instructional efforts, my teachers provided me an entry to Dewey's thought. They opened a door to the kinds of problems and concerns he sought to address and to ways of appreciating the questions that studying his work can generate. The interest they triggered has led to a conversation on my own part with tradition, as embodied in Dewey's arguments and my responses to them. I have shared some of the outcome of that encounter in this book.

Teachers can shape conditions in the classroom that fuel thinking, questioning, and wonder. One of those conditions is the voice of tradition, as represented in the various subjects, themes, and texts in the curriculum. Teachers can engage that voice with the voices of their students by helping students approach the material with thought and care. In the process, teachers can help students appreciate that there are ideas, insights, understandings, emotions, and hopes that exceed what they may have thought possible, accessible, or even capable of being articulated in the first place. That outcome can position students to raise questions about those very ideas, insights, and understandings, questions that might lead to even broader horizons. To recall the terms I used previously, teachers can help students experience genuine lessons—genuine encounters with human achievements and strivings that potentially transform their self-understanding, their knowledge, and how they regard the world with its varied people, objects, and events. Much of this process may be indirect. It may take place quietly, without fanfare, without falling under a spotlight. It will take place over time, and it will often be subtle and unpredictable.

Teachers can prepare themselves intellectually and morally for this work by developing a sense of tradition. They learn about the terms of the practice from their precursors and peers, and from a broad variety of related sources (more on this below). That process can uncover their deepest presumptions about what the work entails and why a person would take it up. At the same time, the process can position teachers to extend, in a critical spirit, the boundaries of the practice. They can reply to tradition in a way that harmonizes their hopes to be of service, in their own distinctive ways, with the obligations inherent in the work. To recall the epigram from Goethe that heads this chapter, "tradition, or what is handed down from the past, confronts us as a *task*, as an effort of understanding we feel ourselves required to make because we recognize our limitations, even though no one compels us to do so. It precludes complacency, passivity, and self-satisfaction with what we securely possess; instead it requires active questioning and self-questioning" (Gadamer, 1960/1996, p. xvi, translators' introduction).

ENGAGING THE VOICE OF TRADITION

In this section, I examine Rebecca Bushnell's study of sixteenth- and early seventeenth-century educational practice in England. Her book is entitled *A Culture of Teaching: Early Modern Humanism in Theory and Practice* (1996). I focus on the book because, although not its avowed purpose, it both illustrates and exemplifies what it means to engage tradition and, in so doing, to cultivate a sense of tradition with respect to education. Bushnell's themes, and her telling remarks on what she learned from undertaking her historical expedition, reveal the vitalizing quality of tradition in teaching. Her inquiry also demonstrates how a person can learn to criticize tradition productively and thereby keep it alive and fruitful for human flourishing.

In simplified terms, humanism as a historical phenomenon conceives humanity as something more, or at least other than, merely a natural or divine entity or creation. Humanism seeks to realize the distinctively human contribution (presuming there is such) to our experience. According to Bushnell, humanism took form, in sixteenth-century England, in the growing interest in teaching the arts of writing and speaking, in reading texts through a historical rather than solely logical lens, and in the close study of ancient Greek and Roman texts (e.g., Plato, Aristotle, Cicero). Those texts were rediscovered throughout much of Europe during that time. Their strong humanistic impulse deeply affected Renaissance art, scholarship, and education.[4]

Through a careful, nuanced analysis, Bushnell (1996) reveals the tensions, the accomplishments, the failures, and the ambiguities that characterized humanist pedagogy at the time. She draws analogies and correspondences with present educational concerns and dilemmas. For example, humanist thinkers and teachers fretted about the status of teachers, whose reputation had risen and fallen (sometimes sharply) during the previous centuries (p. 37). They struggled to shape a substantial and livable notion of teacher authority in the classroom, ever mindful that teachers differ from parents and from acknowledged political or religious authorities. Humanist teachers' authority, Bushnell writes, was "moral rather than inherited." But their power was "circumscribed," in part, by continued ambiguity about what the concept "moral" encompassed with respect to teaching (p. 44). Bushnell shows how these teachers were often "caught in a web of contradictions: like a father and opposed to the father's rule, a monarch in the classroom yet feared as a tyrant, a lover who holds the instrument of pain [the birch used for beatings], a master who is also, in many cases, a servant of the family and the state" (p. 44).

Bushnell examines how humanist educators debated questions of instructional method, whether corporal punishment was legitimate, when to introduce particular academic lessons to the young, how to decide what to teach (a problem created, in part, by the explosion of printing at the time), and whether their mission was to socialize youth into accepted thought or to cultivate truly independent thinkers. Echoing current calls for safe schools and classrooms, some humanist writers urged educators to create "a sanctuary against fear" and "a space of the conscience" in which teachers and students could resist, or at least not just replicate, current social and political mores and ideologies (pp. 43, 44). Like educators today, humanist thinkers and teachers sometimes doubted the efficacy of education, worrying whether political realities rendered "the master free only if he stayed in his schoolroom, [and] the child free only to emulate him there" (p. 72). Bushnell also points out that most formal education was restricted to boys and men, and she documents views and actions that would be criticized today as blatantly sexist. At the same time, she shows that there was serious discussion of girls' and women's education and that occasional provision was made for them, sometimes in the face of established societal mores.

Humanist thinkers wrestled with tradition itself, embodied both in approaches to pedagogy that preceded them (e.g., scholasticism) and in previous forms of the arts they taught (Bushnell attends especially to poetry). They struggled with tensions between imitation and creativity. They went back and forth about the roles of nature and nurture in the development of human beings. Bushnell shows how educational debates became saturated with the languages and images of gardening that also emerged at the time. "When a teacher was compared with a gardener," Bushnell writes,

> it could mean many things ranging from violent mastery to tender regard; similarly, a student was imagined in different ways when compared with a seed, a plant, or soil. On the one hand, such comparisons suggested that the teacher/gardener could plan and cultivate the pupil's mental garden for greater profit. On the other hand, such analogies also conveyed resistance on the child's part, for they granted the child a specific property or nature that the teacher/gardener could not alter. (pp. 75–76)

Bushnell argues that below the surface of these energetic debates reside "two of the most familiar—and potentially conflicting—premises attributed to humanist educational theory: that there is an essential human nature and that each person is particular, with different inclinations or propensities that defy generalization" (p. 102). She rightly suggests that the question of the universal and the particular continues to preoccupy educational thought and practice today, surfacing in everything from debates over multiculturalism, to disagreements about the "canon," to worries about the nature of teacher authority, and more. In these and other ways, Bushnell demonstrates that many of the humanists' concerns and dilemmas prefigure contemporary educational life.

Given the generally ahistorical nature of much current educational theory and practice, Bushnell's project merits attention simply because of its respect for historical origins and precedents. In this light, her work complements the efforts of scholars in the field of educational foundations, especially educational history. But studying educational foundations and history is not a synonym for cultivating a sense of tradition, even though the former can fuel the latter. *An awareness of the past does not, by itself, imply or generate a sense of tradition.* A person must come to grips *with* tradition in order to begin the process of developing a sense *of* tradition. There is a personal dimension involved in this endeavor that cannot be replicated, at least not in precise terms, by another person. Just as no two poets respond to tradition in identical ways, so no two teachers can duplicate each other's odyssey into the practice.

Bushnell's study illuminates these claims. I turn now to her own comments on her project. In them, we witness a scholar/teacher working through her own prejudices as she engages tradition and emerging a different and, in her own eyes, a wiser person. Her experience also attests to the development of a sense of tradition, about which I still have more to say.

Bushnell writes that her orientation toward early modern humanism may itself be humanist (p. 17). But it is not traditionalist, in the sense of dogmatically embracing the views and practices she unearths. She explicitly distances her project from those of conservative thinkers who are either described as "humanists" by some critics or who may characterize themselves with the term. At the same time, Bushnell's posture does not entail a break from the past, nor a search for a standpoint that resides above or beyond it. She resists looking at past or present pedagogies "in terms of a Foucauldian saturation of disciplinary power" (p. 17). According to that perspective, persons and institutions take form and evolve, in part, through responses to what Foucault called "power." No person and no institution holds the reins of power. In Foucault's analysis, power holds the reins on them, in inexorable if not necessarily direct or fixed ways. Educational practice becomes, in part, a matter of constant "surveillance"—of students by teachers (and perhaps by one another) and of teachers by more powerful bureaucratic or political authorities who are in turn under the surveillance of others.

Bushnell replies to this viewpoint by showing that early modern pedagogy was more unsteady "politically, socially, and emotionally" than a Foucauldian perspective allows (p. 18). She discovered that humanist education embodied "unstable terms of rule, control, and autonomy" (p. 181). Rather than clean lines of practice and theory, Bushnell found paradox, ambiguity, deep frustration, and yet also significant innovation and creativity. Early humanists struggled with freedom and control in educational work: "[J]ust as they asked how the poet was free when both a servant to tradition and a master of invention, they also wondered how the student was to be fashioned as 'free' when the teacher was his master and servant, father and mother" (p. 182). "I would never deny," Bushnell emphasizes,

> that the early modern humanist teacher could be boring, brutal, or a fatal combination of both, whether in the town grammar school or the royal nursery. But I have tried to see the other side of humanist pedagogical theory and practice: an insistence on play, pleasure, and kindness, a respect for the child's nature, and an admiration of variety and range in reading, struggling against a will to control, a love of purity, and a belief in hierarchy and exclusivity. (p. 18)

How did Bushnell learn "to see the other side" in the first place? She writes of trying to identify and to take seriously "the best instincts" (p. 17) of early humanist educators. The flip side of that endeavor, she shows, is understanding their worst instincts as well. At the same time, she found it necessary to learn "to understand the humanists' failures sympathetically" (p. 18). This did not mean reading the past in a deliberately favorable manner. Quite on the contrary. As I understand the process, it meant letting the past speak on its own terms to her. She learned to heed the past as much as to read it. Phrased differently, she found that reading the past became a moral endeavor, as she sought to listen to the humanists without distorting their voices. For Bushnell, the task involved attending to the extremes as much as to the typical or the average, to the ways in which early modern education was constraining or liberating, fixed or varied in scope, hardened or supple in form and method (p. 19). "As I read, I encountered the remarkable contradictions and paradoxes often noted as characteristic of Tudor rhetoric: before my eyes, the pedagogical texts oscillated between play and work, freedom and control, submission and mastery" (p. 17). In technical terms, Bushnell steered clear of both traditionalist apologies for past viewpoints and presentist interpretive frameworks that have already, so to speak, put the past in its place.

Bushnell examines early humanist educational practices while acutely mindful of her own and those of her peers in the contemporary educational world. She describes the humanism by which she has learned to guide her work. It is, she tells us, based

> on the belief that people are largely responsible for what happens on this earth; committed to tolerance, attention to the differences among people and the need to treat them with equal respect; shaped by a cheerful acceptance of ambivalence and contradiction; and informed by an almost painful historical consciousness, which sees the past as estranged yet able to illuminate present concerns. (p. 17)

Bushnell's word choice of differences "among" people rather than between them strikes me as telling. In the language I employed in Chapter 2, to speak of differences among people is already to grant them personhood. It is already to say: We are here together, and in one way or another we have to make our way "with equal respect," as Bushnell has come to put it. Differences "between" people, on the other hand, can imply an a priori divide, with persons on one side and those who are rejected as persons on the other. The word choice becomes a significant one for educators. The contrast becomes another lesson to draw from Bushnell's engagement with tradition.

Bushnell describes the terms above as "the values *I learned from and brought to* my reading" (p. 17; emphasis added). I underscore her way of posing the matter because it attests to what Gadamer describes as the conversation with tradition. Bushnell has worked her way through, beyond, and yet also more deeply into her notions of past and present education. Her sustained encounter with early humanist educators has provided her greater clarity about her own educational views, even while shifting those views. That process has deepened her understanding of the current climate of educational debate. It has done so, in part, by quickening her interest in, and what I would call her care for, what is at issue in that debate. She can discern its orienting assumptions better than before. "I have found in writing this book," she concludes, that "we may come to respect again how, at their best, the humanists taught readers to see the power of words to make things happen, not just to represent the world. They may also teach us today to understand better how all texts are tied fast to both the past and the present, ever evolving and yet always rooted in their social uses and transformations" (p. 202). Bushnell succeeds in bringing the voices of past and present into productive dialogue, in such a way that neither has remained the same. And nor has she. It may sound paradoxical to suggest, as she seems to, that one can become clearer, and even more sure, about the realities of paradox, ambiguity, and complexity in a practice like teaching. But Bushnell's response to tradition shows that this outcome may accompany any serious attempt to question the past and to permit oneself to be questioned by it in turn.

READING THE PEDAGOGICAL PAST AND PRESENT

When Bushnell (1996) writes of feeling an "almost painful historical consciousness" (p. 17), I interpret this to mean that she perceives herself as having become more mindful of a continuity—however disharmonious it may sometimes feel—between her precursors and her own stance as an educator today. Her experience suggests that there is nothing sentimental about the sense of tradition, however tempted one might be to gild it in high-sounding phrases. The sense of tradition strengthens and sustains a person's commitment to a practice. But it does so by leading the person to examine and to question, in a philosophical spirit, the terms of that very practice. This questioning respects those who came before, and it helps keep the tradition alive for those who will come after.

I want now to touch on ways in which teachers and teacher candidates can carry on the task of cultivating a sense of tradition. These are not, however, ways in which they can complete the task. The notion of completion, as if it were a matter of earning a license or mastering a technique, is out of place here. As we have seen, the sense of tradition constitutes something other than historical awareness and knowledge per se. It comprises a sensibility or feeling for the sheer facts of human existence, continuity, and change, as expressed and sustained through a practice such as teaching. Cultivating a sense of tradition implies a fundamentally transformative process, not one of simply accumulating information about teaching. In Oakeshott's (1989) evocative language: "A 'picture' may be purchased, but one cannot purchase an understanding of it" (p. 45). Teachers and teacher candidates cannot buy an understanding of teaching. They cannot purchase insight into why the persons they are constitute the most important factor in whatever success they are destined to achieve in the classroom. To cite Oakeshott again: the "ancient Greek exhortation, Know Thyself, meant *learn* to know thyself. It was not an exhortation to buy a book on psychology and study it" (p. 28). Instead, Oakeshott argues, to know oneself means contemplating what people, both in the past and in the present, have made of the "engagement" (p. 28) of cultivating personhood.

This undertaking cannot be scripted, forced, or replicated by others. The process calls on teachers and teacher candidates to be responsive and critical. It can involve abandoning comfortable ideas about teaching, just as it can mean taking aboard counterintuitive insights. The sense of tradition emerges, metaphorically speaking, as a teacher lets him- or herself become freely obedient to the terms of teaching. To be "freely obedient" may sound like an oxymoron. But the idea captures the fact that accepting the terms of teaching creates an opportunity for a person to have a positive influence on students in the first place. In turn, the person can bring those terms alive in a distinctive manner, serving students' flourishing and fueling his or her own sense of fulfillment and meaning.

The sources for developing a sense of tradition in teaching include studying historical precursors as well as commentaries on their endeavors, plunging oneself into recollections by and about contemporary teachers, examining historical inquiries into teaching as it has evolved in recent centuries, and investigating the empirical research literature on teaching. The common denominator in engaging these sources is a blend of listening to and questioning the voice of tradition. To read the testimony of one's precursors in this manner, or to read about them, takes the shape of a quest for meaning. It does not involve asking, How can we explain or categorize what other teachers did? Rather, it involves asking, Should *I* teach as they did, or in the spirit which they embody? Is it possible, and desirable that I follow their example? How can I follow when I feel I must make my own way? How did they make their own way? What should I learn from their example, and how can I learn from it?[5]

These questions are as much about oneself as they are about precursors. They address teachers and teacher candidates. They ask them to think about their motivation and their ability to teach, about their willingness to take the necessary steps to learn how to perform well. The questions draw teachers or would-be teachers into the practice, while also positioning them to undertake the infinitely rewarding task of developing their own styles and signatures. This process involves thinking about concepts and meanings in teaching systematically, just as experienced teachers learn to think about the classroom events of the day or week systematically. If not in so many words, this kind of thinking has been characteristic of the practice of teaching since its inception. To paraphrase Jonathan Lear (1998, p. 8), such an outlook is "open minded." The outlook opens a window, for the teacher or teacher candidate, on what it means to learn to live nondefensively with the questions of how to teach and of how well one is actually doing at any given time.

Let me illustrate the sources I have mentioned by looking briefly at the first category, historical precursors. A familiar place to begin is with figures such as Socrates and Confucius. They lived at almost the same time: Socrates in Greece (469–399 B.C.E.) and Confucius in China (551–479 B.C.E.). Their historical and cultural contexts differed a great deal. Nonetheless, to observe either person in action, as portrayed, respectively, in Plato's dialogues (e.g., *Gorgias, Meno, Phaedo, Protagoras*) and in Confucius's *Analects*, is to witness the genesis of one of the most compelling features of teaching: its capacity, in the midst of human interaction and dialogue, to raise questions and describe possibilities for human expression and growth. Socrates and Confucius complement one another in instructive ways. For example, Socrates often appears to be breaking with religious, cultural, and moral traditions, sometimes sharply so. Confucius, on the other hand, appears to esteem tradition—for example, in the form of *dao* (the Way) or of *li* (ritual). However, listening to their words makes it plain that both figures are challenging what I have described as traditionalism. They neither reject nor embrace, uncritically, the voice of the past, of which they are acutely (and at times painfully) conscious. At the same time, both figures dramatize the moral risks of taking present thought and custom as the sole, much less infallible, source of wisdom and guidance.

Posed in other terms, at first glance the ability of Socrates and Confucius to question and to examine the taken-for-granted seems to pop out of nowhere. Why were they able to do this? How could they guide others, and themselves, beyond a sea of social mores and expectations, even while honoring the place of custom and ceremony? The answer, in part, is that they had precursors in Greece, China, and elsewhere. They did not start from scratch. People before them had begun to articulate something other than a purely traditionalist reaction to human concerns and questions. Nonetheless, they are among the very first human beings we know about who illuminate the power and the potential of teaching as a practice. Perhaps because of their originality, it is no surprise that their example has been subject to caricature and manipulation since they first came upon the scene. This aspect of their fate mirrors the challenge every serious-minded teacher on the globe has had to confront in one way or another: How to hold true to the terms of the practice, while also responding in a reasoned way to pressures that would render the teacher into an instrument of ends conceived apart from the work of education. To study precursors in the light of such issues and questions converts teacher education into something quite different from socialization into an occupation. Instead, such study makes it possible to enter and to take hold of an historically vital practice.

I do not think it possible to cultivate a sense of tradition without engaging seriously works from the past (cf. Higgins, 1998; Proefriedt, 1994). Gadamer (1960/1996), Oakeshott (1989), Shils (1981), and others argue that to read works solely of the present can, in effect, confine one to the always partial, and sometimes short-sighted, outlooks characteristic of any present moment. Such reading can constitute a form of socialization into what may prove to be merely a fashionable point of view. This caution echoes, although it does not imply invoking, the so-called hundred-year rule familiar in the humanities (cf. Shattuck, 1999, p. 4), according to which no work younger than a hundred years old should be in a common core of reading (as contrasted with elective courses of reading). That rule emerged because of a predicament Gadamer (1960/1996) describes as follows:

> Everyone is familiar with the curious impotence of our judgment where temporal distance has not given us sure criteria. Thus the judgment of contemporary works of art is desperately uncertain for the scholarly consciousness. Obviously we approach such creations with unverifiable prejudices, presuppositions that have too great an influence over us for us to know about them; these can give contemporary creations an extra resonance that does not correspond to their true content and significance. (p. 297)

Gadamer does not intend to slap us on the hand for feeling passionate about contemporary works. Quite on the contrary. He is after an important truth, that "to acquire a horizon [of critical understanding] means that one learns to look beyond what is close at hand—not in order to look away from it but to see it better, within a larger whole and in truer proportion" (p. 306).

Plato's dialogues and the writings of Confucius, among many others, can be described as time-honored not because some authoritative body has declared them to be so but because, as Gadamer puts it, the "duration" of their "power to speak directly is fundamentally unlimited" (p. 290; cf. Broudy, 1963). To be sure, any worthwhile text on education from the past is bound to contain particular claims and perspectives educators today would contest. I can think of no rationale, for instance, for adhering to what Aristotle has to say about non-Greeks, slaves, and women. All past works reflect past conditions and beliefs. But they are also something other than mummified remnants of a politically inferior world. They constitute vivid, original sources for deepening a sense of tradition. As Amelie Rorty (1998) points out: "Because we are the inheritors of the history of conceptions of the proper aims and directions of education, that history remains actively embedded and expressed in our beliefs and practices. It provides the clearest understanding of the issues that presently concern and divide us" (p. 2). For example, Aristotle's dynamic analysis of educating human virtue and practical wisdom (in his *Nicoma-chean Ethics*, fifth century B.C.E.) has as much resonance today as any outlook on the moral dimensions of teaching of which I am aware. Aristotle and other pioneering writers on education attempt to move beyond precursors, while also retaining a sense of continuity with their concerns and yearnings. They endeavor to articulate ideas about human possibility and how education can advance them. Any teacher or would-be teacher who takes such texts in hand, and who seeks to "hear" their voice, will discover a source of self-criticism and of criticism of contemporary claims about what teachers should be doing.

They will also discover that that voice is not univocal, a fact that Bushnell (1996), as we have seen, tellingly demonstrates. Rather, the voice of tradition features what Pocock (1968) calls "conflict and contradiction." Teachers in all eras, in all places, have sometimes found themselves torn in different directions, caught in "existential dilemmas of self-determination and self-definition" (p. 217). "A tradition may be a turbid stream to swim in," Pocock emphasizes, "full of backwaters, cross-currents and snags" (p. 217). As we have also observed, however, these very features differentiate tradition from traditionalism. In sum, the kind of reading I have touched on here can provide teachers a feel for the continuity, the innovation, the challenge, and the questioning that have been embedded in the practice of teaching since its very beginnings.

As with these time-honored works, teachers and would-be teachers will find that contemporary accounts written by and about their peers, empirical research, historical studies, and philosophical inquiries into teaching all can raise questions and shed insight on the practice. The works highlight what makes teaching both a distinctive and a difficult endeavor to undertake. John Olson (1992) captures the potential of such work: "Outstanding practice ought to be studied and its documents made into the kind of history which would serve the building of a tradition reflecting the moral basis of practice" (p. 95).

These readings show why we can speak of continuity in the practice of teaching over time, not for all teachers, to be sure, and not for any individual teacher all of the time. The conduct of much teaching in the United States and elsewhere has been in the form of an occupation, job, or function, not of a practice or calling. Moreover, many teachers both today and in the past have been weak, poorly prepared, or uncaring. But to judge from the literature outlined here, there are and have been numberless teachers, most of them unextraordinary and unheroic, who have not abandoned their own agency. These teachers have stayed off the bandwagons and have resisted sacrificing, in the name of expediency or short-term goals, the moral and intellectual meanings in the work. Their generally quiet and steady efforts have kept the practice dynamic and in motion through time.

If approached in a questing spirit, the kind of works I have touched on will, as I have emphasized, address teachers and would-be teachers. The readings will ask them to look within and to ponder their motivation and their abilities, and to look without and to ponder the terms of the practice. This productive conversation with tradition in teaching can be career-long. It can steadily deepen and enrich one's sense of tradition. It can help fashion habits of both self-scrutiny and the critical analysis of public claims about teaching. This undertaking complements ideas I mentioned previously, such as thinking about one's own teachers and talking systematically with peers.

The quest also presumes the main event: namely, that one is a teacher, or is on the road to becoming one. Whether with small children, with adults, or with age groups in between, teaching is what draws a person into the practice. Teaching brings one face to face with the challenges and the opportunities that precursors engaged and have made available. Teaching renders concrete the claims one hears about the positive influence a teacher can have on students. Teaching forces a person to respond to the terms of the work. He or she has to plan, organize, think, speak, listen, pay attention, judge, and do all of these things in ways that broaden, deepen, and enhance students' knowledge, understandings, and outlooks. The readings I have described, conversation with others about them, and criticism of the practice itself can shed continual light on the significance of the work one is undertaking with students.

CONCLUSION: THE SENSE OF TRADITION
AS A SOURCE OF GUIDANCE

> So show him
> something simple which, formed over generations,
> lives as our own, near our hand and within our gaze.
> —Rilke, *Duino Elegies*

In a recent inquiry into the question of whether there is knowledge people should deny themselves, Roger Shattuck (1996) concludes with a call for balance. He reveals the dangers of an unbridled and ethically unconstrained pursuit of knowledge, while also esteeming the often legitimate and necessary need to know. He urges people to cultivate moral wisdom in order to learn to tell the difference between the two impetuses—and even just to recognize their sheer existence. He concludes with a broad word of counsel:

> We need to be faithful to our traditions and our knowledge, to our community and our history. And we also need to be able to respond with guarded flexibility and understanding to challenges to those traditions and that knowledge. To discharge that double duty without fanaticism while firmly maintaining a set of scruples based on reason and experience forms the challenge of an entire lifetime. How can we be faithful and unfaithful at the same time? Over and over again in the tiny decisions of everyday life, we must do just that at every level of action and reflection, through every fluctuation of doubt and faith. (pp. 336–337)

Sustaining a sense of tradition is a project of an entire career. It takes form and it finds expression "over and over again," to use Shattuck's words, throughout the course of one's work in a practice. It spurs a person to be "faithful" to the terms of the practice but "unfaithful" in the sense of criticizing those terms to keep them vital and attuned to concrete human realities. This perspective dramatizes the distinction between traditionalism and a sense of tradition. Traditionalism insists upon unquestioned obedience to past customs and beliefs, while the sense of tradition rejects unquestioned obedience to present customs and beliefs. The sense of tradition makes it possible to learn from past efforts—to learn genuine lessons, as I have posed the matter—while also addressing present concerns and problems. It constitutes something richer and more personal than historical knowledge per se, significant as that is. The sense of tradition embodies a feeling for human time and for human aspirations that span the generations.

I have argued that a sense of tradition offers teachers a standpoint that provides critical distance from both past and present—from both what they have learned about the practice and from what others are telling them comprises the work. The sense of tradition fuels the power to abstract from immediate demands and activities. This notion does not mean sidestepping those activities and demands, but rather placing them against a broader backdrop. Nor does it imply aloofness from students. On the contrary, a sense of tradition helps the teacher retain an educational relationship with students. It provides a source of judgment and an enduring wellspring of remembrance that teaching means serving human flourishing. In an always delicate and unpredictable way, a teacher needs both closeness to and distance from students in order to serve *as* a teacher. Simon Schama (1996) helps captures this point when he observes that "a dispassionate eye is the condition of a compassionate intelligence" (p. 98).

We might say that a teacher and his or her students should be moving closer and closer *apart* and that they should be moving farther and farther *together*.[6] As a teacher listens to students, reads their work, solves problems with them, and leads them in discussion, he or she learns that students think in distinctive ways about the issues, problems, and possibilities in a subject. Ideally, students are themselves becoming mindful of the very same fact. Consequently, teacher and students are, in a manner of speaking, moving closer to one another because they are learning about one another's ways of thinking and acting. But they move closer and closer "apart," in a crucial moral and intellectual sense, precisely because they discern each other's distinctiveness and individuality. And yet, at the same time, they move farther and farther "together" into a subject, into a realm of questions, ideas, issues, ways of reading, speaking, seeing, writing, thinking, feeling, and more.

Teachers also move closer and closer apart, and farther and farther together, as members of a shared practice. I have sought to show in these chapters that a sense of tradition can help teachers appreciate that their work has meaning in its own right, rather than solely because it is a socially sanctioned activity or because it leads to socially approved outcomes. That sense can help all who teach regard their interaction with students as what might be called a scene of learning (cf. Oakeshott, 1989). It can assist teachers in deflecting the pressure to instrumentalize what they do, to see it all as merely a scene of preparation for something else that is no concern of theirs. Moreover, the sense of tradition can help teachers appreciate that the work has its distinctive features that are neither idiosyncratic nor discretionary. In metaphorical terms, the practice and its tradition choose teachers to join it, rather than the other way around. The practice embodies a voice that can question and enlighten all who teach about what the work entails, a voice that can be discerned the moment one begins to take seriously the efforts of precursors. But it is not a voice to heed uncritically. The practice and its tradition can prosper only if teachers learn to reach beyond the ocean of teaching that precedes and surrounds them. Every serious-minded teacher can make this effort, and, in so doing, can affect the shape of the practice and how its tradition will influence those who come after. The sense of tradition in teaching points the way to thoughtful continuity and change among past, present, and future.

⚜ 8 ⚜

The Place of Ideals in Teaching

*I am very glad that I have ideals without knowing
it, and even see them with my eyes.*

—Goethe

*How can there ever be an experience that conforms
to an ideal? For the distinctive thing about an ideal
is that no experience can ever agree with it.*

—Schiller

Do IDEALS AND IDEALISM have a role to play in teaching? Two quick
answers come to mind. The first is that they have no place, or at most a
very limited place. According to this line of thinking, teaching is a well-
defined occupation with well-defined goals. Our romantic impulses may
tell us otherwise. They may lead us to envision teachers as artists and as
transformers of the human spirit. However, a critic might argue, teaching
is not an artistic endeavor because teachers are not artists, save from the
point of view of method and even then only in a metaphorical sense.
Unlike painters at their easels, teachers cannot create whatever they wish
in the classroom. They are public servants beholden to the public to get
a particular job done. Idealism is warranted as a source of motivation,
but teachers' vision had better not take them away from the job itself.
According to this point of view, the only ideal teachers should hold is,
ideally, that of fulfilling their publicly defined obligations in a responsible
and effective manner.

The second answer advances the opposite position. Teachers must
have ideals, and their ideals must reach beyond mere social expectation.
According to this argument, teachers are not bureaucratic hired hands

whose only charge is to pass on to the young whatever knowledge and skills the powers that be have sanctioned. Teachers do play an important role in socializing students into expected custom and practice. However, as teachers, rather than as mere socializers, they also help equip students to think for themselves, to conceive their own ideals and hopes, and to prepare themselves for the task of making tomorrow's world into something other than a tired copy of today's.

Both answers contain truth. Teaching is not an empty cell to be filled in any fashion one wishes. The individual who occupies the role does not own teaching as if it were a possession that can be manipulated to suit personal taste. It is one thing to paint one's own canvases. It is another thing to paint, metaphorically speaking, with the hearts and minds of other people's children. Teachers have publicly defined tasks, ranging from teaching knowledge to treating students with respect. They must uphold these if they are to deserve the right to remain in the classroom.

However, teaching is also more complicated and more important than occupational language alone can capture. Teaching comprises more than a series of discrete tasks whose content and presentation can be prefabricated. Teaching is a moral and intellectual practice whose outcomes cannot just be punched in, at least if we associate teaching with education rather than with a narrow version of training. Moreover, to the extent that teachers exercise autonomy and initiative, their individuality comes to the fore. Issues addressed in previous chapters—person, conduct, and moral sensibility, crafting an environment for teaching and learning, developing a sense of tradition—all point to the ideals and attitudes teachers can bring to their work.

Neither of our initial answers to the question about ideals in teaching is sufficient. Moreover, both answers polarize functional and moral aspects of teaching that, in the final analysis, need to be brought into a working accord. In this concluding chapter, I propose to search for such an accord by taking a different route in thinking about ideals in teaching. Ideals figure importantly in teaching, or so I will argue, but they are ideals of character or personhood as much as they are ideals of educational purpose.

THE PROMISE AND PERILS OF IDEALS

An ideal differs from what falls under the familiar names *goal, purpose,* and *aim*. An ideal also differs from what falls under the names *intention, desire, aspiration,* and *hope*. For example, my goal or purpose might be to earn a degree, to travel somewhere in the world, or to get married. In principle, I could achieve all these aims, as have millions of other people. My intention might be to go to the store this afternoon to ensure that we have dinner on the table tonight. My desire might be to see a student overcome his or her lack of confidence and succeed in the class project. My aspiration might be to plant a garden this year. My hope might be to play a season of basketball without incurring an injury. As with the examples of goals or aims, I can realize all these intentions, desires, aspirations, and hopes, not to mention an uncountable number of others that are part of human life.

However, an ideal connotes something that is either unattainable or, at the very least, not easily attained. A teacher's ideal might be to craft a classroom environment in which every child learns and comes to enjoy learning. An athlete's ideal might be to play the perfect game. An artist's ideal might be to capture down to the finest detail the beauty in a natural scene. A community's ideal might be to bring about conditions in which all its members are healthy and happy. These hopes differ from the usual run of goals, aims, intentions, and aspirations that occupy people in the course of everyday life. Ideals tend to be broader in scope, deeper in meaning, and more demanding (or even awesome, in the original sense of that word) in both the time and the effort entailed in reaching them. Moreover, ideals may be hard to describe, characterize, or pin down, in part because they describe that which has not yet come into being. Dorothy Emmet (1979) suggests that ideals are "transcendental," by which she means something that "is not fully exemplified in experience, and where it is not possible to specify just what it would be like to exemplify it fully" (p. 16).

For these reasons, many people conceive and use the term *ideal* differently than they do terms such as *goals* and *desires*. For example, an ideal can become a measuring rod or standpoint for evaluating present circumstances. The athlete whose ideal is to play a perfect game knows that it cannot really be done. However, the athlete can use the ideal as motivation to intensify his or her training regime. The artist understands that perfecting every detail on the canvas is beyond his or her capability. Nonetheless, the ideal guides the artist's vision and technique, making them richer than they would otherwise be. The community in search of universal happiness appreciates how elusive is such an ideal. Nonetheless, the community can employ the ideal as a source of inspiration and purpose. The sheer act of articulating the ideal can help its members take heart and move forward. The teacher whose ideal is for all students to learn, and to enjoy learning, may not need a tap on her shoulder to remind her of how challenging, or perhaps impossible, the ideal is to realize. The teacher relies on the ideal to strengthen and to broaden her pedagogical efforts. The ideal helps the teacher identify short-term goals and aims. It provides a wellspring, or source of inspiration, for choosing specific instructional activities and curricular materials—those that will help her, in her view, move closer toward realizing the ideal of universal student learning in her classroom.

In sum, ideals point to territory beyond the familiar, the known, the previously attainable. They embody possibilities that the human imagination can generate. Even though they may be out of reach, ideals can provide a source of guidance and courage. They help persons become active rather than merely reactive to life's vicissitudes. To recall the discussion in Chapters 4 and 5, ideals provide a spur to people to design, regulate, or control their environment, rather than leave matters up to chance or unexamined custom.

However, some critics would argue that ideals should have only a limited place in practices such as teaching. They would base their argument not on the occupational language we heard at the start of the chapter. On the contrary, they might agree that such language cannot capture the intensely personal and moral nature of teaching. Their claim would be that ideals are inherently problematic, especially when carried from an individual to a group level. Critics would emphasize two concerns: (1) the power of ideals to develop a momentum of their own and (2) their propensity to lead people to substitute hypothetical goals for real possibilities.

For critics in this camp, the fact that ideals can propel people to action is the very reason to be cautious in how we handle and respond to them. Ideals can inspire people on the basis of passion rather than of careful foresight. Phrased differently, ideals can override reason. The emotion and energy they trigger can substitute for a prudent, but determined, desire to improve conditions. According to this argument, people do not need to be inspired to act beneficently, as if they were like bulls in need of a red flag. Instead, human beings need and deserve an education in thoughtfulness. Ideals grow abundantly and easily—it is not hard to latch onto one, critics might point out—but thought requires nurturance, care, patience, and commitment. Thought helps us identify and differentiate ideals that are worthy and that can enhance the human prospect from those that might lead to harm. Passion alone cannot perform these tasks. Passion can produce evil just as much as it can goodness. History shows what can happen if an ideal embodies injustice in its very form and content. Moreover, people have been "idealistic" or have cited ideals to excuse harmful treatment of others (cf. Taylor, 1989, pp. 518–519). Consequently, critics argue, ideals should not be uncaged without prior thought. Otherwise, they might operate uncritically on the human mind and imagination.

This concern gives rise to a second worry about ideals. People can end up treating ideals as more important than actual human beings. In other words, people might come to prefer the ideal to the real. The ideal is pure, distinct, unadulterated, uncompromised, and untainted. The real is complex, frustrating, unpredictable, opaque, overwhelming in its human variety. As a response, people may focus on the ideal alone, rather than keeping their vision clear in order to appreciate the needs, the circumstances, and the hopes of others. Eventually, they might come to see only the ideal, with potentially harmful results. In a discussion of the virtues and vices of various political ideals and systems, Maurice Merleau-Ponty (1947/1969) shows how people can end up defending the ideal of freedom more than they do actual free men and women (p. xxiv, *passim*). They uphold an ideology, a term sometimes closely related to an ideal, and sing its praises, rather than seek harmonious, just relations with their fellow human beings. George Eliot (1871–72/1985) reminds us that "[t]here is no general doctrine which is not capable of eating out our morality if unchecked by the deep-seated habit of direct fellow-feeling with individual fellow-men" (p. 668). She implies that ideals can isolate and alienate people from others without their even being aware of the cause.

Critics could argue that the history of education provides plenty of examples to bear out their worries. They might spotlight reformist ideals that have generated new programs, plans, and structures for teaching. The reformers tout the new programs as breakthroughs. Many regard the ideals behind them as marvelous, inspiring, even universally embracing. However, argue the critics, the fact that the programs are based in ideals and in the reformist zeal to change things produces harmful consequences. In the absence of sober, careful analysis, the ideals and associated programs may be too narrowly conceived. They may not reflect an adequate study of the many factors at play in any specific attempt to improve education.

Lisa Delpit (1995), for example, suggests that a liberal or democratic education centered around student decision making, initiative, and freedom of expression is splendid—as an ideal. She contends, however, that the ideal has problematic results for some urban Black children (pp. 16–20, *passim*). She argues that many such children are already imaginative and adept at self-expression. But many lack skills of reading, writing, numerating, and more, which in Delpit's view should be given sustained attention since these skills are required for access to sources of opportunity and power, access that some proponents of the ideal perhaps inadvertently take for granted. Delpit does not commend a minimalist back-to-the-basics curriculum, which has at times been the staple educational fare for children of the poor. Rather, I read her as calling for careful consideration of local contexts, circumstances, and communities, an approach that she implies can temper otherwise admirable ideals.

Delpit's claims have generated controversy and debate (see, e.g., Henry, 1998, pp. 96–104). As she acknowledges, there is evidence that minority youth in the American inner city can learn foundational skills while also being challenged with the most liberal, project, or discussion-oriented instructional approaches (cf. Haroutunian-Gordon, 1991; Ladson-Billings, 1994). But the issue of concern here is not the virtue of one pedagogical orientation as compared with another. Critics of ideals would draw from Delpit's work, and from that of others who have called for a second look at various reforms, the lesson that ideals can sometimes lead people to overlook vital human concerns.

Oakeshott (1991, pp. 475–477, *passim*) writes that ideals can have a valuable place in individual lives, spurring people to act better or to strive harder in developing themselves than they otherwise might. However, he argues, ideals can lead to harm when carried uncritically to a social and political level. In some cases, people may wield ideals as if they were weapons, using them to combat the opposition and to mask the exercise of their power and ambition. In other contexts, people may use them to legitimate any number of social and political reforms in which those who are to be reformed often have little say. "Every moral ideal," Oakeshott cautions, "is potentially an obsession" (p. 476; also see Berlin, 1992). Oakeshott suggests that the tragedy of such ideals is that those who act on them often mean well. They are not operating on the basis of malevolent impulse. But ideals become like the proverbial log in their eye, blinding them to the human realities that their ideals simply pass over.

INHABITABLE IDEALS IN TEACHING

Our discussion seems to have reached an impasse. From one point of view, ideals are problematic. To judge from the historical record, they have caused as much harm as good in human affairs. From another point of view, individuals and societies alike appear to need ideals to motivate and to guide their actions. They cannot live without ideals, without images of a better world.

Christine Korsgaard (1996) suggests that such images are built into our human fabric. She speaks of "ideas" we develop about what could be different, with that term based (as I interpret it) in a Kantian use of the German word *Idee*, meaning a picture or image that is generated by reason infused with hope. "It is the most striking fact about human life," she writes,

> that we have values. We think of ways that things could be better, more perfect, and so of course different, than they are; and of ways that we ourselves could be better, more perfect, and so of course different, than we are. Why should this be so? Where do we get these ideas that outstrip the world we experience and seem to call it into question, to render judgment on it, to say that it does not measure up, that it is not what it ought to be? Clearly we do not get them from experience, at least not by any simple route. And it is puzzling too that these ideas of a world different from our own call out to us, telling us that things should be like them rather than the way they are, and that we should make them so. (p. 1)

According to this perspective, ideals, or images of goodness, seem to spring upon us. They emerge from our very nature as social beings dwelling in more or less imperfect association with others. Nobody can fail to observe societal and individual shortcomings. But nobody can deny, Korsgaard argues, that human beings, time and again, have conceived ideals of a better world and have acted on them to bring us closer to, rather than farther from, such a world.

How do things stand with respect to teaching? Can teachers work without ideals? Should educators banish talk of ideals in teaching? Or do ideals play a role in both sustaining and improving practice? If so, what kind of role, and what kind of ideals?

Recent work on teaching suggests that teachers do have ideals and that they take them seriously (see, e.g., Ben-Peretz, 1995; Foster, 1997; Hansen, 1995; Jackson et al., 1993; Johnson, 1990; Kozolanka & Olson, 1994; Schultz, 1997). Many teachers talk and act as if it would be impossible to teach without them. Their ideals appear to vary. For some, the ideal boils down to keeping in mind an image of a growing, educated person, the kind of image examined, for example, in Chapter 3. For others, the ideal pinpoints the personal relationship between teacher and student, a relationship perceived as crucial to establishing an environment in which the student can learn and flourish. For some teachers, their ideal centers around notions of human dignity and social justice. Others are animated by the desire to produce caring, compassionate people. For still others, the ideal pivots around a conception of their discipline and of instructional method, and of implementing that conception as best as they can in the school and classroom. These ideals serve the functions examined previously. They motivate, guide, strengthen, and encourage teachers to perform their best in both the short and the long run.[1]

The teachers' testimony suggests that the critics of ideals may have created an unbalanced picture. Ideals do not automatically blind teachers to the real. On the contrary, the perspectives revealed in the literature suggest that, at least for some teachers, their ideals derive *from* paying attention to the real. Their ideals are securely moored to their understanding and knowledge of students and of the promise of education. Phrased differently, their ideals take form as they teach, as they come to grips with the terms of the practice and with what it means to be responsible for educating the young. In such cases, idealism and respect for reality reinforce one another. The teachers' respect for reality disciplines their idealism by preventing it from flattening out the complexity of education and blocking them from perceiving real constraints and real needs. Their ideals, on the other hand, prevent their sense of reality from unilaterally dampening their hope and vision. Ideals dispose a teacher to be on the lookout for the unexpected and the new in how students respond to the curriculum.

Harriet Cuffaro (1995) describes ideals not as endpoints but as sources of insight:

> The reality of society—the reality of exclusion, inequity, repression, violence, and despair—is far from the ideal. Yet, the ideal is there not as unattainable perfection but to inform the present, to underline what we must attend to, and to help in locating what obstructs the realization of the ideal. An ideal locates the territory of interest and concern, points to desired characteristics and qualities of the landscape, and indicates those features that obstruct the growth of the person and of society. The informing of the real by the ideal focuses the work to be done to lessen the distance between the two. (p. 100)

We might say that in the very best educational practice, the real and the ideal mutually "inform" one another. The teacher strives to establish an environment in which students can learn, while also keeping in view, or letting himself be guided by, images of the kind of flourishing adults students can become. He assists a student struggling with reading while holding onto an image of the student as a successful reader. That image strengthens his resolve and fuels his energy. Over the course of a schoolyear, his imagination propels him to undertake steps to "lessen the distance" between the student's current and future status as a reader. In the long run, the teacher's ideal-in-practice boosts and enriches the student's life chances and, in turn, those of the other people whom the student might one day be in a position to help and to serve. The student might attain such a position only because, long ago and with the help of a teacher, he or she learned how to become a reader.

Teacher educators might interject, perhaps reluctantly and unhappily, that the argument thus far has posed things backwards. They might point out that for many persons new to the field, it is not, metaphorically speaking, reality first and ideals second. Rather, many new candidates enter their professional development programs fired by ideals, in many cases well before they have obtained a sense of the reality of teaching in today's schools and classrooms. To be sure, some candidates take to the work quickly and successfully. They may have worked with young people before, or they may simply be persons who embody idealism wedded to respect for reality. However, teacher educators might emphasize that for many candidates, ideals constitute a mixed blessing. They fuel candidates' enthusiasm. But they may also blind them to pedagogical realities. As a result, when candidates encounter the messiness of working in schools, some feel they have run into a brick wall. In spiritual as much as in practical terms, they do not know how to respond to a mentor teacher who does not share their ideals, to students who do not love learning like they do, to school schedules that make them feel like Charlie Chaplin on the assembly line, and more. In some cases, teacher candidates succumb to the inevitable disappointment that follows in the wake of punctured ideals. Some leave their programs, or they abandon teaching after a brief stint. Others (alas) narrow and harden their sensibility and just try to get through. They may remain in teaching, but they do so in a cynical or even callous state of mind.

Teacher educators familiar with this portrait might add another twist to the concerns I discussed previously about the power of ideals to develop their own momentum and to swamp respect for reality. Teacher educators might tell us about the problems and the pain that can ensue from their own misdirected ideals as teacher educators. In other words, they would have in mind not the often innocent ideals of new candidates, which can, in fact, be focused and matured through a good preparation program and thoughtful classroom experience. Rather, they would caution their fellow educators about rooting out candidates' own ideals and putting in their place ideals those educators themselves prefer. Unless teacher educators undertake a profoundly sensitive and responsible job of instilling such ideals, they may unnecessarily complicate or even compromise their graduates' subsequent teaching. Graduates might enter the field well versed in a particular ideology but inadequately prepared for the difficult moral and intellectual task of letting ideals and human realities mutually inform one another.

I have witnessed the pain that can result from such a process. For example, a first-year high school teacher once telephoned me out of the blue, saying she had recently read something of mine and would like to come talk about it and about some difficulties she was having in the classroom. When she came to my office, she recounted, teary-eyed, her attempts to create a "democratic classroom," an ideal strongly advocated in her teacher preparation program. She had tried to involve her students in everything from creating classroom rules to selecting curricula. They had responded by announcing they wanted to be allowed to chew gum, to have time to visit with friends, to read the newspaper, and the like. The teacher told me that students found her attempts to treat them, to use her term, with respect both "funny" and "weird." It turned out that the teacher had a lot to say about democratic theory but very little about how to balance her ideals with the unfathomably complicated human reality represented by her students and school. She had acted as if she could treat her students as reflective thinkers motivated by high ideals and infinitely sensitive to human differences in personality, need, and viewpoint. Her students may well have had those very impulses, but the latter do not emerge full-blown in our thought and conduct without help from others, including teachers. The teacher and I discussed how to create an environment that invites a focus on learning, including the cultivation of dispositions such as listening critically and giving voice to one's ideas. We contrasted such an environment with one in which teachers expect either too much or too little of students, and of themselves as well.

It would be easy to shake one's head at the naiveté of this first-year teacher. But I do not believe her problem was naiveté. On the contrary, I think she had forgotten what it means to be naive, in the sense given to that term in Chapter 3. I argued there that naiveté, when linked with related qualities of simplicity and spontaneity, denotes a critical innocence, a state of mind not intimidated by others' expectations, by fear, or by cynicism—nor one narrowed by allegiance to an ideology. This spirit of naiveté produces what Italo Calvino (1988) describes as "lightness" in one's approach to the world. Lightness does not mean being light-hearted or casual, nor does it mean embracing a stoic attitude in order to avoid the pain and disillusionment of frustrated ideals. Rather, it facilitates a serious attempt to try to approach other people as they are, rather than solely as what one would wish them to be. This spirit can counterbalance the weight that an ideal or ideology can place on the mind—and consequently on how one regards and treats others. What this spirit requires is careful cultivation and practice. It should not be overrun by unbalanced claims on behalf of one ideal or another. The first-year teacher was not naive. She was in the grip of an ideal. That condition led to considerable pain for her and to confusion and wasted opportunities for her students. (However, I am glad that she did not abandon her ideals, and that was not the intent of the advice I extended. She later reported that her work with students had become much more productive than at the start, a change that I would attribute, in part, to a reawakening of her own sensibility.)

TENACIOUS HUMILITY: AN IDEAL OF PERSONHOOD

The place of ideals in teaching remains ambiguous and uncertain. However, the analysis thus far does not rule out the possibility that good teaching is based on ideals of some kind. Without ideals, the work might be reduced to mere socialization of the young or to a functionalist fulfillment of externally dictated ends. It seems to me that good teaching, at least in many cases, embodies an appreciation for both large and undefinable human possibilities and for ever-present constraints. This posture is neither stoic nor zealous. It implies neither resignation to current pressures and limits nor an arrogant claim that one occupies the moral high ground and can go it alone.

"Tenacious humility" is an apt descriptor for this standpoint. Tenacity implies staying the course, not giving up on students or on oneself. To employ the terms used in previous chapters, tenacity involves fostering and extending one's sense of agency as teacher. It means expanding and deepening one's person, one's conduct, and one's moral and intellectual sensibility. Humility is also an active rather than passive quality. For many people, or so it seems, humility does not come naturally. It has to be worked at, developed, and accepted. For a teacher, humility entails a refusal to treat students as less worthy of being heard than the teacher him- or herself. It means retaining a sense of students' as well as one's own humanity. Humility attests to a grasp on the reality of human differences, institutional constraints, and personal limitations. Tenacity, on the other hand, compels the teacher not to treat those differences, constraints, and limitations as hardened and unchanging.

Murdoch (1970) describes humility as "one of the most difficult and central of all virtues." It is not "a peculiar habit of self-effacement," she argues, but rather makes possible "respect for reality." Murdoch weds humility with freedom, claiming that the latter does not mean "chucking one's weight about" but rather entails "the disciplined overcoming of self" in order to appreciate the reality of others (p. 95). Richard Weaver (1948) notes a family resemblance between humility and what he calls "piety." According to Weaver, piety "is a discipline of the will through respect. It admits the right to exist of things larger than the ego, of things different from the ego" (p. 172).

Tenacious humility helps teachers hold at bay the tempting lure of ideals, theories, and ideologies that purport to "explain" schools and students. Those standpoints can release them from having to deal with complexity and from having to think about, rather than to label, whatever does not fit their outlook. Phrased differently, tenacious humility suggests that there can be ideals that reach beyond the vise of any particular hard-and-fast cluster of beliefs. These are ideals of character or personhood. As such an ideal, tenacious humility can motivate people not to rest on the oars of unexamined belief and expectation. Learning to be tenaciously humble can position persons to alter or to transform their prejudices (which, as we have seen, can also happen in the encounter with tradition). The process can fuel a person's willingness to be self-critical. That disposition becomes crucial if, following Eva Brann (1979, p. 39), an ideology is understood to be a system of ideals and views that is closed to further questioning. (According to Brann, if the set of views is not closed, it constitutes not an ideology but something closer to a philosophy, or an evolving standpoint, or an experimental posture in the world.) I may be dedicated to an ideology, but, cautions John Wilson (1998), "I may not seriously monitor it in the light of reason. The ideology is something I *have*, a kind of personal possession or insurance policy; whereas the monitoring is something that I *do*, not which I *own*" (p. 145). Part of being tenaciously humble is not falling back, uncritically, upon an idealized or ideological "possession" when pressed to listen, to think, to question, to reconsider, to reexamine.

In this respect, tenacious humility supports an ideal of freedom, in a sense captured by Oakeshott (1989). After reviewing possible descriptions of what a person is—for example, an advanced biological entity, a creature driven by the pleasure principle, or a creation of God—Oakeshott writes:

> They may all turn out to be (in some sense) true, or they may all be convicted of some error or obscurity. But with conclusions of this sort we are not now concerned. What concerns us is that each is itself a human utterance expressing a human understanding of the character of a human being, and that the capacity to make such utterances, whether they be true or false, itself postulates a man who is something beside what these, or any other such statements, allege him to be. They postulate what I shall call a 'free' man. (p. 18).

Oakeshott employs the qualifier *free* because, in his view, to the extent that persons can make such "utterances," and can understand them as well as those of other persons, they express a measure of agency and autonomy that reaches beyond biological, social, cultural, or psychological determinants. In Oakeshott's view, human beings are not bound hard and fast to a preordained horizon of meaning and expression. He does not adopt a Cartesian standpoint to capture human autonomy—"I think, therefore I am"—according to which thought, reason, and perspective can operate or originate independently from the social and natural world. But nor does he settle in at the other end of the spectrum and presume, as Alain Finkielkraut (1995) puts it, that "I think, therefore I am from somewhere; by exercising my powers of reflection, I do not affirm my sovereignty, I betray my identity" (p. 25). Oakeshott implies that while persons are from particular places, they can also think about both the places and their particularity. The "utterances" people can make about them both reveal and create additional critical standpoints they can take.[2]

Korsgaard (1996) advances a similar outlook in clarifying the human need to have "practical identities," for example, as parent, teacher, artist, liberal or conservative, and so forth. Korsgaard suggests that such identities are contingent. That is, people are not necessarily predestined by some higher power to develop one practical identity or another. However, she argues,

> What is not contingent is that you must be governed by *some* conception of your practical identity. For unless you are committed to some conception of your practical identity, you will lose your grip on yourself as having any reason to do one thing rather than another—and with it, your grip on yourself as having any reason to live and act at all. But *this* reason for conforming to your particular practical identities is not a reason that *springs from* one of those particular practical identities. It is a reason that springs from your humanity itself, from your identity simply as *a human being*, a reflective animal who needs reasons to act and to live. And so it is a reason you have only if you treat your humanity as a practical, normative, form of identity, that is, if you value yourself as a human being. (1996, pp. 120–121)

From Korsgaard's point of view, a person cannot coherently *not* value his or her humanity and, at the same time, retain a practical identity. At the very least, she suggests, the sheer act of rejecting one's humanity would presume that one is in fact worthy or integrated enough to take such a position. This perspective is an important dimension of her project, which is, in part, to investigate the possibility of human freedom. Like Oakeshott, Korsgaard aspires to a better understanding of what makes persons capable of conducting themselves in moral ways, that is, in ways that cannot be reduced to the playing out of external or internal natural or social forces. As she implies in the passage quoted above, she regards the fact that human beings are capable of asking questions of value as both marvelous and as a sign that the idea of freedom is not a will 'o the wisp.

Tenacious humility sheds light on the terrain of freedom. Its pursuit does not render a person into a hardened or fixed character. Rather, it points to how character or personhood can genuinely emerge and grow, even in the face of any number of societal, cultural, familial, or psychological constraints and forces. Like all ideals, tenacious humility is not attainable in any final or ultimate sense. In metaphorical terms, it is always receding, always just over the horizon no matter how much one strives to realize it in practice. Nonetheless, as an ideal it can, as Cuffaro (1995, p. 100) puts it, "inform" the present. It can position a teacher to think, to feel, and to work in imaginative ways he or she might otherwise not even realize are possible.

Tenacious humility operates as what Emmet (1994) calls a "regulative ideal," a concept that she borrows from Kant but extends beyond his usage. According to Emmet, a regulative ideal sets a direction for conduct or for a given practice. It steers persons away from settling for half-measures or surrogates. While a regulative ideal is not realizable "in particular instances," Emmet writes, it can help set a standard for thought and action (p. 2). She clarifies the two central terms: The "ideal aspect" gives an orientation to an endeavor or mode of conduct, while the "regulative aspect" guides the actual approach (p. 9). In other words, a regulative ideal describes both a destination and how to conduct oneself in striving to reach it. In this respect, a regulative ideal constitutes more than a "principle determining the form of one's reflections" (Wittgenstein, 1980, p. 27e), although that way of conceiving an ideal captures part of its force. A regulative ideal is a guide-in-practice. Moreover, it is dynamic. "The ideal is not sufficiently specific to define the final objective," Emmet (1994) claims, "but we can know enough about it in general to indicate a progression" (p. 9). This is accomplished, she points out, by learning more and more about the nature of the ideal as one moves toward it. Emmet's argument coheres with the idea of a living tradition in which, over time, practitioners both learn about and subtly transform the terms of their practice.

For teachers, the ideal aspect of tenacious humility gives an orientation to their thought and imagination, while the regulative aspect helps guide their concrete approach in the classroom. The ideal aspect, captured in the root terms *tenacity* and *humility*, helps them ponder the persons and teachers they are becoming. That same aspect merges seamlessly with a regulative dimension, as the ideal helps them to plan for and to participate in classroom life in attentive, responsive ways that support students' and their own growth. Teachers do not need a fixed image of tenacious humility, nor a preset plan of action for realizing it in practice. How could they, one might ask, when understanding the nature and meaning of the ideal takes time and experience (and seems always to leave many questions unanswered)? How could teachers spell out an airtight protocol for self-development when they do not know how each group of new students will respond to their curriculum and to each other? Tenacious humility, like personhood itself, emerges through everyday conduct. Teachers can learn more and more about the nature of the ideal, and how to bring it into being, as they engage the terms of the practice.

Like all ideals, tenacious humility invites change. The change is in oneself as teacher and in the way one works with students, peers, administrators, parents, and others concerned with education. The change occurs, in part, in one's sensibility. In Chapter 2, I suggested that a teacher's moral sensibility evolves and enlarges as he or she strives to do right by students and by the vocation of teaching itself. I argued that a moral sensibility is not a possession or goal but is an ongoing, never completed achievement (Oakeshott, 1993, p. 35). The qualifier *moral* is crucial, especially with respect to a practice such as teaching. The moral is something other than a prefabricated list of do's and don'ts that functions, say, like the directions for operating a machine. Such lists often reflect moralism, which is the attempt to dictate to others how they should live. In contrast, the moral comprises, as I have employed the term in this book, treating other people as ends in themselves rather than as merely a means to our ends. The term has to do with making oneself a better person and thereby positioning oneself to contribute to humanity. For Emmet (1979), the moral draws together notions of human purposes, principles of conduct, and feeling. "Moral theories based on only one of these factors," she argues,

> . . . will be in danger of becoming unscrupulous, rigorist, or sentimental. These are designedly perjorative terms for the practical attitudes which can come from truncated moral views, where there is a separation of purpose from principle and principle from purpose, and feeling from both. The separation of purpose and principle can produce swings between moralism and cynicism. The separation of both from feeling can not only produce hardness, but cut moral judgment off from a source of imaginative insight. The appeal to feeling alone can be sentimental if there is no way of criticising and training one's feelings. (p. 11)

Oakeshott (1993) argues that morality constitutes an "endless, practical endeavor resulting in momentary personal failures and achievements and in a gradual change of moral ideas and ideals, a change which is perhaps more than mere change, a progress toward a finer sensibility for social life and a deeper knowledge of its necessities" (p. 44). What I am calling, for short, tenacious humility describes an ideal image of this change that is "more than mere change." It is an image of determination allied with openness, of a commitment to think and to question wedded to action, of stubborn hope embedded in ungrasping conduct toward others. Such a posture can lead to what Oakeshott calls a "finer" sensibility for social life, by which I take him to mean an increased attunement to other people and their individuality. Of equal importance, tenacious humility creates conditions for teacher learning, for a "deeper knowledge" of the "necessities" entailed in good practice.

A critic might ask, at this point, how tenacious humility relates to the host of ideals teachers say guides their work. In addition, the critic might wonder how the ideal relates to the concrete details of teaching. For example, tenacious humility does not seem to offer much advice about what curricular materials to select, how to decide whether to lecture or have small-group discussions, what approach to evaluation to employ, when to take field trips with students, and so forth.

Teachers have described ideals such as fueling societal betterment, producing caring persons, and equipping students for a good life. These are big, broad ideals, familiar and compelling. They can be seen as noble, as mirroring humanity's deepest hopes for a better world. The critic might argue that, in order to work toward such ideals, teachers should develop the disposition of tenacious humility. That is, everything said thus far about tenacity and humility will spur the teacher in the right direction. But, the critic might go on to say, tenacious humility is just that: a disposition, not an ideal. It describes not a desirable condition or state of affairs but a spirit of mind and heart that can enable one to strive for a particular outcome. Consequently, this discussion belongs back in Chapter 2, in the inquiry into person, conduct, and sensibility, not in a study of the place of ideals in teaching.

Here we encounter a question that educators in a pluralist society find hard to answer, and for good reason. Are ideals personal possessions? Phrased differently, can or should teachers use language such as "my ideal," "your ideal," "his or her ideal," "their ideal"? The question is naturally vexing because a pluralist society tends to privilege choice over content. Freedom of religion, freedom of the press, freedom of public expression, and so forth are principles of choice rather than espousals of a particular choice. Those principles do not compel us to agree with other people, but only to acknowledge their right to speak their minds and to enact their beliefs in ways unharmful to those who differ from them. This account reveals, of course, that there is a procedural content underlying such principles, namely, an ongoing agreement to respect other peoples' right to their own choices and values. Whether tacit or explicit, such an agreement is certainly substantial, as persons who live in repressive societies would be the first to point out. In a pluralist society, the principle of choice occupies an important place on the moral dais. A pluralist society also recognizes that there has to be some constraint on choice, as signaled by the term *unharmful* mentioned above. For example, most people are unlikely to welcome into the ranks of teaching a person whose "ideal" is to persuade students to bully their schoolmates. That kind of choice is simply out of bounds. The difficulty boils down to setting reasonable limits or boundaries that respect individual and community aspirations.

In previous chapters, I employed concepts such as "tradition" and "practice" to carve out a boundary within which teachers work. I argued that this boundary constrains what teachers should say and do. However, it does so in such a way that it also opens broad vistas to teacher agency and autonomy. In other words, with constraint comes meaningful freedom, and vice versa. In light of that argument, the ideals that guide teachers do fall within limits. A purely personal ideal may mirror all the dangers of a purely impersonal ideology. An ideal that is subjectively sufficient may be wanting in terms of the objective or nondiscretionary demands of the practice.[3] This prospect does not imply that teachers should henceforth use the language of "our ideals" rather than speak in terms of "my" or "their" ideals. The issue is not one of identifying or forming a party affiliation that would automatically imply that some are in and others are out.

Teachers will differ in the big ideals that guide their work, whether these be to help create a better society or to produce smart and caring people. Such ideals are warranted—for example, as sources of motivation—albeit within limits tailored by the terms of the practice. What teachers can agree on, it seems to me, is an ideal that will enable them to become the kind of person who can indeed have a beneficial, rather than harmful or random, impact on students. Such an ideal will describe at one and the same time a disposition. Tenacious humility is a name for this ideal. It draws a person deeper into the human condition, in part by making it possible for him or her to *become* a person who can help vitalize that condition (although not in heroic or headline-grabbing ways, as I discuss below). Moreover, as an ideal of character or personhood, tenacious humility resolves the worries I examined earlier about how big ideals and ideologies, whether these be conservative or progressive, can blind us to the reality of other people and even lead us to run roughshod over them. Tenacious humility keeps teachers close to the ground. It helps them stay tethered to the terms of teaching, rather than drifting loose and either pursuing idiosyncratic aims (or none at all) or permitting themselves to become a pawn or mouthpiece of others' aims.

What may seem strange about the claims of tenacious humility is the very notion that self-improvement can be guided by moral ideals, rather than by the desire to gain success, self-esteem, contentment, fame, and the like. In contemporary pluralist societies, self-improvement sometimes translates into a highly materialistic project geared toward the pursuit of external rewards. It is not the self per se that is improved but rather one's circumstances and prospects (cf. Pring, 1984, p. 15; see also Taylor, 1985). Phrased differently, whatever work one undertakes on the self is designed to enhance one's opportunities and chances. Such work has instrumental rather than inherent value. Perhaps for these reasons, people often contrast self-development with ideals and idealism, perceiving the latter as other-directed rather than as self-directed. At least in popular talk about them, ideals are often spoken of as selfless rather than as self-oriented, as social rather than as personal, as broad and expansive rather than as pertaining to the comparatively tiny territory any individual life occupies. In such an ethos, it may be difficult to conceive of the possibility that an ideal can motivate one to become a morally better, more engaged person.

But what could compel someone to become a better person and teacher other than an ideal? A quick answer might be the example of other people. A person might yearn to develop the qualities and attitudes of a teacher he or she esteems. "I would like to be like her," the person might say. However, if we take a second look at that desire, more often than not we find that an ideal informs or underlies it. To be like someone is not, after all, to be identical with him or her. Rather, the admired person embodies qualities and attitudes in an ideal, or idealized, way. The admirer wants to get nearer to the ideal. He or she respects what the person stands for and does, not the individual *apart* from those qualities and doings. The admired person *shows* us, or *makes visible*, the possibilities of what we ourselves can become, not just in theory but in our actual lives (cf. Kant, 1785/1990, pp. 18, 25).

Other than an ideal, there are not many candidates for spurring a serious attempt to become a better person and teacher. Blind obedience to someone else's dictates is hardly a recipe for enlightened wisdom. Self-interest will not do, either, because, as we have seen, that motive might simply convert any notion of improvement into a tool or instrument for personal gain, not for personal transformation. As Aristotle (trans. 1962, pp. 169–170 [1144a23–38]) pointed out long ago, such a process might produce a clever or more successful person, with "success" denoting the accumulation of external rewards, resources, and recognition. But that process cannot, in itself, lead one to become a better and wiser person. According to Kant, who also thought such issues through with lucidity, to treat the self as a mere tool for personal satisfaction is no less degrading than using other people as a mere means to one's own ends. From Kant's point of view, a person, including one's own person, is worth more than being treated simply as a vehicle for achieving external rewards. Kant urged his readers to respect humanity both in themselves and in others, which implies taking a nonmanipulative stance toward self and other.

That stance points us back again to tenacious humility. Its cultivation and expression in teaching is not, to borrow terms from Richard Eldridge (1997), an "end-state to be achieved" but rather describes "a modality of action or being with others" (p. 44). Tenacious humility does not tell teachers what materials or instructional methods to employ, all of which are discrete, specific decisions. Rather, in taking tenacious humility seriously as an ideal of personhood, teachers can build into their working lives continuity, or what some scholars call a narrative unity (see Chapter 2). In reaching toward the ideal, teachers will be more likely to make specific educational choices that add up to a meaningful pattern rather than to a haphazard or random series. If they are tenacious about teaching well, and humble in their pretensions, they will be more rather than less likely to become a force for good in students' lives. Striving for this ideal will not prevent teachers from making mistakes and misjudgments. But it will enable them to learn and to keep working to improve. Tenacious humility constitutes a practical, humanizing ideal that can guide both big ideals and everyday practice, keeping them in the service of teaching and learning.

ENACTING TENACIOUS HUMILITY

Tenacious humility describes an ideal that has a long history in guiding men and women along the journey of moral growth and, thereby, making it possible for them to have a beneficial influence on others. Many of these individuals have been teachers, in spirit if not in name. Some are real, others are figures in works of fiction, but no less significant for that given how powerful the moral impact of fiction, and of art more broadly, has been on human beings (cf. Booth, 1988; Dewey, 1934/1980; J. Gardner, 1978; Nussbaum, 1990). The people I have in mind render vivid the meaning of tenacious humility. They attest to the struggles involved in overcoming self-interest, anger at the world, resentment or dislike of others, self-doubt, and more. They are tenacious in seeking meaning in life, which for them is another way of describing self-improvement, but they are not always confident or optimistic about their quest for meaning. Nor are they always successful, in the external sense of that term; they do not always earn public notice or recognition. Moreover, they are distressed and confused by the fact that they do not always have a good influence on others, their hopes notwithstanding. They are humbled by their limitations and by the natural and social constraints placed on their agency and on that of other people. They do not always overcome feelings of envy, avarice, pride, and impatience. In a nutshell, they provide language and images for common, but easy-to-forget, knowledge: that life is both trying and blessed, that dwelling with others is both very difficult and very necessary, and that moral ideals of personhood can help one find the way even when things grow dark.

Such persons are everywhere, although in our busyness we may not recognize them. We may not recognize them because they do not perceive themselves as particularly unusual, much less heroic. But they make a difference in the world. As Wilson (1998) contends, it "is at least arguable that more good gets done by a kind of low-temperature sharing with other people, by the incremental progress of reason and sanity, than by those heroes who spearhead various causes—even perhaps those causes that we approve of" (p. 152). Wilson's claim echoes Eliot's (1871–72/1985) concluding words about the unheroic but infinitely humane Dorothea Middlebrook, the central character in her epic novel *Middlemarch*: "But the effect of her being on those around her was incalculably diffusive: for the growing good of the world is partly dependent on unhistoric acts; and that things are not so ill with you and me as they might have been, is half owing to the number who lived faithfully a hidden life, and rest in unvisited tombs" (p. 896). Like the quality of tenacious humility, teaching is not a heroic endeavor. However, again in a way that reflects the ideal, teachers do not lead "hidden lives." In their roles as teachers, they are public figures working in public settings. Eliot takes care to suggest that the good of the world is only "half owing" (but thank heavens for it) to those whom we never hear about. To whom do we owe the other half? Anyone who recalls a teacher with gratitude already has the beginning of an answer to the question.

There are publicly recognizable persons who incarnate tenacious humility. A short and arbitrary list includes St. Augustine, especially as we see him in his *Confessions*; George Eliot, the authorial imagination and moral voice that informs *Middlemarch* as well as other novels; Etty Hillesum, about whom I will have much to say below; and Malcolm X, especially in light of the spiritual transformations he underwent as recounted in his *Autobiography*. These persons demonstrate, in their conduct and in their sensibilities, that freedom is not a chimera. Phrased differently, they illustrate why persons are "something more" (cf. Kant, 1785/ 1990, p. 80) than the sum of a given set of natural and social forces. They reveal that this something more cannot be predicted or predetermined. Eldridge (1997) illuminates their sense of agency when he writes that "my remembrance of my humanity and its expression or its repudiation, is not something that happens in me; it is not the effect of mental or physical or social substance acting according to their fixed and given natures. It is something that I, animated through my life with others, do" (p. 290).

The persons I have mentioned demonstrate what it means to live, at least in part, by an ideal of personhood or conduct. At first glance, figures like St. Augustine and Malcolm X may seem to contradict this claim. Both appear to be fervently devoted to an ideology, in the one case Christian doctrine, in the other Muslim doctrine linked with racial liberation. However, one reason they have so much to teach persons who are neither Christian, Muslim, nor engaged in liberation struggles is that they push beyond the well-laid out grids of ideology and doctrine, even while appreciating that doing so can be a daunting (even dangerous) prospect. Both undergo profound personal transformations that express their tenacity and their humility and that position them to act in the world with strength and courage. Their ability to question both their lives and their circumstances instantiates the quest to become a certain kind of person, a person who can recognize the face of humanity and act on its behalf. And though St. Augustine took this path somewhat late in life, at least in his reckoning, and though Malcolm X was embarking on a whole new dimension of the quest when his life was cut short, both illuminate why we can speak of and live by ideals of personhood or character.

These men and women fret more about their flaws than flaunt their virtues. They recall the character Levin in Leo Tolstoy's novel *Anna Karenina*. Like Levin, when they reflect on their selves, they become dissatisfied. Their faults and weaknesses seem to stand out like flashing neon lights. But when they are in a position to contribute to human life, to make a positive difference in the balance of good and evil, they act on the opportunity as if doing so were as natural as the sun rising. It has become natural for them, in part, because of their tenacious humility.

I propose that we enter more fully into the world of one of these figures. Doing so will serve several purposes. (1) It will allow me to clarify more sharply, for all who teach, the kind of self-examination and reflection implied by the ideal of tenacious humility. Because this ideal is hard to address, much less define, save in general terms, a biographical account might yield a better grasp on it. (2) The account can show how this inner, reflective process influences the way a person dwells and works with other people—an issue of obvious concern to teachers, given the social nature of their work. (3) The analysis can respond to concerns that tenacious humility, as an ideal of self-improvement, might veer into self-absorption. As Emmet (1994) puts it: "Anyone who tries to live a moral life may properly be interested . . . in thinking about how he or she is getting on, entering into the 'inner court of conscience' for self-examination. But if moral self-improvement is the primary interest, this can lead to inward-looking scrupulosity rather than to outward-looking appreciation of the character of human situations and what one ought to do in them" (p. 26). In other words, tenacious humility as an ideal might lead a person so far inward, metaphorically speaking, that he or she fails to look outward. The moral monitor might become tuned to one's inner dispositions and their growth, rather than to how the people around one are faring. Etty Hillesum shows how this result need not happen.

HARMONIZING THE INNER AND THE OUTER

Hillesum was a young Dutch woman who was taking university courses and supporting herself, in part as a teacher of Russian, in Amsterdam when World War II broke out. She was also Jewish, and for that fact alone she was eventually put to death by the Nazis. The diaries and letters she left behind (Hillesum, 1996) provide a remarkably lucid, accessible portrayal of a person's inner and outer transformation. She reveals how what I have called tenacious humility can lead a person away from mere self-concern into a commitment to assisting others and how this commitment, in a reciprocal dynamic, leads to a more substantial sense of self. In an unheroic but indefatigable way, Hillesum shows how an individual can help take responsibility for a world.

The diaries begin with Hillesum (1996) troubled by self-doubts and self-recrimination. She regards herself as egotistical, as dominated by a "grasping attitude" (p. 17), as needing control of both people and events. This obtains in her love life, in her friendships, and in her intellectual life as a reader and thinker (she is a voracious reader of literature, philosophy, poetry, psychology, and more). "My protracted headaches: so much masochism," she states with brutal frankness; "my abundant compassion: so much self-gratification. Compassion can be creative, but it can also be greedy" (p. 10). Hillesum dreams of becoming a successful writer, but here, too, she second-guesses both her motives and her ability. Her diary is laced with exhortations to herself: "Come on, my girl, get down to work or God help you" (p. 8) . . . "And now to the job at hand!" (p. 10) . . . "And so to work" (p. 19) . . . "And now I really must get down to work" (p. 115).

At times Hillesum despairs because of her ego, her lack of discipline, and her restlessness. She feels the frustration doubly so, for she senses how her faults and her selfishness are blocking what she also knows to be her genuine desire for purpose and meaning in life. Her doubts and confusions make her feel what she calls, when her diary opens, "the emptiness of my quest" (p. 8). She is not sure in what form meaning will arrive, nor is she sure how to strive or prepare herself for it. But in sounding her inner being, she hears repeated echoes of something "deep inside me that is still locked away" (p. 3). She yearns to "roll melodiously out of God's hand" (p. 8). She wants to be "more straightforward" so that she might, as she imagines at one moment, "finish up as an adult, capable of helping other souls who are in trouble, and of creating some sort of clarity through my work for others, for that's what it's really all about" (p. 11). Her talk of straightforwardness, here and elsewhere in her book, complements the idea (cf. Chapter 3) that being straightforward helps a person engage with and contribute to human projects.

Hillesum wrestles with her confidence, with her merit as a person, with whether she is worthy to speak of the serious things she can hardly help writing. As quoted above, she doubts her own sense of compassion for the world. "Even while I write," she broods at one point, " . . . my unconscious is protesting at such expressions as 'purpose' and 'mankind' and 'solution of problems.' I find them pretentious. But then I'm such an ingenuous and dull young woman, still so lacking in courage. No, my friend," she goes on to chide herself, "you are not there yet by a long chalk, you ought really to be kept away from all the great philosophers until you have learned to take yourself a little more seriously" (p. 36).

However, Hillesum thinks, writes, and conducts herself out of this unsteady, conflicted self-conception. As she writes of her friendships, of her family, of the fateful goings-on around her, she learns to accept her own humanity, her own capacity to speak and to act. She regards this not as a choice or as a decision she makes but rather keynotes it as a "momentous discovery" (p. 40). "I will have to dare to live life with all the seriousness it demands," she confesses, "and without thinking that I'm being pompous, sentimental, or affected" (p. 40). "With all the suffering there is," she goes on to say, as if persuading herself,

> you begin to feel ashamed of taking yourself and your moods so seriously. But you must continue to take yourself seriously, you must remain your own witness, marking well everything that happens in this world, never shutting your eyes to reality. You must come to grips with these terrible times and try to find answers to the many questions they pose. And perhaps the answers will help not only yourself but also others. (p. 41)[4]

As Hillesum writes such words, and seeks to act on them, she finds her relationship with others altering. She becomes more "composed" and less grasping (p. 17). She listens better and takes the present moment seriously (p. 19). She discovers she is learning to "channel" her energy and her yearning (pp. 14, 33). She feels she is cutting loose from the anchor of prior self-understandings, which yields a surprising consequence: "And now that I don't want to own anything any more and am free, now I suddenly own everything, now my inner riches are immeasurable" (p. 16; also pp. 30, 40).

To any person who has searched for meaning in life, Hillesum's self-doubts and her attempts to overcome them may strike a familiar chord. What she writes about, in her nuanced, lyrical style, seems so very recognizable. However, my reason for dwelling at length on her witness is that she reveals how a process of inner reflection and self-examination—a process that accompanies tenacious humility—can fund a humane pattern in one's conduct and actions.

As the months roll by (the diary covers the period from March 9, 1941, to October 13, 1942, accompanied by letters from the latter point through September 15, 1943), Hillesum's self-doubts and confusion are replaced by increasing self-understanding and clarity. Her emerging insight begins to express itself both in her deeds and in her philosophy. At first, what might be called her "outward" acts take place on a small scale. But they are no less significant, both for their immediate benefits to others and for what they show to be the products of her inner reflection. She starts with those with whom she lives:

> I have recently made it my business to preserve harmony in this household of so many conflicting elements: a German woman, a Christian of peasant stock, who has been a second mother to me; a Jewish girl student from Amsterdam; an old, levelheaded social democrat; Bernard the Philistine, with his pure heart and his fair intellect, but limited by his background; and an upright young economics student, a good Christian, full of gentleness and sympathetic understanding but also with the kind of Christian militancy and rectitude we have become accustomed to in recent times. Ours was and is a bustling little world, so threatened by politics from outside as to be disturbed within. But it seems a worthy task to keep this small community together as a refutation of all those desperate and false theories of race, nation, and so on. As proof that life cannot be forced into pre-set molds. (p. 12)

Hillesum counsels and consoles other friends and associates as well. I make the obvious point that such acts are "outward" in order to emphasize that *inner* reflection is just as much a form of action (cf. Murdoch, 1970). Hillesum goes so far as to say that "molding one's inner life" should be described as a "deed" (p. 102). She shows that just as working on the self takes effort and often leads to anxiety and frustration, so it is with learning how to act in the world. Preserving peace in her household community, she remarks, "causes a great deal of inner struggle and disappointment, and now and then means inflicting pain on others, and anger and remorse" (p. 12).

As conditions for the Jews worsen, Hillesum finds herself drawn into more public work. In the middle of July 1942 she takes up secretarial duties in the local Jewish Council, an organ created by the Nazis through which Jews were to administer their affairs. The chaotic, unnerving, and often oppressive atmosphere in the Council offices does not throw Hillesum off her moral stride. In part, this is because her environment constitutes something other than merely her surroundings (see Chapter 4). Unlike many of her co-workers, Hillesum responds with patience and energy to any and all human exigencies. To the astonishment of her peers, she places flowers on her desk each day, and she reads poetry during brief moments of respite, this in the very middle of what she characterizes as a madhouse. In early September she voluntarily accompanies the first group of Jews being sent to Westerbork, a transit camp outside Amsterdam where Jews were to be gathered before being shipped to concentration camps. Hillesum turns her back on opportunities to escape and to go into hiding. Instead, she does laundry, handles office duties, administers to the sick, holds the hand of frightened children, comforts old people, serves as a go-between (in the early months when she is allowed to leave the camp) for couples and families trying to stay in touch with each other, and much more. Such acts mirror Hillesum's inner reflections and her emerging convictions about how to lead a life.

"[D]on't hate anything," Rilke urges young poets (1908/1986, p. 35). In likeness, Hillesum comes to believe that hatred destroys a creative response to life and its demands. Early in the diaries, she speaks of how hatred "poisons everyone's mind" (p. 11). "We must not infect each other," she entreats, with "bad moods," resentment, and bitterness (p. 56). Her plea calls to mind why teacher educators counsel new candidates against hanging around in schools with surly-talking teachers for whom teaching is a burden rather than an opportunity. Teacher educators caution that participating in such talk can breed the very apathy (or worse) that underlies it. Nikolai, one of Anton Chekhov's finely drawn characters in his *A Boring Story*, describes how easy it is to demoralize one's life and that of others through heartless, mean-spirited talk. "All this talk about degeneracy [of the younger generation]," he complains, "always makes me feel as if I had accidentally overheard some unpleasant remark about my daughter. What I find so offensive is that these accusations are utterly unfounded and are based on such hackneyed commonplaces and such scarifying phantoms" (Chekhov, 1889/1964, p. 81). "Shut up, will you?" Nikolai finally bursts out at his snide-talking friends. "What are you sitting there like a couple of toads for, poisoning the air with your breath?" (p. 84). Eliot offers comparable commentary in her novel *Middlemarch*:

> [I]n the multitude of middle-aged men who go about their vocations in a daily course determined for them much in the same way as the tie of their cravats, there is always a good number who once meant to shape their own deeds and alter the world a little. The story of their coming to be shapen after the average and fit to be packed by the gross, is hardly ever told even in their consciousness; for perhaps their ardour in generous unpaid toil cooled as imperceptibly as the ardour of other youthful loves, till one day their earlier self walked like a ghost in its old home and made the new furniture ghastly. Nothing in the world more subtle than the process of their gradual change! In the beginning they inhaled it unknowingly; you and I may have sent some of our breath toward infecting them, when we uttered our conforming falsities or drew our silly conclusions. (1871–72/1985, p. 174)

As Murdoch (1970) puts it, "Everyday conversation is not necessarily a morally neutral activity and certain ways of describing people can be corrupting and wrong" (pp. 32–33). Many teachers and other persons in the helping professions would resonate with the perspective articulated by Hillesum, Chekhov, Eliot, and Murdoch. They can attest from experience how easy it can be to dwell on the negative, until such narrowness becomes a crippling habit.

The striking aspect of Hillesum's brief against hatred is that it unfolds in such evil circumstances. "I know that those who hate have good reason to do so," she observes. "But why should we always have to choose the cheapest and easiest way? It has been brought home forcibly to me here [in the transit camp] how every atom of hatred added to the world makes it an even more inhospitable place" (p. 256). "We have so much work to do on ourselves," she believes, "that we shouldn't even be thinking of hating our so-called enemies. . . . I see no alternative, each of us must turn inward and destroy in himself all that he thinks he ought to destroy in others" (p. 212). One day a friend asks angrily, "What is it in human beings that makes them want to destroy others?" Hillesum replies: "Human beings, you say, but remember that you're one yourself. . . . The rottenness of others is in us, too. . . . I really see no other solution than to turn inward and to root out all the rottenness there. I no longer believe that we can change anything in the world until we have first changed ourselves" (p. 84). She acknowledges the necessity of both moral indignation and moral action (more on this below). "But we must know what motives inspire our struggle," she argues, "and we must begin with ourselves, each day anew" (pp. 154–155). "If one wants to exert a moral influence on others," Hillesum concludes, "one must start with one's own morals" (p. 216).

In these and many similar remarks, Hillesum reveals how she has learned, as she hoped she would, to take herself seriously, to see herself as a person with a sense of purpose in life. "I find life beautiful, and I feel free," she remarks at one point, almost by way of a testament of faith; "the sky within me is as wide as the one stretching above my head." She goes on to say:

> Life is hard, but that is no bad thing. If one starts by taking one's own importance seriously, the rest follows. It is not morbid individualism to work on oneself. True peace will come only when every individual finds peace within himself; when we have all vanquished and transformed our hatred for our fellow human beings of whatever race—even into love one day, although perhaps that is asking too much. (p. 145)

Hillesum's witness to humanity is not unprecedented. Its power derives from the energy and the grace of her character and her prose, and from her obviously enriching presence in the lives of many of her contemporaries. But even while granting such things, there are questions to ask about Hillesum's moral posture, questions that can also be posed about tenacious humility.

The historian and critic Tvetzan Todorov (1996), for example, writes with great admiration for Hillesum. "In the midst of the deepest despair," he suggests, "her life glitters like a jewel" (p. 198).[5] But Todorov worries about the political implications of Hillesum's philosophy. "[W]hen danger looms before us," he argues, "we know we cannot avert it with gestures of goodwill. And we are not necessarily wrong. If Hitler's armies are streaming across borders, nothing is gained by making peace proposals. If Stalin decides to put to death all the peasants in the Ukraine, they cannot protect themselves by pitying him" (p. 201). Todorov is troubled by what he characterizes as Hillesum's quietism. In part, his concerns emerge from the contrast between Hillesum and those who actively fought against the Nazis (persons who make up the bulk of Todorov's study). In comparison with such men and women, many of whom were killed in action, Hillesum's pacific approach seems tame. Her diary concludes with the words: "We should be willing to act as a balm for all wounds" (Hillesum, 1996, p. 231). The image is one of healing, of comforting, of restoring a suffering humanity. But Todorov points out that Hillesum's charge presumes damage and hurt as a prior condition. He asks why people should not, instead, get to work on the conditions that lead to wounding and pain in the first place, so that we do not have to be cast in the role of providing a balm (Todorov, 1996, p. 208). Todorov urges us to look elsewhere for a philosophy of life robust enough to combat evil. "[I]n the end," he concludes, Hillesum's "fatalism and passivity lent themselves to the murderous project of the Nazis" (p. 209).

Todorov's criticism could be levied, albeit in modified form, against the claims of tenacious humility. How will striving for this ideal of personhood, a critic might ask, help us solve the nation's many educational and social problems? How will it redress the inequities, the bigotry, the indifference that continue to weigh society down? How will it assist the individual teacher to confront injustice in his or her own school, to deal with cynical or even harmful teachers and administrators, to combat a bureaucracy with an agenda that seems to consist of self-preservation and nothing more? How can we be confident that tenacious humility won't merely perpetuate the status quo?

These questions could easily be multiplied. Rather than answer them directly, let us first see if Hillesum's life contains a response to Todorov's criticism. This seems a sensible course to take, if only because I have suggested that Hillesum illuminates the meaning of tenacious humility as an ideal of personhood. That would mean, *pace* Todorov, that she would also make plain its limitations. In a nutshell, does Hillesum's posture necessarily promote what Todorov calls fatalism and passivity?

Hillesum was keenly aware of how problematic others might find her moral stance. "Many would call me an unrealistic fool," she admits at one point, "if they so much as suspected what I feel and think" (p. 181). But she insists that her philosophy is not one of resignation, apathy, indifference, or helplessness (p. 176). She contends that she is not "a schoolgirl with a 'beautiful soul'" and that she does not seek to "escape from reality into beautiful dreams" (p. 135). She is not an "armchair theorist" (p. 152), she says, for refusing to concede that only the enemy should be perceived as evil. She claims that her intensive study of literature and philosophy, and her writing, have not been a mere pie-in-the-sky rhapsody. Instead, she believes that her reading and her writing have readied her for what she earlier called "adult life," a phrase that she now appreciates means engaging the needs of her surrounding world. "Michelangelo and Leonardo," she states, "[t]hey, too, are part of me, they inhabit my life. Dostoyevsky and Rilke and Saint Augustine. And the Apostles. . . . These writers tell me something real and pertinent" (p. 134).

Throughout her diaries, Hillesum shows how the inner dialogue that contributes to developing tenacious humility incorporates thoughtful study of what others have said and done. She demonstrates why self-examination cannot take place in a vacuum: A person needs sources for reflection and questioning. This idea mirrors the discussion in Chapter 7 about routes for cultivating a sense of tradition in teaching. Hillesum found sources in art, in literature, in philosophy, as well as in the world around her that she perceived with a poet's eye, and she treated them as partners in a living conversation. Just as she shows how reflection can translate into public action, so she discloses how a habit of thoughtful study can expand and deepen one's insight into the human condition. "[T]o let it all soak in," she observes, "that is probably the only right way with literature, with study, with people, or with anything else . . . to let it mature slowly inside you until it has become a part of yourself" (p. 102). We witness this process in Hillesum herself. Before our very eyes, she becomes a person who brings strength and compassion to others. She can justifiably conclude: "After all, it has not been 'literature' and 'aesthetics' alone I have been busy with here at my desk during these last few years" (p. 183).

It seems to me that Hillesum harmonizes word and deed in a manner reminiscent of well-known philosophies of nonviolent action. She does not presume to be an orator or political leader along the lines of a Mahatma Gandhi or Martin Luther King, Jr. But nor is she "merely" a person of goodwill and peace. Consider once more the main lineaments of her life as traced through her diaries and letters. She becomes, as she had hoped, an excellent writer. This accomplishment positions her to be a "chronicler" of her times (pp. 173, 196), to be the "thinking heart of the barracks" (pp. 199, 225). As I argued previously, she thinks and writes herself into a world she realizes she must inhabit and help, to the point of her voluntarily going off to assist others in pain. Her writing becomes directly valuable; for example, the Dutch resistance publishes several of her letters describing life in the camp. She continues to write about her experience to the very end, even while helping others each exhausting, frightening day that comes her way. She goes so far as to fill out a last postcard to worried friends even while the train carrying her to her death lurches out of the camp (she pushed the card through a small window in the cattle car, and it was found and mailed by local farmers).

This pattern of thinking, writing, acting, and helping cannot be captured by terms such as *fatalism* and *passivity*. True, Hillesum's posture will not stop an invading army. There had better be forces prepared to fight in such circumstances. But, crucially in my view, Hillesum's tenacious humility reveals how an individual human being can be a force for good by capitalizing on his or her distinctive character and abilities. *It seems to me that Hillesum employs her talents and the person she has become to the very full*. She shows how an inner searching, and an outer quest for meaning, can lead a person to take the risk of trying to do something for the world without becoming either dogmatic or fanatical in the process. Her determination not to hate and to lash out, but rather to seek the beauty and the human possibility in even the roughest moments, and her desire to become "hardy," but not "hard" (p. 195), are not, as Todorov (1996) claims, "superhuman—and therefore, inhuman" (p. 208). Hillesum's actions may not be of this world as we know it, but that is precisely the point. In their own modest way, Hillesum's acts evoke a more humane world, which I would characterize as a central dimension of the moral life. Hillesum walks with one foot in the world as it is and one foot in the world as it could be. She helps us see the problems and the promise in both.

In sum, the issue does not come down to choosing between Hillesum's view and that of a concerned critic like Todorov. Teachers do not have to either pursue the ideal of tenacious humility or abandon it in favor of a more overtly activist or aggressive stance. In this chapter, I have focused on tenacious humility as an ideal of personhood. But there will be important moments when a teacher needs to contribute to institutional projects of change and reform. One lesson to draw from Hillesum's testimony— and, I hope, from everything I have written in this chapter—is that tenacious humility represents a revolutionary ideal in its own right. Were all teachers to try as hard as they could to be tenacious and humble, were they to strive to enact a full measure of patience, of imagination, of attentiveness in their work with students, nothing less than a quiet transformation would take place in classrooms (as is always happening in some of them). That transformation, in turn, would reverberate throughout society. Again, this is a matter of emphasis, not of a stark choice, because at the same time issues of institutional change, of broad curricular improvement, of wiser assessment practices, and more—including, crucially, support for teachers to enact tenacious humility—remain to be addressed. Teachers have much to offer here, just as do many others in the system. "We have to focus on the *meaning* of practice when we think about changing it," Olson (1992) reminds us. "Changing a practice isn't merely a technical process—it involves considering what the change signifies. That entails dialogue—a conversation between the old and the new" (p. 78). Teachers merit a central role in the conversation precisely because they are the inheritors, and the guardians, of a tradition of practice. With that role comes an obligation, at some level, to participate in institutional reform and improvement. As numerous critics have underscored, however, such endeavors should not cause teachers to lose any more contact time with students than necessary. It would be tragic, and harmful to the long-term health of the practice of teaching, if attempts to change educational institutions diminished rather than enhanced how teachers and students work together.

It seems to me that all who teach can seek a balance that avoids, at one end of the spectrum, self-absorption and passivity, and, at the other end, fanaticism and dogmatism. To recall the terms used previously, it is a balance between respect for ideals and respect for the reality of other people. Moreover, such a posture can only emerge if teachers treat contemplation and self-reflection as seriously as they do their public obligations. "[O]ne must keep in touch with the real world," Hillesum (1996) writes, "and know one's place in it; it is wrong to live only with the eternal truths, for then one is apt to end up behaving like as ostrich. To live fully, outwardly and inwardly, not to ignore external reality for the sake of the inner life, or the reverse—that's quite a task" (p. 25).[6]

CONCLUSION: IDEALS AND THE PRACTICE OF TEACHING

"And back to me came the words I wrote down months ago in one of these notes to myself, words I shall keep writing down time and again, until they are a part of me: Slowly, steadily, patiently" (Hillesum, 1996, p. 99). As we have seen, Hillesum's creed positions her to take advantage of whatever opportunities the immediate moment offers to develop herself and, in what amounts to the same thing, to express her care for humanity. The words she recalls attest to the unheroic, unpretentious, but serious life she learned to lead. And precisely here is the bridge between her stance, adopted generations ago at a grim time in human history, and the stance captured by tenacious humility as an ideal of personhood and teaching. *Slowly, steadily, patiently*: These very terms help frame the process of teaching and learning. Tenacious humility complements the patience and the attentiveness that are hallmarks of the practice of teaching. The ideal affirms the truism that genuine learning, for both students and teachers, cannot be forced or rushed, any more than we can hasten the sunrise or quicken the tide. *Slowly, steadily, patiently*: These words help capture how inner reflection can translate into public conduct that is tenaciously humble. Hillesum's life serves not so much as a model for teachers, since every teacher's self-examination will take him or her in a unique direction, but as showing that inner questioning and scrutiny are possible and that they can shape one's presence as a teacher.

The inquiry into tenacious humility in this chapter suggests that ideals have a place in teaching, even if the nature of ideals makes it hard to specify that place in precise terms. "Big" ideals such as social betterment and enlarging human dignity motivate teachers. But such ideals take their shape from within the terms of the practice. No such ideal trumps, by itself, all that is built into the practice of teaching. The critics who worry about big ideals help us appreciate the dangers of heeding them unchecked by a sense of reality and responsibility. Ideals can become ideological or doctrinaire and can lead teachers away from their educational obligations and cause them to treat their students as a means to an end, whether the latter be political, social, or whatever. The first-year teacher whose woes I recounted earlier illustrates how an otherwise laudable ideal of democratic education can override perception and understanding of students. Her experience attests to why an ideal and a sense of reality and responsibility should mutually inform one another.

Tenacious humility describes an ideal disposition, a moral ideal of character or personhood. Those who take it seriously embark on a quest to become a better person and teacher. They position themselves, thereby, to have that much more positive an influence on students—and perhaps on others, too. They learn to see students for who they are—to listen, question, think, and wonder with them—rather than to see them solely through the lens or the terms of a big ideal. Their tenacious humility guides and disciplines their other ideals, keeping them in the service of teaching and learning.

Tenacious humility reveals the difference between self-improvement and self-absorption or self-indulgence. Etty Hillesum and others mentioned in the chapter are acutely aware of how "the dear self" (Kant, 1785/1990, p. 23) keeps showing up in our human deliberations to demand comfort, ease, and protection from hard and thorny questions. That demand steers people away from others and from associating with them (not to mention helping them). "Will not a tiny speck very close to our vision," writes Eliot, "blot out the glory of the world, and leave only a margin by which we see the blot? I know no speck so troublesome as self" (1871–72/1985, p. 456). These same persons also shed light on the symmetry between self-improvement, understood as a moral undertaking or quest, and what I called in Chapter 3 being object-conscious rather than self-conscious. To be object-conscious is to focus on the world—on the task, opportunity, problem, difficulty, or situation at hand. It can mean focusing on that which is not yet the case, as much as it can mean considering precedent and what else is going on that might be pertinent. Tenacious humility emerges from being object-conscious, from attending to persons and the things of the world, from striving to be that which one is not (yet). Emmet (1979) clarifies the point while shedding additional light on the nature of an ideal. "One has . . . to decide," she writes, "to make the venture of believing that one can come to appreciate situations in greater depth, and this is a venture reinforced through following it rather than one whose correctness can be demonstrated at the start. The start is to change our orientation from preoccupation with our own interests to liberty of spirit to see things disinterestedly" (p. 141). Emmet does not mean that we should strive for a position of pure impartiality, which she suggests is impossible for human beings. The key words in her argument are *preoccupation* and *liberty of spirit*. For teachers, to be preoccupied with students and with teaching transfers energy and focus from the self, conceived as something apart or isolated from what one does, and liberates teachers to "become adults," as Hillesum puts it, who can be a positive influence in the lives of the young.

Must teachers and teacher candidates think and talk about an ideal such as tenacious humility for it to serve its guiding purpose? Or does it function as something unspoken yet felt, as something present but unseen? Is it less a rational or reasoned position than a feeling, a feeling of there being something more that one can do and be, but juxtaposed with uncertainty about what that something more might be? Or does it bring feeling and reason together? Like artists, athletes, and many others, some teachers talk about "getting it right." They have in mind an image of excellence and success in working with students. But when pressed to define the "it," they stutter, they hem and haw, they go back and forth. Or they become excited and enthused, yet offer no airtight definitions. Instead, they provide metaphors for what it means to get it right. They illustrate it with example; they circle around it.

In light of our discussion of ideals, their conduct is not surprising. After all, how can persons define that which they have not experienced? As Schiller states in one of the epigrams that heads this chapter, how could there be an experience that "conforms" to an ideal, when the ideal describes a possibility rather than a present condition? To try to get it right means one has not yet, after all, gotten it right. That means plowing ahead into unknown territory, call it the land of the ideal. No teacher, no artist, no athlete—nobody will ever truly know what it is like to be in such a country. But that becomes a cause for pressing forward, in the literal sense of causing a person to act in the spirit of the ideal. Other motives will doubtless be present, and it seems beyond human capacity to have complete insight into one's purposes and aspirations. In addition, as discussed in previous chapters, every person perceives life through a prism of presumptions, and it is not always easy to become mindful of them. However, as Hillesum (1996), Kant (1785/1990, 1788/1993), and others show, it is possible to think and to talk oneself into acting in better rather than worse ways. As Kant might put it, a person can be the cause of his or her own conduct, rather than ceding that power to natural or social forces. In so doing, Kant argues, the person expresses his or her freedom.

Moreover, it is always possible to characterize the journey toward an ideal, to talk about the character or nature of the process. Part of the quest to become as fully human as one can is learning, all the while, what such a quest entails. As Hillesum discovered, this means taking oneself seriously as the complement to taking other people seriously. She also saw that no person can accomplish such growth alone. People must dwell with others in order to learn how to think, to talk, and to act in such a way that they develop both the tenacity and the humility to push ahead despite doubts, obstacles, and failures. Thus, to characterize the journey—to ponder, discuss, and describe what it means—becomes, in an almost literal way, a route through which human beings form their very character as persons.

Here is where conversation between teachers becomes valuable. To talk about an ideal brings it to life, helps it become sharper, positions it to animate one's conduct. Such talk honors the fact that, at the end of the day, the ideal of tenacious humility serves the human spirit. To talk about tenacious humility, and to read about those whose lives illuminate it, is to discern an orientation, an outlook, a source of meaning and purpose. In this domain, as many have tried to show, argument, explanation, and even knowledge have their limits. The poet and scientist Goethe evokes those limits in the other epigram which heads the chapter. Goethe talks about "see[ing]" an ideal and having it without "knowing" it, by which he means not having an airtight, unchanging grasp of it—but, nonetheless, recognizing its place in the crafting of a life. That recognition points to a kind of wisdom or insight ("seeing into"), not to a form of knowledge per se.

The kind of conversation I have in mind comprises something more than argument, explanation, or an exchange of information, although it includes all of those things. As Oakeshott avers, "A conversation may contain arguments, but is not reducible to arguments" (quoted in Hollinger, 1985, p. xvi). An argument has to be orderly. But in metaphorical terms, that requirement cannot always capture the feeling, the surprising surge within, the breathlessness, the heartbeat one can feel when in the invisible presence of what one could be as a person and teacher. Conversation is a way to render that presence more vivid, more real, and more a source of one's teaching. It can assist a person to take on, and to live, the hopeful images and ideas that, for reasons not always fathomable, loom up in the mind. "My ideas," Hillesum (1996) writes, "hang on me like outsize clothes into which I still have to grow" (p. 37). She envisions what she is not yet able to be. And, just as she understands the need for other people in order to bring her ideas to life, so the philosopher Stanley Cavell (1990) writes of the importance of the friend, "the figure, let us say, whose conviction in one's moral intelligibility draws one to discover it, to find words and deeds in which to express it" (p. xxxii). Teachers in conversation can serve as such friends, providing occasions for one another to talk their way into and forward in their quest to be good people and good teachers.

Notes

CHAPTER 1

1. This sentence reflects an argument by the historian Jacob Burckhardt about what happens when artists feel themselves subjugated to market conditions, with the latter's relentless demand for novelty for novelty's sake. In such conditions, Burckhardt contends, nonartistic considerations overwhelm artistic judgment, and "the historically relevant takes the place of the artistically relevant" (quoted in Gossman, 1997, p. 37).

2. I mention "formal" theories in order to contrast them with informal theories—or, better perhaps, with preconceptions or preunderstandings (cf. Gadamer, 1960/1996)—that persons are always bringing to bear in their contact with the world. Matt Sanger helped me understand the need to make such a contrast.

3. For reviews of this literature, see Hansen (2000), Noddings (2000), Oser (1994), and Sockett (1992).

4. Nor can teaching be "deconstructed" into a facade, if by those terms we understand the project of showing that behind every practice or human endeavor resides a hidden system of interests and power (or a "regime of truth," as it is sometimes called). I share the widely held assumption that a practice such as teaching never operates in a political or social vacuum. Its identity and status are always in question. But as a living practice, it constitutes something other than a mere locus of underlying, deterministic interests or power whose origins reside outside the practice. I try to illuminate why this is so throughout the book.

5. Unless otherwise noted, no quotations I cite that feature solely male or female pronouns embody, in my view, sexist assumptions or views. Also, unless otherwise noted, all italicized words in quoted material in this book reflect the author's emphasis, not mine.

6. For a useful discussion of strong versions of the theory, see Hacking (1999) and D. C. Philips (2000).

7. I am thinking of what might be called, in technical terms, the tradition of the hermeneutics of suspicion (cf. Gadamer, 1984), according to which human affairs and practices rest on (usually) hidden psychological or material forces.

Pioneering and endlessly fruitful work by writers such as Nietzsche, Freud, and Foucault comes to mind here. Raymond Boisvert (1998) contrasts this orientation with what he calls the hermeneutics of recovery, which he claims "challenges the whole notion of thinking in terms of pre-Modern, Modern, and post-Modern" (p. 157). Taylor (1989) shows convincingly how persons might, as he puts it, "retrieve" empowering links with the past.

CHAPTER 2

1. On differences between conduct and behavior, see Dewey (1930), Oakeshott (1989, 1991), and Taylor (1985). Chambliss (1987) argues that "educational conduct" should be understood as the union of educational theory and practice.

2. Cf. Langford (1985). Kant (1788/1993, p. 93, *passim*) calls personhood "personality" and gives this term a deep moral meaning. However, I employ the term *personhood* to steer clear of the contemporary meanings associated with the word *personality*, some of which drain it of moral content.

3. There is a rich literature on narrative and its value in helping us to comprehend human experience. For treatments of the moral power of fictional narratives, see, e.g., Booth (1988), J. Gardner (1978), and Nussbaum (1990). For accounts that embed morality in lived narrative, see, e.g., Hauerwas (1977) and Taylor (1989) as well as MacIntyre (1984). For work on teaching and how to understand it through the lens of narrative, see, e.g., Gudmundsdottir (2000), McEwan & Egan (1995), and Witherell & Noddings (1991). For work on thinking and its relation to narrative, see, e.g., Bruner (1985, 1991).

4. Bricker (1993) and Pendlebury (1990) have employed the concept "situational appreciation" to capture this reflective capacity. See also Garrison's (1997) complementary discussion of what has been called "moral perception."

CHAPTER 3

1. The image differs from a hard-and-fast ideal or ideology, too. Jane Roland Martin (1985) raises pointed questions about ideals of what she calls "the educated person." Such ideals can be based, however unknowingly, on the model or customs of a particular group of people. Martin especially criticizes ideals of an educated person that are, in her view, skewed toward what she characterizes as male or masculine traits. Her critique has sparked controversy, debate, and useful lines of inquiry. It seems to me there is wisdom in the caution it contains about taking on any ideal too hastily. In Chapter 8, I discuss the dangers of ideals in teaching, while also seeking to carve out an inhabitable place for them.

2. Since I have drawn on and will continue to draw on Kant's moral philosophy, I should point out that my interpretation of his philosophy parts company with those that characterize it as rationalistic or deontological. I believe Kant regarded virtue and feeling as necessary complements to reason and principle in

the fashioning of a moral life—in the achievement, especially, of a moral pattern in a life. See his discussion, for example, in his *Lectures on Ethics* and *The Metaphysics of Morals*. His classic *Foundations of the Metaphysics of Morals*, its forbidding title (that is Kant's own description) notwithstanding, reveals his passionate moral sensibility. My outlook has been influenced by recent work by, among others, Richard Eldridge (1997), Barbara Herman (1993), Felicitas Munzel (1999), and Nancy Sherman (1997).

3. My interpretation of spontaneity differs from what Shirley Pendlebury (1995) calls "perceptive spontaneity," by which she means taking delight "in complex particulars for their own sake" (p. 55). A teacher's perceptive spontaneity, says Pendlebury, can yield a lively imagination and a fresh response to new experiences. From her point of view, however, it can be too open, too uncritical, too unreliable a guide for sound educational practice. I will suggest that, when allied with the other qualities I am examining, spontaneity embodies a critical outlook.

4. "Whether you are free or not," Konrad (1981) adds, "will always be de-cided in the very next minute. You could be on a street corner waiting for a bus, in your room waiting for a telephone call, in your bed waiting for a dream. . . . Our freedom is an impatient master; it doesn't give us much time to rest. . . . 'This is what I am; this is what I can do,' we complain. 'You are more, you can do more,' the master says calmly. Make room for light in you, for you are the room and you are the light. When you get tired, the room grows dark" (p. 49).

5. For a recent exchange on the meaning of open-mindedness in education, see P. Gardner (1993, 1996), Gluck (1999), and Hare & McLaughlin (1994, 1998). Hare (1985) addresses how difficult open-mindedness can be, to the extent that persons might become skeptical of its very possibility.

6. In less dramatic terms, Philippa Foot (1978) shows why it may be mis-guided to speak of a "courageous robber." She argues that courage as a virtue, and robbery as an act, do not harmonize. It would be closer to the mark, she implies, to speak of a relentless, cool-headed, or cold-hearted robber.

CHAPTER 4

1. The concept of a stimulus, in this context, is not behaviorist. On the contrary, Dewey's conception of education raises questions about the meaning of a genuine educational stimulus. It calls attention to how a teacher can foster an environment that gives rise to the right kind of opportunities and invitations, those that lead to thinking, experience, and growth rather than to their opposites. Dewey's concept of a stimulus is interactive or, better perhaps, "transactive," a term that highlights organic relations between people and their environment (cf. Dewey & Bentley, 1949). Things, objects, events, *become* stimuli by virtue of what persons are already doing. "Stimuli from the environment," Dewey (1932/1989) writes, "are highly important factors in conduct. But they are not important as

causes, as generators of action. For the organism is already active, and stimuli themselves arise and are experienced only in the course of action. The painful heat of an object stimulates the hand to withdraw but the heat was experienced in the course of reaching and exploring. The function of a stimulus is—as the case just cited illustrates—to *change the direction of an action* already going on. Similarly, a response to a stimulus is not the beginning of activity; it is a *change*, a shift, of activity in response to the change in conditions indicated by a stimulus" (pp. 289–290). People can provoke the very stimuli to which they respond. Their responses can engender new stimuli. Moreover, they can infuse intelligence, purpose, feeling, and hope into this transactive process.

This understanding of the dynamics of stimulus and response contrasts with B. F. Skinner's historically influential conception (for background, see, e.g., Alexander, 1987; Bowers, 1987; Bredo, 1998; Tiles, 1988). Eliyahu Rosenow (1980) writes that "Skinner aims at planning an environment which produces regulated stimuli prearranged in such a way that they modify the individual's behavior as designed by the cultural engineer. His guiding principle is that the behavior thus acquired should be useful both to the individual and to his culture" (p. 221). Skinner denies many aspects of morality, in part because he denies much of what we associate with consciousness. He aims at producing not moral persons per se but a moral environment that will induce people to behave well. Ultimately, in Skinner's scheme, what I described in Chapter 2 as a moral sensibility would become irrelevant to human flourishing.

2. These remarks become all the more provocative when one considers Rousseau's personal failings and mistakes over the course of his life. For example, critics have severely reprimanded him for sending his illegitimate children to a foundling home. As his *Confessions* document, Rousseau was not unaware of his weaknesses and failures (or at least some of them). Moreover, he had tried his own hand at tutoring children and found himself unfit for the task. Yet he learned a great deal from his inadequacy and from pondering what it would have taken to succeed. "I am too impressed by the greatness of a preceptor's duties," he wrote in *Émile*. "I feel my incapacity too much ever to accept such employment from whatever quarter it might be offered to me" (1762/1979, p. 50).

3. Foucault's studies, animated by his evocative interpretive and humane voice, have spawned a veritable industry of like-minded projects across the humanities and social sciences. A helpful place to start with his work is Rabinow (1984). Recent applications of Foucault's perspective to education can be found in Ball (1990), Popkewitz & Brennan (1998), and Rousmaniere et al. (1997).

CHAPTER 5

1. Rosenblatt prefers the term *transaction* to *reader response*, since the latter words connote, for some critics, a highly subjectivist view of reading and interpreting texts; see, for example, her remarks in Karolides (1999, pp. 166–167). Connell (1996) illuminates and raises useful questions about Rosenblatt's viewpoint.

Hans-Georg Gadamer (1960/1996) makes a comparable argument about the human experience of interpretation, which I draw on in Chapter 7 in order to illuminate the teacher's encounter with pedagogical tradition.

2. I enrolled in a course entitled Autobiography and Education: American Lives at the University of Chicago in the fall of 1985. The two teachers, Amy Kass and Ralph Lerner, centered our weekly discussions around these three questions, which they introduced and clarified throughout the term.

3. Hofstadter's (1962) criticism illustrates the view of those who find Dewey's writing convoluted, if not tortuous. I believe Dewey's writing is accessible and appealing, once one gets used to its rhythm and cadence. Dewey's style results from what he was trying to accomplish, which is nothing less than a reconstruction of educational theory and practice (see Alexander, 1987, pp. xii–xiii). Dewey's style is not "bad" in the sense that he was like a painter who should have stuck to sculpting, to theater, or to golf (or who was simply a poor painter). Dewey was like a poet in the sense that a poet is something other than a refugee from prose. A poet writes poetry because that is the only way to express her or his ideas or vision. I believe Dewey was object-conscious, borne along by the questions he confronted—obedient to them, as it were. That led him to abandon many customary frames of understanding, expectation, and expression.

4. This argument applies to lecturing, too. In a good lecture, the audience participates with both thought and feeling, even if the participation is less overt than in a discussion. The lecturer and the audience fuel an environment that positions them to learn from the experience, or, as Dewey might put it, to have an experience in the first place.

5. A feature of our program I value is that a year or so after taking the course I am describing, students enroll in a field-based course in which they return directly to Dewey's philosophy of education. In that course, they read and study works such as Dewey's *Moral Principles in Education* (1909/1975), *Experience and Education* (1938/1963), and "The Relation of Theory to Practice in Education" (1904/1974b). I have taught this course, too, and the educational benefits (and sheer pleasure) of working again with the same students, who have often grown a great deal by then, are enormous.

6. In Chapters 6 and 7, I discuss the value to teachers of developing a sense of tradition. Part of that process is engaging works from other eras (such as *Democracy and Education*) that do not approach education according to contemporary mood or fashion.

7. Students also attest to the nature of teaching indirectly as a pedagogical approach. Here are some additional comments they make about the course: "[The teacher's] major strength is his ability to be a leader without us knowing he is. He really leads us to think about what we say and why we say it. . . . The responsibility for making the class effective was left to the student. Of course there was excellent guidance and the occasional intellectual bucket of ice water thrown on us. His willingness to hear us out was contagious. It made us all more willing to listen, believe, and accept our peers' contributions. . . . He had a very real but almost 'hidden' presence. He allowed the class to basically direct the learning,

but guided us effectively. . . . He lets the class 'drive' itself, along with gently suggesting the direction."

CHAPTER 6

1. Langford (1985) provides a useful distinction between what he calls "critical" and "conservative" traditions. Critical traditions encourage change and innovation; they mirror the idea of a living tradition. Conservative ones discourage or smother movement; they might be dubbed traditionalist traditions. Eisenstadt (1972) makes a comparable distinction between what he calls tradition and traditionality. In this chapter I work with the contrast between tradition and traditionalism, in part because much of the literature I draw on makes extensive use of it (if not always in so many words).

2. This positive answer, however, does not dissolve the tensions between tradition and creativity, tensions that Pelikan (1984, p. 73) argues form an "ineradicable element" in a living tradition.

Bloom's (1975) study, incidentally, is mainly about how those he calls "strong poets" (especially from the Romantic period) appear to elide tradition. They create the impression that they have broken loose from tradition into radically new and liberating terrain. Bloom applauds their artifice. But he also acknowledges that it is artifice and that no poet can ever ignore or completely override the influence of poetic tradition. Far from shattering tradition, Romantic poets gave it a powerful infusion. One reason I have made use of Bloom's insights is that he takes pains to dissociate his stance from anything that could be called traditionalism or an uncritical embrace of the past.

3. For insight into the teacher's "manner" of working, see, e.g., Fallona (1999), Fenstermacher (1990, 1992, 1999), and Richardson & Fallona (1999). On "style" in teaching, see Hansen (1993) and Jackson et al. (1993). For an examination of a related concept, called the "tact" of teaching, see van Manen (1991). I have discussed differences and similarities among manner, style, and tact (Hansen, 2000).

4. Many students in courses I have taught have argued that all mimetic teaching has potentially transformative results. For example, a person being taught how to dance, step by step, might experience so much joy and confidence that he or she attains a whole new presence as a person, even if the teacher never intended such an outcome. For an argument which suggests that the mimetic and the transformative may be irreconcilable, see Boostrom (1997, 1998).

5. Robert Pirsig (1979) explains how instruction in what are often called vocational or technical fields (e.g., motorcycle maintenance) can—and, in his view, should—embody what I have said here about teaching as compared with socialization or acculturation.

CHAPTER 7

1. George Eliot created a forbidding portrait of an antiquarian, Mr. Casaubon, in her novel *Middlemarch*. The novel brilliantly contrasts Casaubon's grim

handhold on the past with the author's subtle, loving, nontraditionalist portrait of a form of community life whose human goodness she hoped would continue to find expression in a rapidly changing world.

2. For a defense against the charge that Dewey gives short shrift to tradition, see, e.g., Alexander (1994/95) and Robertson (1992). For more severe criticisms than mine, see, e.g., Bowers (1987) and Callan (1981).

3. For useful background analysis and criticism, see, e.g., Kerdeman (1998), Warnke (1987), and Weinsheimer (1985). Also see the discussion in Chapter 5 of "transactive" views of reading.

4. "A teacher of classical languages and literatures in Renaissance Italy," Konstantin Kolenda (1995) points out, "was described as *umanista* (contrasted with *legista*, teacher of law), and what we today call 'the humanities,' in the fifteenth century was called *studia humanitatis*, which stood for grammar, rhetoric, history, literature, and moral philosophy" (p. 340).

5. The questions take inspiration, in part, from Alexander Nehamas's (1998) study of individuals he calls "philosophers of the art of living" (p. 4).

6. The first part of this sentence adapts a line from the poet A. D. Hope, cited in Bayley (1998, p. 52).

CHAPTER 8

1. Research on teaching has generated terms that have a family resemblance to ideals. For example, LaBoskey (1994) discusses teacher candidates' "passionate creeds," while Hammerness (1999) examines teachers' "visions." This work complements that of scholars who focus on teachers' "images" of the practice; see, e.g., Calderhead & Robson (1991), Clandinin (1986), Elbaz (1983), Joseph & Burnaford (1994), and Koerner (1989).

As I conceive them, the concepts "ideal" and "image" emphasize different matters, even while they overlap in meaning. In Chapter 3, I described an image of a growing, educated person that can help guide a teacher's work. I understand such an image to be suggestive, nonarbitrary, and, hopefully, compelling in an enduring way. But such an image is less binding, in a manner of speaking, than an ideal in teaching—especially, as I will show, an ideal of personhood. The image focuses on *students'* destinies, while the ideal underscores *the teacher's*, particularly how the teacher's growth is bound up in helping students learn and flourish.

2. Oakeshott's argument also calls into question the sufficiency of the formulation, "I think, therefore my biochemical system is functioning properly." A biochemical system can be understood as a condition that makes thought possible. But the nature and content of thought cannot be reduced, deterministically, to the operation of that system. Oakeshott argues repeatedly that thoughts have reasons, not causes (e.g., 1989, pp. 19–20, 35). As Socrates puts it in Plato's *Phaedo* (99b): "Fancy being unable to distinguish between the reason for a thing, and the condition without which the reason couldn't be operative!"

3. Karl Hostetler (1997, pp. 74–105) provides a useful example of the prob-

lems that can arise when a teacher's personal ideals interfere with carrying out the tasks that accompany the role.

4. Hillesum seems to have been much influenced by the poet Rilke, whose work (especially *The Book of Hours* and *Letters to a Young Poet*) she refers to often. "Don't search for the answers," Rilke (1908/1986) writes in response to a young poet, "which could not be given to you now, because you would not be able to live them. And the point is, to live everything. *Live* the questions now. Perhaps then, someday far in the future, you will gradually, without even noticing it, live your way into the answer" (pp. 34–35). Compare also Hillesum's image of rolling "melodiously" out of God's hand with Rilke's poetic, metaphorical appeal to God: "Don't you sense me, ready to break / into being at your touch?" (Rilke, 1905/1996, I, 19).

5. Todorov's metaphor may be an intentional reference to Kant, much of whose moral philosophy Hillesum embodies in her conduct (for example, the idea of treating other people as ends in themselves rather than merely as means to our ends). At one point, Kant (1785/1990) says that even if a good will was thwarted in its efforts to perform goodness, it would still "sparkle like a jewel all by itself" (p. 10).

6. I recall a moment, as I was writing notes in the margin of Hillesum's book, when I stopped and looked at my words, and then looked back at her's, and had the sudden feeling of a dialogue taking place. I felt the shared condition of being on a quest for meaning, for I understand her as showing that the quest can happen and can lead to a real issue. Perhaps my reaction attests to the intimacy generated by reading what, after all, is a diary. Nonetheless, it struck me, at that moment, that Hillesum's words were alive, expressing the vibrancy of her spirit and hopes. Her words seemed to carry palpable intellectual and moral weight, of which she herself was not fully aware. In short, I found myself not "just" reading, but also wondering, imagining, waiting, remembering, and more. With these thoughts in mind, I then wrote in the margin words from Rilke—"Look, I am living. On what?" (Ninth Duino Elegy)—and I answered, in the margin: *on this*. My experience, doubtless familiar to readers everywhere (and not just of books), fueled the analysis in Chapters 6 and 7 of person, practice, and tradition in teaching.

References

Abbott, A. (1988). *The system of professions*. Chicago: University of Chicago Press.

Abrams, M. H., Donaldson, E. T., Smith, H., Adams, R. M., Monk, S. H., Ford, G. H., & Daiches, D. (Eds.). (1962). *The Norton anthology of English literature* (Major Authors edition). New York: Norton.

Allan, G. (1993). Traditions and transitions. In P. Cook (Ed.), *Philosophical imagination and cultural memory* (pp. 21–39). Durham, NC: Duke University Press.

Alexander, T. M. (1987). *John Dewey's theory of art, experience and nature: The horizons of feeling*. Albany: State University of New York Press.

Alexander, T. M. (1994/95). Educating the democratic heart: Pluralism, traditions and the humanities. *Studies in Philosophy and Education, 13*, 243–259.

Applebaum, B. (1995). Creating a trusting atmosphere in the classroom. *Educational Theory, 45*(4), 443–452.

Aristotle. (trans. 1962). *Nicomachean ethics* (M. Ostwald, Trans.). New York: Macmillan.

Arnold, P. J. (1997). *Sport, ethics, and education*. London: Cassell.

Baier, A. (1983). Secular faith. In S. Hauerwas & A. MacIntyre (Eds.), *Revisions: Changing perspectives in moral philosophy* (pp. 203–221). Notre Dame, IN: University of Notre Dame Press.

Baker, B. (1998). Child-centered teaching, redemption, and educational identities: A history of the present. *Educational Theory, 48*(2), 155–174.

Ball, S. J. (Ed.). (1990). *Foucault and education: Disciplines and knowledge*. London: Routledge.

Bayley, J. (1998, July 27). Elegy for Iris: Scenes from an indomitable marriage. *The New Yorker*, pp. 45–61.

Benner, P. (1994). The role of articulation in understanding practice and experience as sources of knowledge in clinical nursing. In J. Tully (Ed.), *Philosophy in an age of pluralism: The philosophy of Charles Taylor in question* (pp. 136–155). Cambridge, UK: Cambridge University Press.

Benner, P., & Wrubel, J. (1989). *The primacy of caring: Stress and coping in health and illness*. Reading, MA: Addison-Wesley.

Ben-Peretz, M. (1995). *Learning from experience: Memory and the teacher's account of teaching*. Albany: State University of New York Press.

Berlin, I. (1992). *The crooked timber of humanity: Chapters in the history of ideas*. New York: Vintage.

Bloom, H. (1973). *The anxiety of influence: A theory of poetry*. New York: Oxford University Press.

Bloom, H. (1975). *A map of misreading*. Oxford, UK: Oxford University Press.

Bloom, H. (1998). *Shakespeare: The invention of the human*. New York: Riverhead.

Boisvert, R. D. (1998). *John Dewey: Rethinking our time*. Albany: State University of New York Press.

Boostrom, R. (1997). Teaching by the numbers. In N. C. Burbules & D. T. Hansen (Eds.), *Teaching and its predicaments* (pp. 45–64). Boulder, CO: Westview.

Boostrom, R. (1998). "Safe places": Reflections on an educational metaphor. *Journal of Curriculum Studies, 30*(4), 397–408.

Booth, W. C. (1988). *The company we keep: An ethics of fiction*. Berkeley: University of California Press.

Bowers, C. A. (1987). *Elements of a post-liberal theory of education*. New York: Teachers College Press.

Brann, E. T. H. (1979). *Paradoxes of education in a republic*. Chicago: University of Chicago Press.

Brann, E. T. H. (1999). The American college as *the* place for liberal learning. *Daedalus, 128*(1), 151–171.

Bredo, E. (1998). Evolution, psychology, and John Dewey's critique of the reflex arc concept. *Elementary School Journal, 98*(5), 447–466.

Bricker, D. C. (1993). Character and moral reasoning: An Aristotelian perspective. In K. A. Strike & P. L. Ternasky (Eds.), *Ethics for professionals in education* (pp. 13–26). New York: Teachers College Press.

Broudy, H. S. (1963). Historic exemplars of teaching method. In N. L. Gage (Ed.), *Handbook of research on teaching* (pp. 1–44). Chicago: Rand McNally.

Bruner, J. (1985). Narrative and paradigmatic modes of thought. In E. Eisner (Ed.), *Learning and teaching the ways of knowing* (pp. 97–115). Chicago: National Society for the Study of Education.

Bruner, J. (1991). The narrative construction of reality. *Critical Inquiry, 18*, 1–21.

Buchmann, M. (1989). The careful vision: How practical is contemplation in teaching? *American Journal of Education, 98*, 35–61.

Buchmann, M., & Floden, R. E. (1993). *Detachment and concern: Conversations in the philosophy of teaching and teacher education*. New York: Teachers College Press.

Burbules, N. C. (1993). *Dialogue in teaching: Theory and practice*. New York: Teachers College Press.

Burbules, N. C., & Densmore, K. (1991). The limits of making teaching a profession. *Educational Policy, 5*, 44–63.

Burbules, N. C., & Hansen, D. T. (Eds.). (1997). *Teaching and its predicaments*. Boulder, CO: Westview.

Bushnell, R. W. (1996). *A culture of teaching: Early modern humanism in theory and practice*. Ithaca, NY: Cornell University Press.

Calderhead, J., & Robson, M. (1991). Images of teaching: Student teachers' early conceptions of classroom practice. *Teaching and Teacher Education, 7*, 1–8.

Callan, E. (1981). Education for democracy: Dewey's illiberal philosophy of education. *Educational Theory, 31*(2), 167–175.

Calvino, I. (1988). *Six memos for the next millennium* (P. Creagh, Trans.). Cambridge, MA: Harvard University Press.

Carr, D. (1999). Is teaching a skill? In R. Curren (Ed.), *Philosophy of Education 1999* (pp. 204–212). Champaign, IL: Philosophy of Education Society.

Carr, W. (1995). *For education: Towards critical educational inquiry*. Buckingham, UK: Open University Press.

Cassirer, E. (1945). *Rousseau, Kant, Goethe* (J. Gutmann, P. O. Kristeller, & J. H. Randall, Jr., Trans.). Princeton, NJ: Princeton University Press.

Cavell, S. (1990). *Conditions handsome and unhandsome: The constitution of Emersonian perfectionism*. Chicago: University of Chicago Press.

Chambliss, J. J. (1987). *Educational theory as theory of conduct*. Albany: State University of New York Press.

Chekhov, A. (1964). A boring story. In *Lady with lapdog and other stories* (D. Magarshack, Trans.). London: Penguin. (Original work published 1889)

Clandinin, D. J. (1986). *Classroom practice: Teacher images in action*. London: Falmer.

Connell, J. (1996). Assessing the influence of Dewey's epistemology on Rosenblatt's reader response theory. *Educational Theory, 46*(4), 395–413.

Cranston, M. (1991). *The noble savage: Jean-Jacques Rousseau 1754–1762*. Chicago: University of Chicago Press.

Cua, A. S. (1998). *Moral vision and tradition: Essays in Chinese ethics*. Washington, DC: Catholic University of America Press.

Cuffaro, H. K. (1995). *Experimenting with the world: John Dewey and the early childhood classroom*. New York: Teachers College Press.

Delpit, L. (1995). *Other people's children: Cultural conflict in the classroom*. New York: The New Press.

Dewey, J. (1930). *Human nature and conduct*. New York: The Modern Library. (Original work published 1922)

Dewey, J. (1933). *How we think*. New York: D. C. Heath & Co.

Dewey, J. (1963). *Experience and education*. New York: Collier. (Original work published 1938)

Dewey, J. (1974a). The need for a philosophy of education. In R. D. Archambault (Ed.), *John Dewey on education* (pp. 3–14). Chicago: University of Chicago Press. (Original work published 1934)

Dewey, J. (1974b). The relation of theory to practice in education. In R. D. Archambault (Ed.), *John Dewey on education* (pp. 313–338). Chicago: University of Chicago Press. (Original work published 1904)

Dewey, J. (1975). *Moral principles in education*. Carbondale: Southern Illinois University Press. (Original work published 1909)

Dewey, J. (1980). *Art as experience.* New York: Perigee. (Original work published 1934)

Dewey, J. (1989). Theory of the moral life. In J. A. Boydston (Ed.), *John Dewey, the later works 1925–1953: Vol. 7. Ethics* (pp. 159–310). Carbondale: Southern Illinois University Press. (Original work published 1932)

Dewey, J. (1997). *Democracy and education.* New York: The Free Press. (Original work published 1916)

Dewey, J., & Bentley, A. (1949). *Knowing and the known.* Boston: Beacon.

Dillon, J. T. (1994). *Using discussion in classrooms.* Buckingham, UK: Open University Press.

Donald, J. (1992). *Sentimental education: Schooling, popular culture and the regulation of liberty.* London: Verso.

Donoghue, D. (1998). *The practice of reading.* New Haven, CT: Yale University Press.

Downie, R. S., & Telfer, E. (1980). *Caring and curing: A philosophy of medicine and social work.* London: Methuen.

Eisenstadt, S. N. (1972). Intellectuals and tradition. *Daedalus, 101*(2), 1–19.

Elbaz, F. (1983). *Teacher thinking: A study of practical knowledge.* New York: Nichols.

Eldridge, R. (1997). *Leading a human life: Wittgenstein, intentionality, and romanticism.* Chicago: University of Chicago Press.

Eliot, G. (1985). *Middlemarch.* Harmondsworth, UK: Penguin. (Original work published 1871–72)

Elkins, J. (1996). *The object stares back.* San Diego: Harcourt Brace.

Ellsworth, E. (1997). *Teaching positions: Difference, pedagogy, and the power of address.* New York: Teachers College Press.

Emerson, R. W. (1990). Experience. In R. Poirier (Ed.), *Ralph Waldo Emerson* (pp. 216–234). Oxford, UK: Oxford University Press. (Original work published 1844)

Emmet, D. (1979). *The moral prism.* London: Macmillan.

Emmet, D. (1994). *The role of the unrealisable: A study in regulative ideals.* New York: St. Martin's Press.

Epstein, J. (Ed.). (1981). *Masters: Portraits of great teachers.* New York: Basic Books.

Fallona, C. (1999, April). *Manner in teaching: A study in observing and interpreting teachers' moral virtues.* Paper presented at the annual meeting of the American Educational Research Association, Montreal, Canada.

Fenstermacher, G. D. (1990). Some moral considerations on teaching as a profession. In J. I. Goodlad, R. Soder, & K. A. Sirotnik (Eds.), *The moral dimensions of teaching* (pp. 130–154). San Francisco: Jossey-Bass.

Fenstermacher, G. D. (1992). The concepts of method and manner in teaching. In F. K. Oser, A. Dick, & J.-L. Patry (Eds.), *Effective and responsible teaching: The new synthesis* (pp. 95–108). San Francisco: Jossey-Bass.

Fenstermacher, G. D. (1999, April). *On the concept of manner and its visibility in teaching practice.* Paper presented at the annual meeting of the American Educational Research Association, Montreal, Canada.

Finkielkraut, A. (1995). *The defeat of the mind* (J. Friedlander, Trans.). New York: Columbia University Press. (Original work published 1987)

Fishman, S. M., & McCarthy, L. (1998). *John Dewey and the challenge of classroom practice*. New York: Teachers College Press.

Foot, P. (1978). *Virtues and vices*. Berkeley: University of California Press.

Foster, M. (1997). *Black teachers on teaching*. New York: The New Press.

Friedson, E. (1994). *Professionalism reborn*. Chicago: University of Chicago Press.

Gadamer, H.-G. (1984). The hermeneutics of suspicion. In G. Shapiro & A. Sica (Eds.), *Hermeneutics: Questions and prospects* (pp. 54–65). Amherst: University of Massachusetts Press.

Gadamer, H.-G. (1996). *Truth and method* (2nd rev. ed.) (J. Weinsheimer & D. G. Marshall, Trans.). New York: Continuum. (Original work published 1960)

Gardner, J. (1978). *On moral fiction*. New York: Basic Books.

Gardner, P. (1993). Should we teach children to be open-minded? Or, is the Pope open-minded about the existence of God? *Journal of Philosophy of Education, 27*(1), 39–43.

Gardner, P. (1996). Four anxieties and a reassurance: Hare and McLaughlin on being open-minded. *Journal of Philosophy of Education, 30*(2), 271–276.

Garrison, J. (1996). A Deweyan theory of democratic listening. *Educational Theory, 46*(4), 429–451.

Garrison, J. (1997). *Dewey and eros: Wisdom and desire in the art of teaching*. New York: Teachers College Press.

Gluck, A. L. (1999). Open-mindedness versus holding firm beliefs. *Journal of Philosophy of Education, 33*(2), 269–276.

Goffman, E. (1961). *Asylums: Essays on the social situation of mental patients and other inmates*. New York: Doubleday Anchor.

Gossman, L. (1997). Burckhardt between history and art: *Kulturgeschichte, Kunstgeschichte, Genuss. Common Knowledge, 6*(1), 17–43.

Gotz, I. L. (1988). *Zen and the art of teaching*. Westbury, NJ: J. L. Wilkerson.

Grant, R. W. (1996). The ethics of talk: Classroom conversation and democratic politics. *Teachers College Record, 97*(3), 470–482.

Graubard, S. R. (Ed.). (1978). Rousseau for our time [Special issue]. *Daedalus, 107*(3), 1–206.

Green, T. F. (1994). Public speech. *Teachers College Record, 95*(3), 369–387.

Greene, M. (1989). The teacher in John Dewey's works. In P. W. Jackson & S. Haroutunian-Gordon (Eds.), *From Socrates to software: The teacher as text and the text as teacher: 89th yearbook of the National Society for the Study of Education, Part I* (pp. 24–35). Chicago: University of Chicago Press.

Gudmundsdottir, S. (2000). Narrative research on teaching. In V. Richardson (Ed.), *Handbook of research on teaching* (4th ed.). Washington, DC: American Educational Research Association.

Hacking, I. (1999). *The social construction of what?* Cambridge, MA: Harvard University Press.

Hammerness, K. (1999, April). *Visions of delight, visions of doubt: The relationship between emotion and cognition in teachers' vision*. Paper presented at the annual meeting of the American Educational Research Association, Montreal, Canada.

Hansen, D. T. (1993). The moral importance of the teacher's style. *Journal of Curriculum Studies, 25,* 397–421.

Hansen, D. T. (1995). *The call to teach.* New York: Teachers College Press.

Hansen, D. T. (1998). The moral is in the practice. *Teaching and Teacher Education, 14,* 643–655.

Hansen, D. T. (1999). Understanding students. *Journal of Curriculum and Supervision, 14,* 171–185.

Hansen, D. T. (2000). Teaching as a moral activity. In V. A. Richardson (Ed.), *Handbook of research on teaching* (4th ed.). Washington, DC: American Educational Research Association.

Hare, W. (1985). *In defense of open-mindedness.* Kingston, Ontario, Canada: McGill-Queen's University Press.

Hare, W., & McLaughlin, T. H. (1994). Open-mindedness, commitment and Peter Gardner. *Journal of Philosophy of Education, 28*(2), 239–244.

Hare, W., & McLaughlin, T. H. (1998). Four anxieties about open-mindedness: Reassuring Peter Gardner. *Journal of Philosophy of Education, 32*(2), 283–292.

Haroutunian-Gordon, S. (1991). *Turning the soul: Teaching through conversation in the high school.* Chicago: University of Chicago Press.

Hauerwas, S. (1977). *Truthfulness and tragedy.* Notre Dame, IN: University of Notre Dame Press.

Hendel, C. W. (1934). *Jean-Jacques Rousseau, moralist* (Vol. 2). London: Oxford University Press.

Henry, A. (1998). *Taking back control: African Canadian women teachers' lives and practices.* Albany: State University of New York Press.

Herman, B. (1993). *The practice of moral judgment.* Cambridge, MA: Harvard University Press.

Higgins, C. R. (1998). *Practical wisdom: Educational philosophy as liberal teacher education.* Unpublished doctoral dissertation, Columbia University, New York.

Hillesum, E. (1996). *An interrupted life: The diaries, 1941–1943, and letters from Westerbork* (A. J. Pomerans, Trans.). New York: Henry Holt.

Hofstadter, R. (1962). *Anti-intellectualism in American life.* New York: Vintage.

Hollinger, R. (1985). Hermeneutics and pragmatism. In R. Hollinger (Ed.), *Hermeneutics and praxis* (pp. ix–xx). Notre Dame, IN: University of Notre Dame Press.

Horton, J., & Mendus, S. (1994). Alasdair MacIntyre: *After Virtue* and after. In J. Horton & S. Mendus (Eds.), *After MacIntyre: Critical perspectives on the work of Alasdair MacIntyre* (pp. 1–15). Notre Dame, IN: University of Notre Dame Press.

Hostetler, K. D. (1997). *Ethical judgment in teaching.* Boston: Allyn & Bacon.

Hoy, D. C. (1978). *The critical circle: Literature, history, and philosophical hermeneutics.* Berkeley: University of California Press.

Huizinga, J. (1955). *Homo ludens: A study of the play element in culture.* Boston: Beacon. (Original work published 1944)

Iheoma, E. O. (1997). Rousseau's views on teaching. *Journal of Educational Thought,*
    31(1), 69–81.

Jackson, P. W. (1986). *The practice of teaching.* New York: Teachers College Press.

Jackson, P. W. (1992). *Untaught lessons.* New York: Teachers College Press.

Jackson, P. W., Boostrom, R. E., & Hansen, D. T. (1993). *The moral life of schools.*
    San Francisco: Jossey-Bass.

Johnson, S. M. (1990). *Teachers at work: Achieving success in our schools.* New York:
    Basic Books.

Joseph, P. B., & Burnaford, G. E. (Eds.). (1994). *Images of schoolteachers in twentieth-*
    century America. New York: St. Martin's Press.

Kant, I. (1960). *Religion within the limits of reason alone* (T. M. Greene & H. H.
    Hudson, Trans.). New York: Harper & Row. (Original work published 1793)

Kant, I. (1963). Conjectural beginning of human history. In L. W. Beck (Ed.), *Kant:*
    On history (L. W. Beck, Trans.) (pp. 53–68). New York: Macmillan. (Original
    work published 1786)

Kant, I. (1990). *Foundations of the metaphysics of morals* (L. W. Beck, Trans.). Engle-
    wood Cliffs, NJ: Prentice Hall. (Original work published 1785)

Kant, I. (1991). On the common saying: 'This may be true in theory, but it does
    not apply in practice'. In H. Reiss (Ed.), *Kant: Political writings* (H. B. Nisbet,
    Trans.) (pp. 61–92). Cambridge, UK: Cambridge University Press. (Original
    work published 1793)

Kant, I. (1993). *Critique of practical reason* (L. W. Beck, Trans.). Upper Saddle River,
    NJ: Prentice Hall. (Original work published 1788)

Karolides, N. J. (1999). Theory and practice: An interview with Louise M. Rosen-
    blatt. *Language Arts, 77*(2), 158–170.

Kerdeman, D. (1998). Hermeneutics and education: Understanding, control, and
    agency. *Educational Theory, 48*(2), 267–278.

Koerner, M. (1989). *Teachers' images of their work.* Unpublished doctoral dissertation,
    University of Illinois at Chicago.

Kolenda, K. (1995). Humanism. In R. Audi (Ed.), *The Cambridge dictionary of philoso-*
    phy (pp. 340–341). Cambridge, UK: Cambridge University Press.

Konrad, G. (1981). Letter from Budapest. *New York Review of Books, 27*(17), 49.

Korsgaard, C. M. (1996). *The sources of normativity.* Cambridge, UK: Cambridge
    University Press.

Kozolanka, K., & Olson, J. (1994). Life after school: How science and technology
    teachers construe capability. *International Journal of Technology and Design*
    Education, 4(3), 209–226.

Labaree, D. F. (1992). Power, knowledge, and the rationalization of teaching: A
    genealogy of the movement to professionalize teaching. *Harvard Educational*
    Review, 62, 123–154.

LaBoskey, V. K. (1994). *Development of reflective practice: A study of preservice teachers.*
    New York: Teachers College Press.

Ladson-Billings, G. (1994). *The dreamkeepers: Successful teachers of African American*
    children. San Francisco: Jossey-Bass.

Lampert, M. (1990). When the problem is not the question and the solution is not the answer: Mathematical knowing and teaching. *American Educational Research Journal, 27*(1), 29–63.

Langford, G. (1978). *Teaching as a profession: An essay in the philosophy of education.* Manchester, UK: Manchester University Press.

Langford, G. (1985). *Education, persons and society: A philosophical inquiry.* London: Macmillan.

Lear, J. (1998). *Open minded: Working out the logic of the soul.* Cambridge, MA: Harvard University Press.

Lortie, D. C. (1975). *Schoolteacher.* Chicago: University of Chicago Press.

Loukes, H. (1976). Morality and the education of the teacher. *Oxford Review of Education, 2*(2), 139–147.

MacIntyre, A. (1984). *After virtue* (2nd ed.). Notre Dame, IN: University of Notre Dame Press.

Martin, J. R. (1985). *Reclaiming a conversation: The ideal of the educated woman.* New Haven, CT: Yale University Press.

Mauss, M. (1985). A category of the human mind: The notion of person, the notion of self. In M. Carrithers, S. Collins, & S. Lukes (Eds.), *The category of the person: Anthropology, philosophy, history* (pp. 1–25). Cambridge, UK: Cambridge University Press.

McCarty, L. P. (1997). Experience and the postmodern spirit. *Educational Theory, 47*(3), 377–394.

McEwan, H., & Egan, K. (Eds.). (1995). *Narrative in teaching, learning, and research.* New York: Teachers College Press.

McIntyre, D., Hagger, H., & Wilkin, M. (1993). *Mentoring: Perspectives on school-based teacher education.* London: Kogan Page.

Merleau-Ponty, M. (1969). *Humanism and terror: An essay on the communist problem* (J. O'Neill, Trans.). Boston: Beacon. (Original work published 1947)

Mounce, H. O. (1973). Philosophy and education. *The Human World, 13,* 11–20.

Munzel, G. F. (1999). *Kant's conception of moral character: The "critical" link of morality, anthropology, and reflective judgment.* Chicago: University of Chicago Press.

Murdoch, I. (1970). *The sovereignty of good.* London: Ark.

Nehamas, A. (1998). *The art of living: Socratic reflections from Plato to Foucault.* Berkeley: University of California Press.

Nicholls, J. G., & Hazzard, S. P. (1993). *Education as adventure: Lessons from the second grade.* New York: Teachers College Press.

Noddings, N. (1993). *Educating for intelligent belief or unbelief.* New York: Teachers College Press.

Noddings, N. (2000). The caring teacher. In V. A. Richardson (Ed.), *Handbook of research on teaching* (4th ed.). Washington, DC: American Educational Research Association.

Nussbaum, M. C. (1990). *Love's knowledge: Essays on philosophy and literature.* Oxford, UK: Oxford University Press.

Oakeshott, M. (1989). *The voice of liberal learning: Michael Oakeshott on education* (T. Fuller, Ed.). New Haven, CT: Yale University Press. (Original essays published between 1949 and 1975)

Oakeshott, M. (1991). *Rationalism in politics and other essays*. Indianapolis, IN: Liberty Press. (Original essays published between 1932 and 1991)

Oakeshott, M. (1993). *Religion, politics, and the moral life* (T. Fuller, Ed.). New Haven, CT: Yale University Press. (Original essays published between 1925 and 1955)

Olson, J. (1992). *Understanding teaching: Beyond expertise*. Milton Keynes, UK: Open University Press.

Oser, F. K. (1994). Moral perspectives on teaching. *Review of Research in Education, 20*, 57–127.

Oyler, C. (1996). *Making room for students: Sharing teacher authority in Room 104*. New York: Teachers College Press.

Pelikan, J. (1984). *The vindication of tradition*. New Haven, CT: Yale University Press.

Pendlebury, S. (1990). Practical arguments and situational appreciation in teaching. *Educational Theory, 40*(2), 171–179.

Pendlebury, S. (1995). Reason and story in wise practice. In H. McEwan & K. Egan (Eds.), *Narrative in teaching, learning, and research* (pp. 50–65). New York: Teachers College Press.

Peshkin, A. (1991). *The color of strangers, the color of friends: The play of ethnicity in school and community*. Chicago: University of Chicago Press.

Peters, R. S. (1981). *Essays on educators*. London: George Allen & Unwin.

Philips, D. C. (Ed.). (2000). *Constructivism in education: Opinions and second opinions on controversial issues. 99th yearbook of the National Society for the Study of Education, Part I*. Chicago: University of Chicago Press.

Philips, D. Z. (1979). Is moral education really necessary? *British Journal of Educational Studies, 27*(1), 42–56.

Pirsig, R. M. (1979). *Zen and the art of motorcycle maintenance: An inquiry into values*. New York: Morrow.

Plievier, T. (1966). *Stalingrad* (R. Winston & C. Winston, Trans.). New York: Time Inc. (Original work published 1947)

Pocock, J. G. A. (1968). Time, institutions and action: An essay on traditions and their understanding. In P. King & B. C. Parekh (Eds.), *Politics and experience: Essays presented to Professor Michael Oakeshott on the occasion of his retirement* (pp. 209–237). London: Cambridge University Press.

Popkewitz, T. S., & Brennan, M. (Eds.). (1998). *Foucault's challenge: Discourse, knowledge, and power in education*. New York: Teachers College Press.

Popper, K. R. (1963). *Conjectures and refutations: The growth of scientific knowledge*. New York: Basic Books.

Preskill, S. (1998). Narratives of teaching and the quest for the second self. *Journal of Teacher Education, 49*(5), 344–357.

Pring, R. (1984). *Personal and social education in the curriculum*. London: Hodder & Stoughton.

Proefriedt, W. A. (1994). *How teachers learn: Toward a more liberal teacher education*. New York: Teachers College Press.

Rabinow, P. (Ed.). (1984). *The Foucault reader*. New York: Pantheon.

Rappaport, R. A. (1971). Ritual, sanctity, and cybernetics. *American Anthropologist, 73,* 59–76.

Reagan, T. (1996). *Non-Western educational traditions: Alternative approaches to educational thought and practice.* Mahwah, NJ: Erlbaum.

Richardson, V., & Fallona, C. (1999, April). *Classroom management as method and manner.* Paper presented at the annual meeting of the American Educational Research Association, Montreal, Canada.

Rilke, R. M. (1986). *Letters to a young poet* (S. Mitchell, Trans.). New York: Vintage. (Original work published 1908)

Rilke, R. M. (1989). Archaic torso of Apollo. In *The selected poetry of Rainer Maria Rilke* (S. Mitchell, Trans.). New York: Vintage Books. (Original work published 1908)

Rilke, R. M. (1996). *Rilke's book of hours* (A. Barrows & J. Macy, Trans.). New York: Riverhead Books. (Original work published 1905)

Robertson, E. (1992). Is Dewey's educational vision still viable? In G. Grant (Ed.), *Review of Research in Education 18,* 335–381.

Rorty, A. O. (1997). The ethics of reading: A traveler's guide. *Educational Theory, 47*(1), 85–89.

Rorty, A. O. (Ed.). (1998). *Philosophers on education: New historical perspectives.* London: Routledge.

Rorty, R. (1983). Method and morality. In N. Haan, R. N. Bellah, P. Rabinow, & W. M. Sullivan (Eds.), *Social science as moral inquiry* (pp. 155–176). New York: Columbia University Press.

Rosenblatt, Louise M. (1978). *The reader, the text, the poem: The transactional theory of the literary work.* Carbondale: Southern Illinois University Press.

Rosenow, E. (1980). Rousseau's *Emile,* an anti-utopia. *British Journal of Educational Studies, 28*(3), 212–224.

Rousmaniere, K. (1997). Good teachers are born, not made: Self-regulation in the work of nineteenth-century American women teachers. In K. Rousmaniere et al. (Eds.), *Discipline, moral regulation, and schooling: A social history* (pp. 117–133). New York: Garland.

Rousmaniere, K., Dehli, K., & de Coninck-Smith, N. (1997). *Discipline, moral regulation, and schooling: A social history.* New York: Garland.

Rousseau, J.-J. (1979). *Émile, or On education* (A. Bloom, Trans.). New York: Basic Books. (Original work published 1762)

Ryan, A. (1998). Deweyan pragmatism and American education. In A. O. Rorty (Ed.), *Philosophers on education: New historical perspectives* (pp. 394–410). London: Routledge.

Schama, S. (1996, April 1). The Flaubert of the trenches. *The New Yorker,* pp. 97–98.

Schultz, D. R. (1997). *Toward wisdom in practice: A study of teachers' pedagogic judgments.* Unpublished doctoral dissertation, University of Illinois at Chicago.

Schwab, J. J. (1978a). Eros and education: A discussion of one aspect of discussion. In I. Westbury & N. J. Wilkof (Eds.), *Science, curriculum, and liberal education:*

Selected essays by Joseph J. Schwab (pp. 105–132). Chicago: University of Chicago Press.

Schwab, J. J. (1978b). The "impossible" role of the teacher in progressive education. In I. Westbury & N. J. Wilkof (Eds.), *Science, curriculum, and liberal education: Selected essays by Joseph J. Schwab* (pp. 167–183). Chicago: University of Chicago Press.

Seixas, P. (1993). Historical understanding among adolescents in a multicultural setting. *Curriculum Inquiry, 23*(3), 301–327.

Shalem, Y. (1999). Epistemological labor: The way to significant pedagogical authority. *Educational Theory, 49*(1), 53–70.

Shattuck, R. (1996). *Forbidden knowledge: From Prometheus to pornography.* New York: St. Martin's Press.

Shattuck, R. (1999). The need for core. In S. Lee & A. Speight (Eds.), *Tradition and innovation* (pp. 1–7). Lanham, MD: University Press of America.

Sherman, N. (1997). *Making a necessity of virtue: Aristotle and Kant on virtue.* Cambridge, UK: Cambridge University Press.

Shils, E. (1958). Tradition and liberty: Antinomy and interdependence. *Ethics, 68*(3), 153–165.

Shils, E. (1981). *Tradition.* Chicago: University of Chicago Press.

Simpson, D. (1997). The cult of "conversation." *Raritan, 16*(4), 75–85.

Smeyers, P. (1995). Education and the educational project II: Do we still care about it? *Journal of Philosophy of Education, 29*(3), 401–413.

Sockett, H. (1992). The moral aspects of the curriculum. In P. W. Jackson (Ed.), *Handbook of research on curriculum* (pp. 543–569). New York: Macmillan.

Sockett, H. (1993). *The moral base for teacher professionalism.* New York: Teachers College Press.

Taylor, C. (1985). *Philosophical papers, I: Human agency and language.* Cambridge, UK: Cambridge University Press.

Taylor, C. (1989). *Sources of the self: The making of the modern identity.* Cambridge, MA: Harvard University Press.

Taylor, C. (1992). *The ethics of authenticity.* Cambridge, MA: Harvard University Press.

Tiles, J. E. (1988). *Dewey.* London: Routledge.

Todorov, T. (1996). *Facing the extreme: Moral life in the concentration camps* (A. Denner & A. Pollak, Trans.). New York: Metropolitan Books.

Tom, A. (1984). *Teaching as a moral craft.* New York: Longman.

Van Manen, M. (1991). *The tact of teaching: The meaning of pedagogical thoughtfulness.* Albany: State University of New York Press.

Warnke, G. (1987). *Gadamer: Hermeneutics, tradition and reason.* Stanford, CA: Stanford University Press.

Weaver, R. M. (1948). *Ideas have consequences.* Chicago: University of Chicago Press.

Weil, S. (1986). The *Iliad* or the poem of force. In S. Miles (Ed.), *Simone Weil: An anthology* (M. McCarthy, Trans.) (pp. 162–195). New York: Weidenfeld & Nicolson. (Original work published 1941)

Weinsheimer, J. C. (1985). *Gadamer's Hermeneutics: A reading of "Truth and Method."* New Haven, CT: Yale University Press.

Will, F. L. (1985a). Reason, social practice, and scientific realism. In R. Hollinger (Ed.), *Hermeneutics and praxis* (pp. 122–142). Notre Dame, IN: University of Notre Dame Press.

Will, F. L. (1985b). The rational governance of practice. In R. Hollinger (Ed.), *Hermeneutics and praxis* (pp. 192–213). Notre Dame, IN: University of Notre Dame Press.

Williams, B. (1981). *Moral luck: Philosophical papers 1973–1980.* Cambridge, UK: Cambridge University Press.

Wilson, J. (1993). *Reflection and practice: Teacher education and the teaching profession.* London, Ontario, Canada: Althouse.

Wilson, J. (1998). Seriousness and the foundations of education. *Educational Theory, 48*(2), 143–153.

Winch, C. (1996). Rousseau on learning: A re-evaluation. *Educational Theory, 46*(4), 415–428.

Witherell, C., & Noddings, N. (Eds.). (1991). *Stories lives tell: Narrative and dialogue in education.* New York: Teachers College Press.

Wittgenstein, L. (1980). *Culture and value* (G. H. von Wright, Ed.; P. Winch, Trans.). Chicago: University of Chicago Press. (Posthumous)

Wokler, R. (1995). *Rousseau.* Oxford, UK: Oxford University Press.

Wolfe, A. (1993). *The human difference: Animals, computers, and the necessity of social science.* Berkeley: University of California Press.

Yamamoto, K. (Ed.). (1979). *Children in time and space.* New York: Teachers College Press.

Zahorik, J. (1996). Elementary and secondary teachers' reports of how they make learning interesting. *Elementary School Journal, 96*(5), 551–564.

Author Index

Subject Index

Growing person (*Continued*)
  open-heartedness, 45, 52–53
  open-mindedness, 44, 51–52, 69, 76, 93,
    110, 136, 150, 195
  plasticity, 57, 89
  "readiness," 61
  responsibility (intellectual and moral),
    44, 53–54, 55–56, 58, 76, 93, 113
  seriousness, 45, 54–55, 113, 190
  simplicity, 45, 46–47, 81, 89, 95, 136, 166
  spontaneity, 45, 46, 47–48, 66, 89, 110,
    112, 166, 195
  straightforwardness, 44, 45–46, 76, 93
  See also Persons

Humanism, 144, 148, 199

Ideals, 30, 158–160, 162–163, 167, 172, 199
  "big" ideals, 18, 172–173, 187–188
  of coherence, 16
  vs. cynicism and jadedness, 181–182
  dangers of, 157, 158, 160–162, 165–166,
    178, 183–184
  vs. ideology, 161, 162, 165, 166, 168, 173,
    186, 188, 194
  vs. "images," 15, 17, 43, 194, 199
  of personhood or character, 18, 170, 172,
    173, 174, 187
  and realism, 103, 164, 184, 187
  as source of insight, 164–165
  of teachers, xi, 157–158, 163, 164, 172,
    184, 186, 187
  See also Teachers, Tenacious humility
Indirect teaching. *See* Teaching
Instruction. *See* Teachers, Teaching

Middlemarch (G. Eliot), 176, 182, 198
Mind, nature of, 25–26, 27, 82–83, 180–181
Moral, conceptions of the, 32–33, 49–50,
  66, 69, 77, 171–172, 186, 188

Nicomachean Ethics (Aristotle), 153

Object-conscious vs. self-conscious, 50–51,
  70, 93, 95, 188–189

Persons, conceptions of, 21–22, 25–26, 27–
  28, 29–30, 31, 71, 148, 194
  and freedom, 27–28, 47–48, 50, 66–67,
    110–111, 122, 167, 168–170, 195, 199

and indirect influence on others, 33–39,
  41–42, 61, 62, 73–75, 107–108
and narrative unity in a life, 31, 194
  See also Growing person
Practice, idea of a, 9, 13, 16, 117–118,
  153–4. *See also* Teaching

Rational (moral) faith, 50, 67, 113
Rationalism, 12–13
The Republic (Plato), 63–64

Sense of tradition
  cultivating, 116, 143–144, 146, 148, 149–
    154, 185
  and curriculum, 142–143, 151–153
  vs. historical knowledge, 116, 137, 138–
    139, 146, 149
  and human time and remembrance, 115,
    116, 123, 132, 138
  moral contours of, 123–125, 127, 131–
    132, 147–148
  as an overall orientation, 115, 121–122,
    126
  provides a critical standpoint, 7, 17–18,
    115, 125, 126, 127, 128, 132–133, 136,
    149, 155
  as source of guidance, 6–7, 115, 126,
    154–156
  See also Tradition
Situational appreciation, 194
Social construction, theory of, 8–9, 11, 12,
  13, 15
  and deconstruction, 193
  and hermeneutics of suspicion, 193–4
Students
  closeness to and distance from teachers,
    155–156
  moral receptivity to teachers, 33–38
  personal agency, 37, 43, 57, 69–70, 75,
    101–102

Teacher education, 73–75, 85–86, 134, 197
Teachers
  authority, 94, 108, 144, 146–147
  as a "community of adherents," 116
  as a "community of hope," 120, 136
  as a "community of interpretation," 116
  conduct, 28–31, 76, 158, 194
  creed, x–xii
  and humanism, 144–146

About the Author

DAVID T. HANSEN is on the faculty of the College of Education, University of Illinois at Chicago. He serves as coordinator of the college's secondary teacher education program, and he has chaired the university's Secondary Teacher Education Advisory Committee. Hansen is the author of *The Call to Teach* (1995), co-author (with Philip W. Jackson and Robert E. Boostrom) of *The Moral Life of Schools* (1993), and co-editor (with Nicholas C. Burbules) of *Teaching and Its Predicaments* (1997). He has been an active member of the American Educational Research Association, serving as Program Chair of Division B, Curriculum Studies, in 1995, and of the Philosophy of Education Society. Hansen's work focuses on the philosophy and practice of teaching.

DATE DUE

DEC 04 2009			